Social Transformation of Naxal Affected Areas:
(A Sociological Study)

Social Transformation of Naxal Affected Areas:

(A Sociological Study)

Rakesh Rai

GYAN

The Publication of this thesis was financially upheld by ICSSR and the responsibility of the facts stated, opinions expressed or conclusions reached are entirely that of the author and ICSSR accepts no responsibility for them.

ICSSR Consultant

Professor S.L. Sharma, P-3, University Campus, University of Rajasthan, Jaipur 302055.

First Published, 2018

Published by

Gyan Publishing House
5, Ansari Road
Daryaganj, New Delhi-110002
Phone: 9811692060
E-mail: books@gyanbooks.com

Printed at: G. Print Process, Delhi.

Cataloging in Publication Data—DK
Courtesy: D.K. Agencies (P) Ltd. <docinfo@dkagencies.com>

Rai, Rakesh, 1983- **author.**
Social transformation of Naxal affected areas : a sociological study based on Sonbhadra District, U.P. / Rakesh Rai.
pages cm
Includes bibliographical references.
ISBN 9788121213561

1. Naxalite movement—Social aspects—India—Sonbhadra (District)
2. Social problems—India—Sonbhadra (District)
3. Rural development—Government policy—India—Sonbhadra (District)
I. Title.

HX395.S66R35 2017 DDC 303.37209542 23

In the Holy Memory

of

My Father

Late Dr Baikunth Rai

Contents

List of Tables

Acknowledgement

I pay my sincere regards and heart felt gratitude to Professor Jaikant Tiwary, Head, Department of Sociology, Banaras Hindu University, Varanasi my revere guide for his scholarly and invaluable guidance and support and Patience by which he has shared my dilemmas at every step during my research work and personal life. His versatile academic and administrative personality inspired me to pursue this endeavor within the stipulated time under his able super vision.

I am highly indebted to my maternal uncle, Dr Bansh Narayan Rai and my brother Rajesh Rai for his consistent suggestions in drafting of this dissertation.

I express my gratitude to Professor Manjeet Kumar Chaturvedi, Professor Rajendra Rai and Professor Sohan Ram Yadav, Department of Sociology, B.H.U. for all his in valuable suggestions. His scholarly and galvanising teaching inspired me at every step.

I acknowledge the valuable suggestions and comments offered by Professor P.N. Pandey, Professor Salim, Professor A.K. Kaul, Professor A.K. Joshi, Professor J.N. Singh, Professor A. K. Pandey, Dr Kumud Ranjan, Dr Anuradha Bapuly, Dr D.K. Singh, Kalpana and other faculty staff of the Department of Sociology. I would like to thank Mr Badal Patra, Vijay, Bal Karanji, Office Assistant of the Department of Sociology and Social work, B.H.U. for his technical help in preparing the dissertation.

My family members always supported my Just and Unjust Endeavours in life. I really don't have the words to express my feelings towards them. I express my gratitude to my mother Raj Kumari Rai for her continuous support. I owe my special thanks my Bhabhi Nidhi

Singh for her immense support with a sense of responsibility at every stage. On this occasion, I would like to mention the name of my lovely niece and nephew Aryan, Arush, Pari and Pihu who provided me the deepest emotional and mental satisfaction at the time of stress. I want to offer my gratitude and respect to my relatives who always motivated me to pursue the doctoral work and stood next to me during the tension of personal and social life and their blessings always provided me a great relief.

I wish to express my sincere thanks to Dr Manish Tiwari, Assistant Professor, Arya Mahila College, B.H.U. and Dr Rajiv Kumar Singh (PDF, ICSSR) for their help in understanding the Naxal Movement and Social Transformation and for increasing my knowledge of Naxalism and Social Transformation.

I am indebted for sincere efforts put by my friends Dr Krishna, Dr Brijendra Singh, Dr Awadesh, Parijat Pradhan, Manoj, Ram Dhanee, Naresh, Brijesh, Mrs Swati, Vivekanth, Vikas Sharde, Ramesh Singh and Ashutosh Tiwari.

I wish to put on record the unmatched support and co-operation which I received from the respondents of the sampled households of Sonbhadra District during data collection and field survey.

Last but not least, I would like to thank Anil Kumar Srivastava and Chitrankana, Chitransh Typing and Shorthand Institute.

I owe all the errors in completion of this dissertation.

— **Rakesh Rai**

Preface

Gandhi ji was the architects of social transformation in India. His dreams were to give autonomy (Decentralisation) to our villages. He advocated his noble theory of "Hind Swaraj". He suggested that India must do away with basic necessities of life. It is also said that when the first draft of India's constitution was referred to him, he tore it off that it did not contain anything about Gram Swaraj and social Transformation in Indian Social Structure.

After Independence Indian Government take initiative to transformed the Indian Society launched various policies and plans for the welfare of weaker and marginalised section of society such as CDP, PRI"s ,Green revolution, Zamindari Abolition act, etc. but its benefit not reached to rural population at grass root level and it created atmosphere against the state. Many state governments brutally suppressed the anti state movement. People realised only radical communist model can solve their problem, to curbed the naxalite and communist movement launched both strategic and development model to solve the naxal menace in tribal and rural region of country.

1

Introduction

India's independence represented for its people the start of an epoch that was imbued with a new vision. In 1947, the country commenced its long march to overcome the colonial legacy of economic underdevelopment gross poverty, near total illiteracy, wide prevalence of disease and stark social inequality and injustice.

The first and the most important task was to preserve, consolidate and strengthen India's unity, to push forward the process of the making of the Indian Union and to buildup and protect the nation-state as an instrument of development and social transformation. In India many programme launched for weaker and marginalised sections upliftment such as Community Development programmes, Green revolution Zamindari Abolition Act, Panchayati raj, but its benefit has not reached to rural people at grass root level, and it created atmosphere against central and state government in late 1960's. During this anti state agitation many intellectual, youth, peasants, workers, etc. consider that only rule change from white elite people to the hand of brown elite class people, who are only different in colour but not in taste.

In Indian Social System, during that time many changes occur such as upliftments of women status, increased literacy, decline in mortality and fertility rate, social mobility etc. But real social transformation not occur and people specially in north and eastern India think that only communist model of state can solve their problem and they get whatever only by the help of 'Barrel of Gun' in the Indian democratic setup and this lead to the emergence of naxalite movement in India.

After emergence of naxalism in India, many social transformations occur in rural and backward areas of country which are discussed in present research work especially in context of the new changes and development occurred after 1990's in India. It is not surprising that in the countries of Third World, especially Indian context which is yet in the process of social transformation from primary sector "Socio-Economic to Secondary and Tertiary Sector. Economic Development is a big challenge, especially in naxal affected rural areas of Sonbhadra District.

Poverty, unemployment, migration, bonded labour, starvation death, exploitation of weaker sections; socio-economic disparities are the main issue and challenges which cannot be solved even after attaining Independence 64 years ago. As a result, the problem of naxalism even today after completing its 45 years of journey still today emerged as the biggest internal security problem. Today, it is not a Socio-economic ideological based movement but it changes its paradigm and it becomes weapon in the lands of Maoist who used it time by time to gain political power and run parallel government and bargaining Indian government on many issues.

Without solving the naxal violence problem in India social transformation is not possible in backward areas of country. It required a strong political will power, bilateral talk, socio-economic development and also using weapons if necessary in some urgent situation.

Concept of Social Transformation

The term 'Transformation' has been coined in social sciences from vocabulary of physics, especially from the 'laws of thermodynamics'. It denotes replacement of one stage into another in a time span. When the replacement of the former stage by the latter is such in depth that it makes meaningful difference the phenomenon may be referred as transformation.

Tiwary, J.K. (1994), in his study of social transformation in India, explained the concept of social transformation how it is related to mode of production, political economy and land reform; how state intervention measures bring social change in social life and social institutions.

Maheswari (1985): Considers social transformation as an interminable process to bring about improvement in the economic and social life of the rural poor.

Yogendra Singh (1990): The term 'social transformation' has multidimensional connotation. It comprehends enormous diversity in analysis among the various disciplines of social sciences. We feel that the concept can be grasped more vividly if it set in motion under specific historic context of social forces, ideology and national policy.

These contexts lead us to identification of social transformation in contemporary rural India. The scenario of transition in rural society especially in post-independence era suggests that the process of planned development has created diverse patterns of social transformation in its different regions. It is difficult to comprehend all such patterns in a limited manner. However, the major trends evolving out of the varied patterns may be summarised as under:

1. The transition of *Agrarian Society* from subsistence base to market based agrarian sector.
2. The introduction of modern technology techniques and devices to transform the existing loose scattered and under developed colonial agrarian economy into a well knit compact one and its organic integration into the total national economy.
3. The emergence of complex network of various association and institutions within the agrarian society having close links with and being shaped by external influences.
4. Emergence of power blocks which try to work within the constitutional frame wing a combination of protests through mass action, appeals to bureaucracy and courts and even lobbying centres of power.
5. State intervention in adopting different measures to strengthen certain communities, groups or classes on the one hand and weaken others on the contrary.

6. Emergence of dominants groups like neo-rich peasants, intermediary castes, etc. and their tightened, hold over avenues of political power and the use of public resources.

Desai (1985): defined social transformation as-"an approach which, by better utilisation of local resources and by creating infrastructural facilities for economic and social development aims at and at improving the quality of life of the rural population, especially the rural poor, by creation of expanded employment and income opportunities for them."

Routray, J.K. and Patnaik M (1982): He mentions the path of social transformation in various phases. Each phase is characterised by its own distinctive complexity of phenomena and structure and function to him, the approaches to social transformation are linked together in the following ways:

(A) Physical environment (Structural Arrangement Changes in Shape and Form:

It is guided mainly by

1. Transport networks
2. Irrigation networks
3. Power networks.

(B) Economic transformation: (Shifting from primary to secondary and Tertiary activities)

It is guided by technology with respect to structural variation in resource endowments.

(C) Social- cultural transformation: It is guided by the cross Interaction of physical and economic factors with the degree of Modernisation. The phenomenon includes:

1. Occupational mobility
2. Gradual replacement of caste system by class system.
3. Religious mobility
4. Ascriptive to Achieved society.

Kumar Ravindra (1983)-defines the concept of social transformation, that the creation of physical infrastructure, facilities in rural areas through the Industrialisation of the areas building roads, schools, hospitals etc...Creating growth centres with trickle down effect will serve the purpose, while others argue that creating organised employment in rural areas with reasonable facilities will automatically lead to their social transformation.

Cropp (1972): defined social transformation as a process which aims at Improving the well being and self realisation of people living outside the urbanised areas through collective efforts.

Harris (1986): defined it as policy and process which has emerged as a distinct field of research since the inception of new strategy for development planning by the World Bank, UN Agencies.

Social transformation in rural context denotes the successive changing patterns conceived in rural set, in its structure, function, form and character both in positive and negative direction.

Social transformation of rural areas does not mean urbanisation of villages or ruralisation of cities.

The realm of rural transformation rather covers wider perspectives i.e. rural to urban transformation as well as transformation in socio-economic and political structure of rural society.

The process of social transformation is an outcome of various factors such as state Intervention measures, role of civil society, people's participation etc.

After Independence, State embarked upon development programme of nation building such as creation of Infrastructure development, development of Basic and heavy Industries, growth of modern agricultural power, transportation, communication poverty-alleviation programme, land reforms, Zamindari Abolition Act, tenancy reform, Green revolution, building-up a network of transport links, facilities, standardisation of weight and measures, etc. Social transformation also enunciated by introducing affirmative action reservation and other upliftment programmes to weaker and marginalised section of society.

But these programmes of social transformation would provide the initial stimulus and the people will actively and willingly co-operate in these programmes.

It was assumed that the benefits of these programmes will percolate down to the rural poor of society. All these assumptions proved to be wrong in the coming years, the programme was also ambitious both in terms of financial outlays and targets and expectation of people because of these, all over hopes were belied and it generated general apathy, resistance and unrest among the rural poor.

All this, lead to genesis and emergence of naxalite movement in India, especially the Eastern part of country where mostly population is dalits, tribal's and minorities. Sonbhadra, is also one of the backward naxal-affected district which also faces naxal menace in last two decades because here also government measures and social transformation is not reached to down trodden section of society.

Theories of Social Transformation

1. Marxist Theory of Social Change-

Marxism is an economic and socio-political worldview and method of socio-economic inquiry that centres upon a materialist interpretation of history, a dialectical view of social change, and an analysis and critique of the development of Capitalism.

Marxism was pioneered in the early to mid 19th century by two German philosophers, Karl Marx and Frederic Engel's. Marxism encompasses Marxian economist theory, a sociological theory and a revolutionary view of social change that has influenced socialist-political movement worldwide.

The Marxian analysis begins with an analysis of material conditions taking at its starting point the necessary economic activities required by human society to provide for its material needs. The form of economic organisation or mode of production is understood to be the basis from which the majority of other social-phenomena-including social relation, political and legal systems, morality and Ideology-arise (or at least by which they are greatly influenced). These social relations form the superstructure of which the Economic systems forms the base. As the forces of production, mostly notable technology improve existing form of social-organisation become inefficient and stifle further progress. These inefficiencies manifest themselves as social- contradiction in society in the form of class struggle. Under the Capitalist mode of production this struggle materialises between the minority who own the means of production, the bourgeoisie and the vast majority of the population who produce goods and service the proletariat, taking the idea that social change occurs because of the struggle between different classes within society who are under contradiction against each other. The Marxist analysis leads to the conclusion that Capitalism oppresses, the proletariat, the inevitable result being a proletarian revolution.

Marxism views the emergence of a socialist system as a historical inevitability that arises from the obsolescence of capitalism and the corresponding social revolution where private property in the means of production would be superseded by co-operative ownership. The hypothetical system of socialism would succeed capitalism as the dominant mode of production when the accumulation of capital can no longer sustain itself due to falling rates of profit in real production relative to increasing productivity. A socialist economy would not base production on the accumulation of capital but would instead base production and economic activity on the criteria of satisfying human needs that is production would be carried out directly for use.

Eventually, socialism would give way to communist stage of history, a classless, stateless system based on common ownership and free access, super abundance and maximum freedom for individual to develop their own capacities and talents. As a political movement Marxism advocates for the creation of such a society.

A Marxist understanding of history and of society has been adopted by academics studying and in India the left extremist movement-naxalism which is one form of Maoist movement based on the Ideology of Marx-Stalin Mao-Zedong is becoming one of the biggest challenges related to internal security to our country. To deals with this problem their is need of understanding Marxist theory and its implementation and find out the loopholes why this problem emerged as biggest internal security and what measures we takes to solve this problem. We also evaluated the various measures and programmes launched by state and civil society to solve this menance there is also need to bring proper implementation of these programmes in a right direction with transparency and accountability. So that we know the real changes occur and what social transformation occurs in after naxal emergence in that particular area.

2. Capitalist Theory of Social Transformation

During the course of the eighteenth and nineteenth centuries there was a gradual movement in Europe and in the states that European had founded for the reduction of trade barriers, in particular restriction on production and labour, the use of non-standard weights and measures restriction on the formation of new businesses and the curtailing of royal prerogatives that interfered with the conduct of commerce.

Two parallel doctrines emerged to describe and justify this process. One was the legal doctrine that the rightful owner of land or exerciser of a property right was the one that could make the best economic use of it, and that this principle must be reflected in the property laws of each nation. The other was the political doctrine of *laissez-faire* economic namely that all coercive government regulation of the market represents unjustified and that economies would perform best with government only playing a defensive role in order to ensure the operation of free markets.

The next major revision of the theoretical basis of the capitalism began in the late 19th century with the expansion of corporation and finances the Globalisation of production and the markets and the increasing desire to tap the productive capacity of the capital sectors of economics in order to secure the market and resources required to continue economic growth. The state came to be viewed by many, particularly by the wealthy, as a vehicle for improving business conditions, securing market and gaining access to scarce materials, even when such objectives could only be achieved through military force.

A theory of capitalism describes the essential features of capitalism and how its functions. The history of various such theories is the subject of this conception of what constitutes capitalism has changed significantly over time, as well as being dependent on the political perspective and analytical approach adopted by the observer in question.

Adam Smith: Focused on the role of enlightened self interest (the invisible hand) and the role of specialisation in promoting the efficiency of capital accumulation. Any Rand maintained that capitalism is thc only morally valid socio-political systcm bccausc it allows people to be free to act in their rational self-interest, and asserted that no politico/economic system in history has ever proved its value so eloquently or has benefited mankind so greatly She defined it as a social system based on the recognition of Individuals rights in which all property is privately owned and adduced that capitalism is the unknown ideal; people not knowing its nature, with the tacit compliance and silence of those who know better and being its foundations battered by a flood of altruism which is the cause of modern world collapse.

The first theorist of what we commonly refer to as capitalism is usually considered to be Adam Smith and his 1776 work, ***an inquiry into the nature and causes of wealth of nations***. Theorised that within a given stable system of commerce and evaluation individuals would responds to the incentive of earning more by specialising their production. These individuals would naturally without specific state intervention direct that industry in such a manner as its produce may be of the greatest value. This would enable the whole economy to become more productive and it would therefore be wealthier, similar view advanced by David Hume.

His systematic treatment of how the exchange of goods or a market would create incentives to act in the general interest became the basis of what was then called political economic and later economics. It was also the basis for a theory of law and government which would gradually supersedes the mercantilist regime that was then prevalent capitalism change the society, bring social transformation in all sphere of life primarily on agriculture industry, family, social institution etc.

Later industrial revolution in the textile industry and cotton cloths production in England, India earlier is famous for its cotton and silk cloths all over world but after invention and technology. Innovation India change it production unit into consumption only, Indian cotton silk goods not competitive to British machine made goods which are more cheaper and better than comparison to Indian goods. James Watt Steam Engine, also provide ground to British Industrialisation and the remote and isolated areas comes in the main stream society cultural sphere.

In India, Lord Dalhousie was called as the father of modern technology and communication network. In 1853 first Indian Railway steam engine runs. Railways broken the traditional social boundary and many caste people travelled together by railways, improved transportation helped in carrying messages as well as people, it assimilated the whole population. In the agriculture and farming sector also revolution come with new methods and technology leads to more food production, specially cash and commercial crop which is good for both consumer and markets.

This change in agricultural sector gives benefit to only big landholder only. With capitalist mode of production many new factories and industrial unit setup and it leads to both urbanisation and industrialisation people migrated from rural areas to urban areas.

The crowding population into cities has always faced problems of housing, health and sanitation. Many social bonds were dissolved. Many more restraints which life in a village community imposed broken down the relationship on the other hands men became freer to develop their capabilities.

The industrial society was divided into classes of Have's and Have's not, many time class conflict also emerged in the society. It also affected the old handicraft and village industry, people becomes unemployed and lived a marginalised life, they migrated to cities and work as labourer.

Role of old laws, customs, tradition, mores and folkways reduced its importance, as an agency of social control in modern capitalist society. In their places constitution, laws agencies become important and act as agents of social control.

3. Socialist Theory of Social Transformation

Socialism is an economic system in which the means of production are publicly or commonly owned and controlled cooperatively or a political philosophy advocating such a system. As a form of social organisation socialism is based on cooperative social relations and self management, relatively equal power relations and the reduction of elimination of hierarchy in the management of economic and political affairs.

Socialist theories are based upon production for used and the direct allocation of economic inputs to satisfy economic demands and human needs, accounting is based on physical quantities of resources, some physical magnitude, or a direct measures of labor time. Goods and services for consumption are distributed through markets and distribution of income is based on the principle of individual merit contribution. State socialist form of socialism advocates for the nationalisation of the means of production distribution and exchange as a strategy for implementing socialism; while social democrats advocated public control of capital within the frame work of market economy.

Modern socialism originated from an 18th century intellectual and working class political movement that criticized the affects of Industrialisation and private property on society. Utopian Socialist such as Robert Owen (1771-1858) tried to find self sustaining communes by secession from a capitalist society.

Friedrich Engel's and Karl Marx advocated the creation of a society that allows for the widespread application of modern technology to rationalised economic activity by eliminating the anarchy of capitalist production that results in Instability and cyclical crisis of overproduction. Socialist holds that capitalism is an illegitimate economic system, since it serves the interests of the wealthy and allows the exploitation of lower classes. As such, they wish to replace it completely or at least make substantial modification to it, in order to create a more just society that would guarantee a certain basic standard of life. A primary goal of socialism is social equality and a distribution of wealth based on one's contribution to society, and an economic arrangement that would serve the interest of society as a whole.

Planned Economy: Model of Socialism

In which production to the needs of the community, would distribute the work to be done among all those able to work and would guarantee a livelihood to every man, woman and child.

Planned economy combines public ownership of the means of production with centralised state planning. This model is usually associated with the centralised Soviet style command economy. This model is popular in communist state.

India's Socialist model is state directed. After independence, Nehruvian Socialist model of development adopted. This leads to creation of license raj, the elaborate licenses, regulation and the accompanying red tapism.

Nehru and his advisers embarked on a programme of planned development that focused on Agrarian reform as well as Industrialisation from the 1950's to the 1970's a series of land reform laws were as in the states that were intended to bring about changes.

The first important legislation was the abolition of the Zamindari system which removed the layer of intermediaries who stood between the cultivators and the state.

Among other major land reform law that was introduced were tenancy regulation and abolition act and land ceiling acts.

There laws imposed an upper limit on the amount of land that can be owned by a particular family.

These laws not only boost agricultural growth but also to eradicated poverty in rural areas and bring about social justice.

Land reforms have not only a limited impact on rural society and the agrarian structure in most regions. In contrast the green revolution of the 1960's and 1970's brought about significant changes in the areas where it took place, it give benefited to big landowners who have amount to invest on modern technology and rest poor small farmers are victims of green Revolution and modern technology.

In India, Socialistic model of development of Social transformation can popular and important even today. When we change our Economic policy after 1991, we even today talk about social welfares' model, where many programs and policy launched to uplift the social, economic condition of weaker and marginalised section of society.

4. Neo Liberal Theory:

The term embedded liberalism refers to the economic system that dominated the non-communist global economy from the end of World Ward-II to the 1970's.

David Harvey: argues that at the end of World War-II the primary objective was to develop an economic plan that would not lead to a repeat of the great depression during the 1930s. Harvey notes that under this new system free trade was regulated under a system of fixed exchange rates anchored by the US dollar's convertibility into gold at a fixed price. Fixed exchanges rates were incompatible with free flows of capital. Harvey argues that embedded liberalism led to the surge of economic prosperity that came to define the 1950s and 1960s.

Across much of the world, the work of John Maynard Keynes which sought to formulate the means by which governments could stabilise and fine tune free markets, became a high influential approach. Within the developing world, several developments-among them decolonisation a desire for national Independence and the destruction of pre-war global economy and the countries could not effectively. Industrialize under free market system encouraged economic policies that were influenced by communist, socialist and import substitution.

Thirty year of golden age of liberalism come to an end in 1960s. The 1970s were defined by an increased accumulation of capital, unemployment, inflation (or stagflation as it was dubbed), and a variety of fiscal crises. He notes that "the embedded liberalism that had delivered high rates of growth to at least the advanced capitalist countries after 1945 was clearly exhausted and no longer working. A number of theories concerning new system began to develop, which led to extensive debate between those who advocated" social democracy and central planning on the one hand and those concerned with liberating corporate and business with liberating corporate and business power and re-establishing market freedoms on the other. Harvey notes that, by 1980, the latter group had emerged as the leader, advocating and creating a global economic system that would become known as Neo-liberalism chronic economic crisis throughout the 1980s, and the coupes of the communist block at the end of 1980's helped foster political opposition to state interventionism in favour of free market reform policies. From the 1980's onward, a number of communist and socialist countries initiated various neo liberal market reform, such as socialist Federal Republic of Yugoslavia under the direction of Ante Marko Vic (United the Country's collapse in the early 1990's) and the people republic of China under the direction of Deng Xiaoping.

Changes occurred from the 1970's to the 1980's started off withy most of the democratic world government focused primarily in the primacy of economic individual rights, rules of law and roles of the governments in moderating relative free trade. It was almost considered national self determination at the time.

Stances of organised labour shifted when governments of Ronald Reagan and Margaret Thatcher took strong stances to breakdown trade barriers entirely to reduce government power; thus allowing the market to be more important. Therefore industries will increasingly shift globally with integrated knowledge boosting the economy.

Neo liberation in India: Changes and development in rural society

The policy of liberalisation, that India has been following since the late 1980's, have had a very significant impact on agriculture and rural society. The policy entails participation in the world trade organisation (WTO), which aims to bring about a more free international trading system and requires the opening up of Indian markets to imports. After decades of state supports and protected markets, Indian farmers have been exposed to competition from the global market. For Instance, we have all seen imported fruits and other food items on the shelves of our local stores-items that were not available a few years ago because of import barriers. Recently, India has also decided to import wheat, a controversial decision that reverses the earlier policy of self-reliance in food grains. And bring back bitter memories of dependency on American food grains in the early years after independence.

These are indicators of the process of globalisation of agriculture, or the incorporation of agriculture into the larger global market a process that has had direct effect on farmers and rural society. For instance, in some regions such as Punjab and Karnataka, Farmers enters into contract with multinationals companies (such as PepsiCo) to grow certain crops such as tomatoes and potatoes) which the companies then buy from them for processing or exports. In such 'contract farming systems, the company identifies the crop to be grown, provides the seeds and other inputs, as well as the know-how and often also the working capital. In return, the farmer is assured of a market because the company guarantees that it will purchase the produce at a pre-determined fixed price. Contract farming is very common now in the production of specialised items such as cut flowers, fruits such as grapes, figs and pomes grantees, cotton, and oilseeds. While contract farming appears to provide financial security to farmers, it can also lead to greater insecurity as farmers become dependent on these companies for their livelihoods. Contract farming of export-oriented products such as flowers and gher kins also means that agricultural land is diverted away from food grain production. Contract farming has sociological significance in that it discharges many people from the production process and makes their own indigenous knowledge of agriculture irrelevant. In addition, contract farming caters primarily to the production of elite items, and is because it usually requires high doses of fertilisers and pesticides it is often not ecologically sustainable.

Another and more widespread aspect of the globalisation of agriculture is the entry of multinationals into this sector as sellers of agricultural inputs such as seeds, pesticides and fertilisers. Over the last decades or so, the government has scaled down its agricultural development programmes, and agricultural extension agents have been replaced in the villages by agents of seed, fertiliser and pesticide companies. These agents are often the sole source of information for farmers about new seeds or cultivation practices and of course they have an interest in selling their products. This has led to the increased dependence of farmers on expensive fertilizers and pesticides which have reduced their profits, put many farmers into debt, and also created an ecological crisis in rural areas.

Which farmers in India for centuries have periodically faced distress due to drought, crop failures, or debt, the phenomenon of farmer suicide appears to be new. Sociologists have attempted to explain this phenomenon by looking at the structural and social changes that have been occurring in agriculture and agrarian society. Such suicides have become ' matrix events that is, a range of factors coalesce together to form an event. Many of the farmers who have committed suicides were marginal farmers who were attempting to increase their productivity, primarily by practicing green revolution methods. However, undertaking such production meant facing several risks, the cost of production has increased tremendously due to a decrease in agricultural subsidies, the market are not stable, and many farmers borrow heavily in order to invest in expensive inputs and improve their production. The loss of either the crop (due to spread of disease or pests excessive rain fall or drought) and in some case the lack of adequate support or market price, means that farmers are unable to bear the debt burden or sustain their families. Such distress is compounded by the changing culture in rural areas in which increased income are required for marriages, dowries, and to sustain new activities and expenses such as education and medical care, (Vasavi, 1999a).

Neo liberal Change and Development in Indian Industrial Sector

Since the 1990's, however, the government has followed a policy of liberalisation, privatisation and globalisation. Private companies, especially foreign firms, are encouraged to invest in sectors earlier reserved for the government, including telecom, civil aviation; power etc. licenses are no longer required to open industries. Foreign products are now easily available in Indian shops. As a result of liberalisation, many Indian companies have been bought over by, multinationals. At the same time some Indian companies are becoming multinational companies. An instance of the first is when, Parle drinks were bought by the Coco Cola. Parley's annual turnover was Rs.250

crores, while Coco Cola's advertising budget was Rs. 400 crores. This level of advertising has naturally increased the consumption of Coke across India replacing many traditional drinks. The government is trying to sell its share in several public sector companies, a process which is known as disinvestment. Many government workers are scared that after disinvestment, they will lose their jobs. In modern foods, which was set up by the government to make healthy bread available at cheap prices, and which was the first companies to be privatized, 60 per cent of the workers there forced to retire in the first five years. In global world, outsourcing is done; many companies are reducing the number of permanent employees and out sourcing their work to smaller companies or even to homes. For developing countries like India providing cheap labour because small companies have to compete for orders from the big companies, they keep wages low, and working conditions are often poor. It is more difficult for trade unions to organize in smaller firms. Almost all companies even government ones, now practices some form of outsourcing and contracting. But the trend is especially visible in the private sector. In India, a job security is biggest challenge in the society. Some economists debate that liberalisation and privatisation world wide appear to be associated with rising income inequality.

At the same time as secured employment in large industry is declining, the government is embarking on a policy of land acquisition for industry. These industries do not necessarily provide employment to the people of the surrounding areas, but they cause major pollution. Many farmers, especially adivasis (Tribal), dalits who constitute approximately 40 per cent of those displaced are protesting at the low rate of compensation and the fact that they will be forced to become casual labour living and working on the footpaths of India's big cities.

Naxalbari Movement

The Naxalite Movement (1967-71)

The term naxalite (from naxalbari) has continued to symbolise any assault upon the assumptions and institutions that hole up the established order. It has became part of the common speech all over India and it has found today a place in the modern vocabulary of world revolution.........obituaries of the movement have always been proved pre-mature in their pronouncements. If the movement was continued in one part of the India, and declared 'crushed' it soon erupted in another, sometimes a much unexpected corner of the country. Naxalbari was followed by Srikakulam, Debra Gopiballavpur; Debra Gopiballavpur by Birbhum-So it went on.

The agrarian society of West Bengal experienced a vehement Peasant up rise in May 1967 in the naxalbari thana of the Darjeeling district of the state. Indeed, the naxalbari movement marked the emerged of the new era in the history of peasant struggle in India.

Over the years though the naxalite movement had spread over to various parts of the country. Several areas of Andhra Pradesh and West Bengal had become the important strong holds of this movement in late sixties and early seventies. The naxalite movement was, however, not a sudden at burst of discontent of the peasantry in India. This arm struggle of the peasantry like all other peasant struggle in the history rather than a genesis on their increasing poverty, unemployment, landlessness, indebtness, malnutrition, ailments, illiteracy and various other forms of the social and economic insecurities.

The growing class inequalities and caste segregation in the agrarian society put added disadvantage to the issue of survival and subsistence of the poor peasantry of rural India.

Agrarian Social Structure in the pre-naxalite movement in West Bengal

India inherited a stratified, stagnant, disintegrated agrarian society from the Britishers. The attainment of Independence, according to the national commission on agricultural, created the essential pre-condition for restructuring of the rural economy with a view to putting it on the path of progress and accelerated development. The situation called for far reaching structural reforms in the agrarian system and basis changes in the socio-economic relations of production. To this end the government of India introduced an elaborated land reform program. The draft first five year plan recognised that:

> "The future of land ownership and cultivation constitute perhaps the most fundamental issue in the national development. Sooner

> or later, the principle and objectives of land reform cannot but influence policy in other sections as well form social aspect...... a policy for land may be considerate adequate in the measures in which now and in the coming years, it reduces disparities in wealth and income, eliminate exploitation provides security for tenants and workers and finally promises equality of status and opportunity to different section of the rural population (Govt. of India, 1952).

Thus to ensure economic development with social justice the main objectives of land reforms have been:

(a) Abolition of intermediaries between the state and the cultivators.

(b) Imposition of ceiling restriction on land holding.

(c) Distribution of surplus vested land among the rural poor.

(d) Conferment of ownership rights on the tillers of the land and

(e) Consolidation of land holding and increase in agricultural production.

As a part of this development strategy the community development program was launched in 1952 "to secure fullest development of the material and human resources on an area basis and thereby raise the rural community to higher levels of living with the active participation of and on the initiatives of the people themselves. (Govt. of India 1974).

However, all over India there had been a gap between the land reform, ideology and implementation of the same in this period. Neither the intended beneficiaries were made aware of these laws nor had a political will of the state to take popular initiative for the implementation of these laws. Even where he tenants were aware of their rights they were generally in too weak a position both socially and economically to insist on their right. (Panel on land reform committee, 1956). It was widely recognised that the lack of political will of the political parties in the state power was the key factor for the poor implementation of the land reform laws and the landlords in alliance with the police and local administration could easily deny the poor peasants their rights (Das Gupta, 1984).

All these, in general led to malafide land transfer and termination of the share croppers by the landowners. Though the intermediaries were apparently abolished the influence of the old landlords remained unquestioned in the rural power structure. This process of rural transformation made a large section of the rural poor the peasants, share-croppers, tenants, agricultural labourers and artisans downwardly mobile and poorer. The all India credit committee, in its report in 1968, pointed out the "Emergence of sharp polarisation between classes in two rural areas" (Govt. of India, 1968).

According to the National Sample Survey in 1953-54, 61.24 per cent marginal cultivators (owning less than 1.0 hectare) occupied only 6.23 per cent of the total cultivated area. While 9.77 medium (owning 4.05 to 10.12 hectare) and large cultivators (owning 10.13 hectare) controlled more than 65 per cent of lands. The small and semi-medium cultivators (owning 1.01 hectare to 4.05hectare) occupying 25.64 of the households had control over 28.49 per cent of cultivated area. This depicts the pattern of agrarian inequality as inherited by independent India from the British. Even after the two decades of implementations of the land reform laws there had not been any substantive change in the agrarian scenario. The 1971-72 figures showed the agrarian some of late 1960s of rural India whereby around 63 per cent of the marginal cultivators occupied less than 10 per cent of the cultivable lands. The upper strata of the hierarchy, represented by the medium and large cultivators, occupying around 10 per cent of the house-hold had control over 53.67 per cent of the cultivable lands. The small and semi medium cultivators occupying 27.43 per cent of the household occupied 36.60 per cent cultivable lands. The marginal increase of the percentage marginal, small/ medium cultivators and a marginal increase in the areas of their operational holding; marginal decline in the percentage of the medium and large cultivators with a decline in their area of operational holding to not really indicate any substantive change in the persisting. Inequalities in the agrarian setup. It is significant that the concentration ratio in the areas of insignificant holding for the marginal cultivators and land ownership for the big and medium cultivators has remained more or less the same over these years. Again malafied land transfer has played a crucial role in this change, rather than the real distribution for surplus vested land.

As indicated earlier decline in the landless household was caused not a much by the distribution of surplus vested land, but by the malalfide land transfer. The land owners effectively transferred some portions of their lands in the name of their landless family members or relatives to evade the ceiling restriction many of the landowner also resorted to self cultivation. This resulted into the decline in the percentage of leased out area over the years and consequent large scale eviction of the share croppers and tenants.

Table 1.1: Percentage Distribution of Household and Area Owned by Sizes of Landholding Class in Rural India in 1953-54, 1961-62, 1971-72

Size of Land holding	*House Hold/Area Owned*					
	1953-54	**1961-62**	**1971-72**	**1953-54**	**1961-62**	**1971-72**
Marginal less than (1.0 ha.)	61.24	60.06	62.62	06.23	07.59	09.76
Small (1.01-2.02 ha)	13.14	15.16	15.49	10.09	12.40	14.68
Semi Medium (2.03 to 4.04)	12.5	12.86	11.94	18.40	20.54	21.92
Medium (4.0ha to 10.12)	09.17	09.07	07.83	29.11	31.23	30.76
Large (10.13 ha to ha at)	03.60	02.85	02.12	36.17	28.24	22.91
(Source NSS)	1953-54	1961-62	1971-72			
Total	**100**	**100**	**100**	**100**	**100**	**100**

This uneven pattern of landholding severally affected the social relations of the agrarian society. The social lives of the share croppers, agricultural labourers, poor peasant, artisans were conditioned by:

- Vicious indebtedness with high rate of interest.

Table 1.2: Changes in the Landless and Leased out Households in 1953-54, 1961-62 and 1971-72

	1953-54	1961-62	1971-72
Landless household	23.09	11.68	09.64
Per cent of Area ceased out the total area owned.	11.42	04.43	05.77

Source: Sarvekshanam Oct. 1987.

- Primordial dependency on the big landowners for employment and livelihood security.
- Predominant use of conventional agricultural technology.
- Poor wage.
- Gender based wage variation as a rule.
- Low productivity of their land and labour.
- Illiteracy and lack of occupational mobility.

While such extreme situation of agrarian inequality was prevailing India faced the situation of rapidly worsening food shortage. In 1964 Indian imported as much as 10 million tones of food grains from U.S.A. The food problem had become so grave that many foreign experts predicted that millions would starve to death in India in 1970s. (Maheswari, 1985). All through 1966 and 1967, rumbling of discounted reverberated throughout the Indian country side reports poured into newspapers office of horrors of chronic malnutrition, deaths from starvation, self-annihilation by hungry and disparate peasant. In this scenario while the small peasants could hardly produce any marketable surplus, the big landlords often took advantage of general short supply of food grain surplus produce in the market gradually at a huge profit.

As against this backdrop, when the district committee of the CPI Darjeeling district, West Bengal radicalised their position and grave a call for arm struggle against the landless and the state a large section of the poor peasantry, especially from the scheduled caste and the scheduled tribes joined the movement.

Genesis of Naxalite Movement and its First Phase:

In the truncated Bengal that remained as India's share after independence, the congress party government that came to power under the Chief Minister ship of Dr Bidhan Chandra Roy initiated radical land reform legislation. The West Bengal Estate acquisition Act (1953) was intended to abolish the Zamindari and other intermediary systems and the West Bengal land reform Act (1955) to put a ceiling on landholding, to allow 60 per cent of the produced share to the share croppers and to put restriction on the eviction of share croppers except for self-cultivation by the land owners. Often, however, these far reaching proposals merely remained in the statute books. Initially, the tenants were either unaware of the new legislation or were too weak both economically and socially to insist on their rights. (Report of the panel on the land reform committee 1956). There was widespread malafide land transfer resulting in the eviction of share croppers, their lapse into the category of agricultural labourers, and loss of tenure ship and employment security to the agrarian down trodden. It was also obvious that the political will to implement the egalitarian legislation was lacking (Ghosh and Dutta, 1977) 164 Bardhan and Rudra 1980; 1945, Das Gupta, 1984).

According to the report of the National sample survey of 1954-55, which was unaffected by the ceiling restriction, 20.5 per cent of the households were landless 65.5 per cent of the households had land less than 5 acres of land and occupied only 34.5 per cent of the total land; whereas 5.4 per cent households occupied as much as 40 per cent of the total land. Share croppers constituted 16 per cent of the rural house holds. In 1961-62, the proportion of landless households dropped significantly to 12.6 per cent, while share cropper households came down to 2.9 per cent households owning more than 10 acres of land came down to 4.1 per cent and the areas they owned also came down to 27.7 per cent. Again in 1971-72, the proportion of landless and sharecropper house holds came down to 10.8 and 2 per cent respectively, while the percentage of households owning more than 10 acres of land was reduced to 2.5 acres and they occupied only 8.9 per cent of the total land. The proportion of households owning less than 2.50 acres of land and owning between 2.50 to 9.90 acre changed from 52.9 and 21.2 per cent, respectively, in 1954-55 to 66.8 and 19.9 per cent respectively in 1971-72 significantly enough, in the period under review their area of land holding also had increased from 15.8 to 27.7 per cent and from 44.2 to 53.4 per cent, respectively.

The period between 1947 and 1967 was marked by deteriorating socio-economic status of the lowest section of the agrarian hierarchy of West Bengal though apparently the extent of the landlessness had decreased and the proportion of small and medium cultivators had increased. The upper strata still managed to hold on their socio-economic privileges.

The difficulty posed by the abolition of the intermediary system was skirted by the big landowners (The old intermediaries and their allied) by resorting to malafide land transfer in the names of family members and relatives. In the absence of adequate legal protection sharecropper still had to put up with eviction, low share in the crops they had raised, low wages (in the case of agricultural labourers) and increasing indebtedness. Pressure on land had mean-while increased enormously due to sluggish industrial development, bleak alternative sources of employment for the rural people, and increasing immigration from East Pakistan (now Bangladesh). Census data show that in 1961, of the total main workers 38.5 per cent were cultivators and 15.30 per cent were agricultural labourers, while in 1971, the percentage of cultivators came down to 32 per cent and that of agricultural labourers rose sharply to 26 per cent (census of India, 1961, 1971) obviously a rapid shift was taking place, indicating a heightening of disparities in the rural society. While the economic condition of the poor peasantry was deteriorating, the political happenings of West Bengal a new turn. In 1964, there was a split in the communist party of India (CPI) leading to the formation of the Communist party of India (Marxist) CPI (M), by the breakaway group. In February 1967 the fourth general election brought the 20 years of unbroken rule by the congress party to an end, and an alliance of 14 political parties came to power with the two communist parties CPI and CPI (M) as its constituents.

In late May, 1967 the vehement peasant struggle and armed uprising in the naxalbari thana of Darjeeling district marked the emergence of a new era in peasant movement in West Bengal. The 'naxalbari movement' initially was launched under the Darjeeling district committee of the CPI (M) under the broad Marxist Leninist Maoist ideological framework and opted for mass struggle and seizure of power by the guerilla war fare. The uprising underwent a long-drawn-out struggle between the force organised by the naxalites and the Zamindar police combine. The naxalite leadership provided a forum to form the all India co-ordination committee of communist revolutionaries in November, 1967, and later in mid 1969 the communist party of India (Marxist Leninist) (CPI (M-L)) formed.

The naxalite movement derives its name from a small village naxalbari on the tri-junction of India, Nepal and what was then East Pakistan, where tribal took up arms against the oppression of the landlords in 1967. The movement spread like wildfire to different parts of country. Some of the finest brains and the cream of India's youth in certain area left their homes and colleges to chase the dream of a new world, a new social order, two decades had passed since the dawn of independence and yet large segments of the Indian population peasants, workers and tribal continued to suffer the worst forms of exploitation. The peaceful political process it was felt would not be able to bring about the necessary change because vested interests controlled the levers of power, regulated the wheels of Industry and had a feudal stranglehold over the predominantly agrarian economy. An armed struggle was the only way out, they thought.

The Santhals tribes of naxalbari, armed with bows and arrows forcibly occupied the land of the Kulaks and ploughed them to establish their ownership. Demonstrations were organised against persons holding paddy in their godowns. In many cases, the entire stocks were lifted and disturbed or sold locally at cheaper rates. There were violent clashes between March and May 1967, nearly a hundred incidents were reported to the police. The situation progressively deteriorated. After some dithering, the West Bengal Government ordered the police to take action. The movement was squashed, but "naxalbari exploded many a myth".

The naxalite movement, drawing inspiration from the Maoist Ideology, had a meteoric phase for about two years from the formation of the party till the end of June, 1971. The ripples starting from naxalbari spread in ever widening circles to practically all parts of the country. The only areas which remained untouched were the north-eastern states and the union territories of Goa, Pondicherry, and Andaman and Nicobar Islands. The dominant Strand of the movement was the annihilation of class enemies. It was viewed as a "higher form of class struggle and the beginning of guerilla war". Charu's assessment was that "every corner of India is like a volcano" about to erupt, that "there is the possibility of a tremendous upsurge in India", and he therefore called upon the cadres to start as many points of armed struggle as possible. "Expand any where and every where was his message. Such expansion was particularly noticeable in Srikakulam in Andhra Pradesh, Debra-Gopiballavpuri in West Bengal, Mushahari in Bihar and Palia in Lakhimpur district of U.P.

The Naxalite violence was at a peak from about the middle of 1970 to the middle of 1971. It is estimated that there were a total of about 4,000 incidents in the country from the middle of the 1970 to the middle of 1971. The bulk of these were from West Bengal (3,500) followed by Bihar (220) and Andhra Pradesh (70).

The political parties realised the emergence of a new force. The government became conscious of a new threat not only to law and order but to the very existence of the democratic structure of the country.

The Decline

The Government of India organised Joint Operation by the army and the police in the bordering districts of "West Bengal, Bihar and Odisha which were particularly affected by naxalite depredations. The operations were undertaken from July 1 to August 15, 1971 and were code-named operation Steeplechase. The broad Strategy of the security forces was to surround as large area as possible and seals the routes of entry and exit. The army formed the outer cordon and the CRPF the inner ring. The local police, which was generally accompanied by a magistrate, carried out thorough search of the area. Suspected naxalites were arrested, illicit weapons, ammunition and explosives seized. Wherever possible, simultaneous action was taken in the neighbouring area also so that the naxalite sneaking out were caught while attempting to escape. These operations covered Midnapur, Purulia, Burdwan and Birbhum districts of West Bengal; Singhbhum, Dhanbad and Santhal Parganas of Bihar and Mayurbhanj of Odisha.

The operation achieved the desired results, though not to the extent anticipated by the administration. The organisational apparatus of the naxalites in the aforesaid districts was thrown out of gear and the party activists fled from their known hideouts to other places in search of safety, violence registered a drop. Incidents of arms-snatching fell down. Above all, it restored the confidence of the people in the strength of the administration. Charu-mazumdar was also arrested by the Calcutta police detectives on July 16, 1972. A few days later, he died. Charu's death marked the end of a phase of naxalite movement. The period following his death witnessed red division and fragmentations in the movement.

The Revival: Second Phase

The formation of people's war group in Andhra Pradesh subsequently in 1980 under the leadership of Kondapalli Settharamaih gave a new lease of life to the movement. The PWG's programme included:

- Redistribution of land
- enforcing payment of minimum wages to the farm labour
- imposing taxes and penalties
- holding people's court
- destroying government property
- kidnapping government functionaries
- attacking policemen
- Enforcing a social code.

The PWG is believed to have redistributed nearly half a million acres of land across Andhra Pradesh. Its activists also insisted on a hike in the daily minimum wages and the annual fee for Jeetagadu (year long labour). The poorer sections found that what the politicians had been talking about and the government promising year after year could be translated into a reality only with the intervention of naxalites. Gora Kala doras (lord of the Bushes) is now the naxalites came to be known in the interior areas. Kidnapping to secure the release of its own cadres was frequently resorted to by the PWG activists. The cause cerebra was the kidnapping of six IAS officers including a principal secretary of the state government and collector of East Godavari District on December, 27, 1987 while they were returning from a tribal welfare meeting Pulimatu in the district. The State Government decided to play safe and released the eight naxalites in Rajamundary Jail. The PWG got tremendous propaganda mileage out of the incident.

The revolutionary writers of the Jana Natya Mandali, the cultural front of the PWG, greatly helped in preparing the environment in which the naxalite ideology found ready acceptance. Its moving spirit was Gummadi Vittal Rao, better known as Gaddar. He was a Balladeer who fought the establishment with the power of his songs. The people's war group gradually spread its organisational network to the coastal and Rayal Seema districts in the state. It extended its tentacles to the adjoining area of Maharashtra, Madhya Pradesh and Odisha and made a dent even in the bordering districts of Karnataka and certain pockets of Tamil Nadu.

The Andhra Pradesh government banned the PWG and its six frontal organisation in 1992. At the same time, the state police, assisted by the central para military forces, under took well organised counter insurgency operations. As a result, 248 naxalites were liquidated and 3,434 activists were apprehended in 1992. The arrest of Kondapally Seetharamaih and other important leaders meant further setback to the PWG. There was demoralisation among the ranks and about 8,500 Naxals surrendered before the authorities.

In Bihar, the Maoist communist centre, another major naxalite formation, perpetrated acts of violence. Its organisational network extended to most of the central Bihar districts. During the six year period from 1987 to 1992, there were eight major incidents in Gaya, Chatra and Aurangabad districts in which 42 Rajputs, 40 Bhumihars, 5 Muslims, 1 BJP M.P. and 3 Policemen's among others were killed what began as a fight for social and economic justice actually degenerated into a caste conflict with a veneer of class struggle. The MCC ran virtually a parallel judicial system in certain pockets. These were described as Janadalat or people's court where they would even shorten an accused by six inches-beheads him, in other words.

Present Position: Third Phase:

The present phase-we could also call it the third phase of the movement commenced with the holding of the ninth congress of the people's war group in 2001. When it was decided to militarize the armed component of the party by giving more sophisticated weapons to the people's Guerilla Army. The total number of incidents of violence and Resultant deaths in the country during the last five years has been as follows:

Year	Total Incidents	Deaths
2001	1,208	564
2002	1,465	482
2003	1,597	515
2004	1,533	566
2005	1,594	699

The Ministry of Home affairs, government of India, admits the spread of naxalite movement to 76 districts in 9 states of the Union, namely, Andhra Pradesh, Bihar, Madhya Pradesh, Maharashtra, Odisha, Chhattisgarh, Jharkhand, Uttar Pradesh and West Bengal. It further concedes that the people's war and the MCCI are trying to increase their influence and operations in some parts of the states of Tamil Nadu, Karnataka and Kerala and also in some new areas of the states already affected.

The Disturbing Features of the Movement are:

- Spread over a large geographical area.
- Increase in potential for violence.
- Unification of PW and MCCI.
- Plan to have a Red corridor.
- Nexus with N.E. Insurgents and Nepalese Maoists.

The Government of India has already expressed concern over the spread of the naxalite movement over a huge geographical area. The Prime Minister has described naxalite movement as the single biggest threat to the internal security of the country.

According to the institute for conflict management, the movement has actually spread over 165 districts in 14 states and that the home ministry's assessment in this regard is an understatement. The naxals potential for violence has increased substantially with their acquisition of sophisticated weapons and expertise in the use of improvised explosive devices (IEDs.) They are said to be in possession of at least 6,500 regular weapons including AK 47 rifles and SLR's.

The movement got a tremendous boost when its two major components, the people war (PW) and the Maoist communist centre of India (MCCI) decided to merge on March 21, 2004 only. The unified party was called the Communist Party of India (Maoist). The merger, apart from augmenting the support base of the movement, has given it the character of a pan Indian revolutionary group. The naxals' plan to have a compact revolutionary zone stretching from Indo Nepal border to the Dandakaranya region is likely to get a fillip with the unification of their ranks.

The naxalite groups 'Nexus with the other extremist organisations has added to the complexity of the problem, there are indications that the PWG cadres received training in the handling of weapons and IEDs from some ex LTTE cadres. They have also some understanding; with the National Socialist Council of Nagaland (I-M) for supporting each other's cause. Some batches of CPML-party Unity also appear to have received arms training under the guidance of United Liberation Front of Assam. The Communist Party of India (Maoist) has also worked out a strategic alliance with the communist party of Nepal (Maoist).

Situation in States

Andhra Pradesh: Andhra Pradesh has gradually emerged as the epicenter of the lift wing extremism in the country. The PWG set up a people's Guerilla Army in December, 2000, "to strengthen the political power of the people and to defeat the efforts of the state and the Central Government to check the (revolutionary) movement.

The most audacious attack by the PWG took place on October 1, 2003, when they tried to assassinate the Chief Minister of Andhra Pradesh, N. Chandra Babu Naidu, on a forest road between Tirupati and Tirumala in Chitoor district while he was proceeding to attend the Brahmotsavam celebrations. Claymore Wines hit the car of the Chief Minister; the bulletproof armour over the car however saved him. Four other including the state's information technology minister, B.Gopalakrishna Reddy, sustained serious injuries. The PW claimed responsibility for the attack, saying that it was "to eliminate a person who has been perpetuating state sponsored violence."

Peace talks were held between the people's war group and the state government of Andhra Pradesh during June-July 2002 at the initiatives of 'committee' of concerned citizens'. Three rounds of talks were held but unfortunately there was no agreement on the substantive issue. The PWG called off the talk in July 2002 in protest against the allegedly killing of their cadres in 'Fake encounters'. Second rounds of peace talk were held from October 15 to 18, 2004 at Hyderabad but there were no fruitful discussions. The government took strong exception to the naxals moving about with arms in towns and cities. The naxalites annihilation of Narsi Reddy, Congress MLA and eight others in a major attack on August 15, 2005 in Mehboob Nagar proved to be the proverbial last straw. The peace process ended abruptly and government reimposed the ban on the communist party of India (Maoist) and its front organisations.

Bihar and Jharkhand: The naxalite movement in Bihar in Bogged down in caste based Jealousies and rivalries. On January 5, 2005, the naxalites killed the superintendent of police; Munger by blowing up his Jeep. Six other policemen were also killed. Lately the Maoist Communist Centre has shifted its focus to the Jharkhand region, which was carved out of Bihar on November 15, 2000. The naxalites are said to be active in 15 out of the 22 districts of Jharkhand. They have been particularly targeting the police and the paramilitary personnel.

Madhya Pradesh and Chattisgarh: In Madhya Pradesh, following the bifurcation of the state in November 2000, naxalite violence is now confined to Balalghat, Mandla, Dindori, and Sidhi districts only, The Madhya Pradesh Transport Minister Lakhiram Kavre, was annihilated on December 15, 1999 in retaliation to the killing of four top PWG leaders.

In Chhattisgarh, Naxalite violence is concentrated mainly in the Bastar Area and in Rajnandgaon, Jashpur and Sarguja districts. The state government has been trying to mobilise the tribal's through 'Salwa Judum' (Peace Mission). This is being vehemently opposed by the Naxalites, and they have been recklessly killing the Judum activists. The latest carnage took place on July, 16, 2006 when Maoist Slaughtered 27 tribal's in a relief camp in Dantewada district.

West Bengal: Naxalite violence in West Bengal is at a low pitch compared to the other states. This is to be attributed to the success of operation Baraga under which sharecroppers were registered and given permanent and inheritable rights on cultivation of their plots covering a total area of 11 Lac acres. Besides, 1.37 lac acres of ceiling surplus and benami lands were acquired by the state government and distributed among 25 lac landless and marginal cultivators. The land reforms have seen the emergence of a new class loosely termed 'rural rich' and weakened the social and political power enjoyed by the landlords in the country side. There is some Naxalite activity nevertheless in Midnapur, Bankura and Purulia district.

Recent year, issue of SEZ in Singur, Nandi gram and naxalite strong hold in Jangalmahal areas in West Bengal, again provided strong ground for naxalite to increase their stronghold in the West Bengal.

Odisha: Odisha witnessed a qualitative increase in naxalite violence during 2000 and 2001. The MCC has established its presence in the northern districts while the PWG has consolidated its hold over the southern districts. The formation of Andhra-Odisha border special zonal committee gave fillip to left wing extremism in the state, recent year government policies and its result in the form of displacement of people specially tribal and role of private player like

POSCO and Vedanta group provide ground to mobilised people by the naxalite groups against government machinery and state actors.

Maharashtra: Gadchiroli is particularly affected, though there are incident in Bhandara, chandrapur, Gondia and Nanded district. In 2009-2010 naxalite killed 28 policemen in Maharashtra. Specially adjoining areas of Odisha and Chhattisgarh states.

Karnataka: In Karnataka, naxalites have been active in the Kudremukh area following government move to evict the tribal's from the forests. On February 11, 2005, naxalites killed 6 policemen of the Karnataka state reserve police in Tumkur district.

Uttar Pradesh: Uttar Pradesh has witnessed stirrings of naxalite activities in the eastern belt in Sonbhadra, Gorakhpur, Ghazipur, Ballia, Chandauli and Mirzapur districts. On November 20, 2004 naxalites blew up a police jeep in the forests of Chandauli with a land mine killing of 13 PAC and 4 police personnel's.

The factors which gave rise to naxalism in the country are, unfortunately, very much present day also. The extent of poverty in the country continues to be Abysmal land reforms remain a neglected area. Unemployment figures are high, forest law and displacement of people in the name of development is another issue. Tribals have been getting a raw deal. Governance, particularly in remote areas, is poor.

Governments have prepared a comprehensive 14 point plan to deal with the problem. There is special emphasis on the socio-economic development of the affected areas, and the state governments have been asked to ensure speedy implementation of land reforms. Infrastructure is being developed and there are plans to provide employment to the youth in the remote, backward areas. The National Tribal Policy seeks to protect the rights of tribal's. How far these measures produce the intended results, however, remains to be seen.

Naxal Strategy and Methods of Action:

1. Organisational structure phase.
2. Guerilla warfare phase.
3. The mobile warfare phase.

I. Organisational Phase: In this, Maoist using Intellectual as well as Military cadres both. Intellectual mobilised the masses; weaker and marginalised section of society through debate and discussion, university like Hyderabad, Jawaharlal Nehru, and Banaras Hindu University is the centre of this movement, Maoist cadres on other side, killed the rich landlord, bureaucrats, moneylender and gain support from weaker section of society.

In this revolutionary strategy, headed by committed cadres, these units in doctrinate people considered impressionable. The propaganda chiefly revolves around administrative lapses, misdeeds by political party workers and the exploitative structures in the society.

II. Guerilla Warfare Phase: This phase puts the revolutionaries and the 'enemy' (state) on an equal footing in the fight for control over a particular area. During this phase, the main line of action is to attack the 'enemy', targeting among others police patrols teams or a person identified as a 'class enemy'.

In those areas, which passed through the organisation phase of the revolution in the late 1980s or early 1990s, the Maoist unit is already running parallel administration at the village level-the gram rajah Committee (GRC's), and village defence Committee (VDCs). Till this stage, the naxalites had confined their activity to remote villages, but as their influence spreads, semi-forest areas and plains are also being covered. A well- defined military structure would have already been put in place with Local Guerilla Squads (LGSs) and area committees working in tandem with the GRC's and VDCs.

In most of these villages, the Maoists have succeeded in using the ultimate weapon, terror, applying psychological pressure until all resistance is dissipated. A series of killings of political activists, 'Police informants' and ambushes on police patrols, attacks on police stations, elimination of 'signal targets' have created a situation where unrest reigns supreme. And, to the great advantage of the Maoists is the law enforcement agencies' total inability to control the violence and extend even a modicum of security to the populace. The only way out for the people is to co-operate with the naxalites, especially when given the carrot and stick option of persuasion and intimidation.

III. The Mobile Warfare Phase: This phase, according to the Maoist strategy, begins in areas where the revolutionaries had defeated the state forces, established complete control and had demarcated its area.

The recent year incidence in which C.R.P.F personnel and police men killed in different parts of country , specially Chhattisgarh, Odisha, Uttar Pradesh, Maharashtra and Jharkhand states shows that they change their strategy and attacking methods and created more trouble and violence in the states.

Recently new methods adopted by naxallite

(I) Hijacking of Train: New Face of Red Terror: Recently, naxalite attack the railway department properties, many incident such as stoppage of Bhubaneswar-New Delhi Rajdhani train, on 27 October 2009, attack on Muzaffapur Narkatiyaganj Railway track, Gyaneshwari Express incident which destination station between Howrah and Mumbai are the recent years target by the Maoist, this shows that their ideological movement is change it track of Mao-Lenin-Marx ideology and they totally believed in gaining political power by terrorizing common people and state machinery.

(II) C.R.Z to SEZ: In August 2001, meeting held between the leaders of Indian and Nepali Maoist party in Siliguri district of West Bengal. naxalite have designs of establishing a compact Revolutionary Zone (CRZ) starting from Nepal and going through Bihar, Jharkhand, Chhattisgarh and Andhra Pradesh. According to them, they have already been able to achieve 75 per cent of this plan when these naxalite engaged in expansion of their area, same time government of India bring New Economic Policy of Special Economic Zone (SEZ)- in which Government gives concession and other facilities for development, but SEZ created problem in Singur, Nandi gram, Kalinga nagar areas, and it provided ground to the naxalite and they start mobilising people against government policies and programmes.

In many tribal areas, especially in Chhattisgarh and Odisha, displacement of local people also created strong ground against government and big private player. Naxalite mobilised on the issue of development and displacement to the local peoples specially marginalised section of society.

(III) Urban Area: New Naxal Strategy: Earlier we thought and considered that naxalites have strong hold and base in rural and backward areas but recent year incident and arrest of leader like Kobad Gandhi on Sep, 2009 shows that their base is also gaining strength in urban areas.

Last year killing of Maoist Azad and Pandey by Hyderabad Police and support of intellectual in recent years shows that naxalite gained strong bases in urban areas and it created more problem in coming years.

(IV) Child Cadets: Mostly Children of 13 years to 16 years are part of naxalite movement today, because they are easy target to mobilised, rural poverty and economic disparity in backward areas; motivate children to join Maoist movement. Naxalite formed Children Liberation Army (CLA) they mostly used as spy in the respective areas, provided them arms training also.

(V) Liberated Area: According to government report 55 districts of country are under this category where naxalite have strong hold and they run parallel government. This area where tribal population mostly lived supports the naxalite.

(VI) Relation with Other Extremist Outfit: Naxalite also have relationship with Chinese and Nepali Communist Party cadres and they also getting training from L.T.T.E, Bodo, ULFA and other separatist organisations, shows that their ideology changes from socio-economic equality demands to political power gained in the recent years and they also acted as anti state actor today.

(VII) Cyber Warfare: They used, at possible extent; make use of computers and the internet to further the military objective of the revolution.

(VIII) Central Intelligence: Since, the enemy is centred in the big cities, it is very important that our party develops a network to obtain and analyse political and military intelligence at higher level. Besides human intelligence we can make use of the internet and other modern electronic means for gathering information by entering the enemies' networks. For this it is necessary to allocate separate responsibilities.

Urban party organisation may provide contact and individual for this work however, once they are assigned to this work they do not maintain any links with the local organisation. Such networks are led and directed by the highest bodies of the party.

(IX) United Front against Hindu Fascist Forces: An important call of the 9th Congress is, to build a broad united front of all secular forces and persecuted religious minorities, such as Muslims, Sikhs, and Christians against the Hindu fascist's forces. To gain support of minorities and secular forces, they adopted this new strategy.

(X) Front against Globalisation, Liberalisation and Privatisation: The line of action for building anti-globalisation fronts should rely primarily on the working class, while rallying around all other sections in the struggle against the imperialist's policies.

Other classes and sections of importance we should try to draw into the anti globalisation front are the peasant's organisations and the farmers' bodies, slum bodies, student organisation, intellectuals, writers and cultural activists, pro-people environmental groups, teachers and other middle class employees associations etc..

The scope of the anti-globalisation movement is so large that it includes practically all classes who are part of the strategic united front.

Relationship between social transformation and poverty in naxal affected areas

It is not surprising that in the countries of third world, including India, which is yet in the process of social transformation from primary sector economy to secondary and tertiary sector economy. Development and social transformation is a big issue, especially in rural areas of naxal affected states.

Poverty, unemployment, migration, bonded labour, starvation death, exploitation of weaker section; socio-economic disparities are the main issue and problem which cannot be solved even after attaining independence 64 years ago. As a result, the problem of naxalism, even today after completing 45 years of Journey still today emerged as the biggest internal security problem, presently, it is not socio-economic ideology based movement but it change it paradigm and it become weapon in the hand of Maoist who used it time by time to gain political power and run parallel government and bargaining with Indian government on many issues.

Measures of State Intervention and Rural Transformation

Rural transformation has been one of the major objectives of development planning in India. The concept of 'Rural Transformation' has been interpreted in two ways. In a narrow sense, it refers to social change occur in rural areas through the development of activities based mainly in the rural areas such as agriculture, animal husbandry, village crafts and industries, rural infrastructure, technology, communications and innovations etc. The broader view of rural transformation is not only large in scope and coverage but also with respect to its approach to the problem. Its focus is directly on the well being of the people in rural areas. In broader sense it includes changes in social, political, economic, cultural, technological and structural aspects with a view to improving the quality of life of the rural people. Rural transformation is a multi-dimensional concept involving a multi-disciplinary approach the concept has been defined in various ways. Desai (1988) defined it as "an approach which, by better utilisation of local resources and by creating infrastructural facilities for economic and social development aims at improving the quality of life of the rural population, especially the rural poor, by creation of expanded employment and income opportunities for them."

Maheswari (1985): considers rural transformation as "Interminable process to bring about improvement in the economic and social life of the rural poor.

Cropp (1972): Also defined "as a process which aims at improving the well being and self realisation of people living outside the urbanised areas through collective efforts.

Harris (1986): views it as policy and process which has emerged as a distinct field of research since the inception of new strategy for development planning by the World Bank and U.N. agencies.

In all such expressions the term rural transformation refers to distinct state interventions in the economics of underdeveloped countries and one which is at once broader and more specific than agricultural development. The expression rural transformation may also be used, however, to refer to processes of change in rural societies, not all of which involve action by governments. In this case the activity of rural development, a form of state intervention must be considered simply as one of the forces concerned-although it is one which has become of increasing importance.

There is a long tradition of thought which conceptualizes the 'state as existing 'outside of' or 'above society', and in the line of this tradition there are good many writers who treat the activity of rural transformation as if it were conducted by the state in the interest of society as a whole. Nevertheless, the reality is not always alike some recent studies (such as Lipton, 1977; Epstein, 1978', Dhanagare, 1988, Tiwary, 1994 among others). It reveals that rural development programmes implemented by the state serve the interests of some groups and class and not others, and that their real effects may be very different from what is claimed for them or from the rhetoric surrounding them. It is in this contradictory context that an attempt is made here to evaluate the state interventions in rural development programmes, in India. Our objectives are to analyze whether the state's measures of rural development have been successful enough to bring about rural transformation? To what extent they have reduced inequalities in income, employment, access to public goods and services and how much potential they are in alleviation of poverty in rural society and bring social transformation in naxal affected areas, especially in Sonbhadra district of eastern Uttar Pradesh.

Rural Development Measures

After getting independence India attempted to eliminate the colonial legacy of underdevelopment and social backwardness by adopting various measures to reshape the economy, social structure and cultural life. In newly emerged independent states have been trying to follow a path of rural development. Under the rubric of this path of rural development, measures of various types have been adopted by state in India.

After independence, state embarked upon general development programmes (GDPs) of nation building such as creation of infrastructure, development of basic and heavy industries, growth of modern-agriculture, power and transport, etc. The rural development measures included:-

1. Laws in the form of land reforms, enforcing zamindari abolition, ceilings, tenancy reforms, land redistribution; co-operatives; scale down of debts', consolidation and reconstitution of extremely fragmented and subdivided units of land;
2. Steps to provide irrigation and power facilities standardisation of weights and measures building up of a network of transport and communication facilities.
3. Provision of necessary inputs in the form of seeds, fertilisers, improved, agricultural implements, pesticides and insecticides as well as a framework of research and experimental centres to improve the productivity of agriculture and augment production.

Further, with a view of generating an adequate framework for rural development, special development programmes (SDPs) were launched by state in different phases. In the Initial phase, the SDPS created an infrastructure of administrative and social institutions which took the form of community development programmes (CDPs) national extension service (NES), panchayati raj institutions (PRIs) and network of administrative offices starting at the bottom from Gramsevaks to Sarpanchs, block development officers to ministry in the states and the centre. A large scale network of educational and health institution were also inaugurated.

The GDPs and SDPs of the era were based on state's assumption that these measures would help in rural reconstruction. It was assured that these programmes of rural development would provide the initial stimulus and the people will willingly and actively co-operate in these programmes. The rural development, bureaucracy created under CDPs and PRIs will be development oriented and cater to the needs of the poor masses. It was also assumed that the benefits of these programmes will percolate down to the rural poor. All these assumptions proved to be wrong in the coming years. The programmes were also ambitions both in terms of financial outlays and targets and expectations of the people, because of these, all our hopes were belied and it generated general apathy, resistance and unrest among the rural poor.

This resulted in the need of evolving a new policy for containing and repressing the poor but also giving a small section out of them some relief as well as generating a sense of participation in overall rural development. Hence, the kits of measures were elaborated. The measures, which were worked out to be included in the new policy of rural development have been enumerated by Desai (1985, 7-8) as follows:

1. More zealous implementation of land reform and ceiling measures;
2. Concerned efforts to distribute the surplus land which was not adequately distributed;
3. Elimination of the loopholes in the land records to avoid malpractices pursued by influential groups in rural area;
4. Effort to place the financial allocation to the middle and poor farmers to enable them to take profitable production.
5. Greater attention on organizing farming and other varieties of cooperatives.
6. Crash scheme for rural employment.
7. Small farmer's development agencies to make them available the inputs, including credit, for utilizing the technology and practicing intensive agriculture.
8. Programmes for marginal farmers and agricultural labourers to enable them gainful participation in production.
9. Drought prone area programme for chronically drought affected areas.

Table-1.3: Various Development Programes Undertaken Since Independence

Sl.No.	*Programme/Plan/Institution*	*Year of Beginning*	*Objectives/Description*
1.	Community Development Programme (CDP)	1952	Overall development of rural areas with people's participation.
2.	Khadi and village industries commission (KVIC)	1957	This programme is launched for providing income generation.
3.	Panchayati Raj Institutions (PRI)	1959	Launched to Increased the participation of people at grass root level democracy.
4.	Intensive agriculture development programme (IADP)	1960-61	To provide loan, seeds, fertilizer tool to the farmers.
5.	Intensive agriculture area programme (IAAP)	1964-65	To develop the special harvests.
6.	High yielding variety programme (HYVP)	1966-67	To increase productivity of food grains by adopting latest varieties of inputs for crops.
7	Green Revolution	1966-67	To increased the food grains, especially wheat production.
8.	Nationalisation of 14 Banks	July 1969	To provide loans for agriculture, rural development and other priority sectors.
9.	Rural electrification corporation	July 1969	Electrification in rural areas.
10.	Scheme of discriminatory interest rate	April 1972	To provide loan to the weaker sections of the society at a concessional interest rate of 4 per cent
11.	Drought prone area programme (DPAP)	1973	To try an expedient for protection from drought by achieving environmental balance and by developing the ground water.
12.	Crash scheme for Rural employment (CSRE)	1972-73	For rural employment.
13.	Command area development programme (CADP)	1974-75	To ensure better and rapid utilisation of irrigation capacities of medium and large projects.

(Contd...)

14.	Twenty point programme (TPP)	1975	Poverty era diction and raising the standard of living.
15.	National Institution of Rural Development	1977	Training, Investigation and advisory organisation for rural development
16.	Desert Development Programme (DDP)	1977-78	For controlling the desert expansion and maintaining environmental balance.
17.	Food for work programme	1977-78	Providing food grains to labour for the works of development.
18.	Training rural youth for self-employment (TRYSEM)	August, 15,1979	Programme of training rural youth for self employment.
19.	Integrated rural development programme (IRDP)	October,2,1980	All round development of the rural poor through a programme of asset endowment for self-employment.
20.	Development of women and children in rural areas (DWCRA)	September 1982	To provide suitable opportunities of self employment to the women belonging to the rural families who are living below the poverty line
21.	Rural landless employment guarantee programme (RLEGP)	August,15,1983	For providing employment to landless farmers and labourers.
22.	Council for advancement of people's action and rural technology (CAPART)	Sep.1, 1986	To provide assistance for rural prosperity.
23.	Jawahar Rozgar Yojana	April, 1989	For providing employment to rural unemployed.
24.	Employment assurance scheme (EAS)	Oct.,2, 1993	To provide employment of at least 100 days in a year in villages.
25.	National social assistance programme	1995	To assist people living below the poverty line.
26.	Annapurna Yojana	March, 1999	To provide 10kg. food grains to senior citizen (who did not get pension).
27.	Swarna Jayanti Gram Swarozgar Yojana	April,1999	For eliminating rural poverty and unemployment and promoting self-employment.

(Contd...)

28.	Antyodaya Anna Yojana	Dec. 25,2000	To provide food security to poor.
29.	National food for work programme	Nov.14,2004	Programme to intensify the generation of supplementary wage employment
30.	Janani Suraksha Yojana	April, 14,2005	Providing care to expectant mothers.
31.	Bharat Nirman programme	Dec.,162005	Development of rural infrastructure including six components: Irrigation, water supply, housing road, telephone and electricity.
32.	National rural employment guarantee scheme (MNREGA)	Feb., 2,2006	To provide at least 100 days wage employment in rural area.

10. Special schemes of non-agricultural nature like afforestation, minor irrigation, soil and water conservation, road building, drainage, embankments etc.
11. Area development schemes or special area planning such as DPAP, DADP, CADP, HADP, TADP.
12. Employment oriented schemes such as TRYSEM, NREP, JRY, MNREGA etc.
13. Education and welfare oriented schemes like FTE, CPWPC, ICDS, and NVY etc.
14. Bringing together different programmes under a scheme of integrated rural development.

The various programmes of rural development launched by the state from time to time broadly can be categorised into four main groups on the basis of (a) Income generation (b) Employment orientation (c) education and welfare, and (d) Area development. The table reveals the major rural development programmes undertaken so far in different plan periods since independence.

Approaches to Rural Development

The approaches to rural development are linked to the state's strategy of rural development in the best possible direction. The approaches which have been experimented and adopted in rural India could be enumerated as under:

Multipurpose Approaches

The community development programmes started in 1952, aimed at developing to the fullest extent, the material and human resources of an area through the co-operative and multipurpose efforts of the people and the active help of the state. It was essentially an educational and an organisational process because it was concerned with changing the attitudes and practices which stood in the way of social and economic improvements.

Democratic Decentralisation Approach

Together with community development programmes and extension services, Panchayati-raj institutions, by contribution significantly to the formulation and implementation of local development plans, have provided a new dimension to rural development and have introduced a structural change of high importance in the district administration. It signified decentralisation of administration and democratic participation.

Trickle Down Approach

The rural development programmes in its early phase, were based on state's assumption that economic growth will reach the rural poor automatically through the trickle down effect. However, by the 1970's it was realised that the assumption was wrong for certain kinds of growth improved social Justice, but others did not, so it started redesigning the programmes within it's financial capabilities to impact directly on social justice. The discussion at the theme suggested that the methodology the experience and micro level knowledge of programmes designed for the poor is now available. The problem that remains, as Paul Straiten said is how to mobilise the political elite for such social priorities and create a balance between economic growths on the one hand and social justice on the other.

People's Participation Approach

Rural development administration signified not merely working for the people but working with the people. It signified administration by participation. In the context of rural development, people's participation has a specific notion. By people we mean here those who have been victims of their exclusion from development process and those who are likely to emerge as the beneficiaries of participation. Participation is meant as the introduction of a new set of people into decision making process with regard to resource allocation or resource distribution The capacity to enlist maximum mass participation was considered the key factor of rural development administration and this was attempted in several ways; through extension of community development programmes, promotion of cooperatives of all types, voluntary organisations, joint councils, village panchayats, etc.

Target Group Approach

It was realised that inspite of large attempts the rural development programmes could not remove inequalities in income of rural communities and as such they did not improve the conditions of rural poor.

Area Development Approach

In rural development programmes, special attention was given to different areas with specific problems and as such special area development approach was adopted viz. DPAP, CADP, HADP, TADP, DADP etc. The programmes were conceived and implemented within the frame of special area planning. Besides, an integrated area development approach was adopted which refers to two types of Integration: functional and spatial, which are inter-related:

Microlevel Planning

Micro level planning, particularly at the block level was evolved to take care of other problems facing the villages within the block. Its main objectives, according to Dantawala working committee are:

- Optimum utilisation of growth potential of the area leading to increase in income and employment.
- Ensuring the development of weaker sections of society.
- Fulfillment of the minimum needs of the people.
- Building up social and Economic infrastructure.
- Reorientation of the existing institutions/organisations in order to protect the interests of the poor.
- Building up of appropriate organisations of the poor especially to protect them from exploitation.
- Promotion of progressively more egalitarian structure of ownership of assets.
- Increasing the duration and productivity of employment of the poor and under employed in their present occupations inter-alia through upgrading of technology, imparting of skills and setting up of non-exploitative institutions of credit, marketing and extension and
- Alleviating residential employment through employment on public works.

Integrated Rural Development Approach

The concept of IRDP seeks to correct most deficiencies of conventional approaches to rural development. IRDP, besides incorporating all the elements of rural development, places greater emphasis on the distributive aspects of development. This is largely due to the fact that the IRDP concept has emerged out of frustration on the failure of past development policies with built-in biases against the poor. It derived further impetus from the new thinking on development which sought to establish that growth and distributive justice are not necessarily contradictory concepts and that some measures of equality, far from showing the rate of economic growth, accelerates it. The approach aims at reaching those at the lowest rung of rural society whose opportunities are grossly limited. Actively involve them in the decision making process so that they may make substantial progress in making their lives more economically productive and socially rewarding within egalitarian system.

An Appraisal of Rural Development Measures

An inquiry into state interventionism and its overall impact makes us obvious that rural development measures could have very limited significance on rural society in general and rural poor in particular. Because of some basic weaknesses in policy formulation, implementation and procedural lacunae, these measures could not bring any decisive impetus to rural transformation. An attempt has been made in this section to evaluate in brief, the impact and effectiveness of rural development measures in the process of rural transformation in India.

Land Reform

According to planning commission, land reforms have two specific objects; (a) to remove such impediments to increase in agricultural production as arise from agrarian structure inherited from pasts and (b) to eliminate all elements of exploitation and social injustice within the agrarian system, to provide security for the tiller of the soil and assure equality of status and opportunity to all section of the rural population.

Tiwary (1994;95): argues that due to basic weakness in policy formulation, implementation and procedural lacunae, the measures of state intervention could not bring any decisive impetus us to some of the major programme. Such as land ceiling have been implemented in a Tandy and improper manner in our country only 7.35 million acre areas of ceiling surplus land were vested in the state (March, 2002) of which 5.39 million acres were distributed among 5.65 million beneficiaries. Even distribution was not done correctly. In many cases beneficiaries with "Patta" in land did not get physical possession of the land allotted to them old owners continued to possess and enjoy the usufruct of these lands. Worse still are the cases of the same vested land being distributed to different sets of beneficiaries at different points of time, ofcourse giving no physical possession to any one of them. It only made the poor to fight the poor so that the erstwhile land lords could lord over their former estates.

Land holding after several decades of implementation of ceiling laws still remains highly skewed. In 1994 tiny holding constituted 78 per cent of the total operational holding and commanded 32 per cent of the area. Thus 22 per cent of operational holding controlled 68 per cent of the arable land while figures clearly justify further reduction of land ceiling and rationalisation of various categories and rationalisation of various categories of land for ceiling purposes under the pressure of neoliberal economic policies different states are doing the opposite by enhancing the ceiling limits in the name of commercialisation and modernisation of agriculture. Thus the possibility of getting a parcel of land by the landless for minimal livelihood and household food security is becoming dimmer by the day. Apparently, in different parts of the country indifferent depressed and oppressed groups, there are keys of dry powder waiting for fire to set in. But the flaming brush fire is not taking place as there is a lack of country-wide political mobilisation among the landless and the deprived. Instead of being united on the basis of class, the poor are fragmented along caste, ethnic, religious and other divisive lines. Moreover, land strangle tend to differ for different interest groups. Landless strive for land ownership. Tribal's and indigenous groups strive for the protection of their traditional right on forest and other livelihood resources. Marginal and small farmers strive not only to retain their land but also to make it more productive and to acquire and, or to enhance their political power and influence, Thus with dissatisfaction all around there being no coalescing of interests and objectives, no combined determined movement was possible to seriously there at then the establishment.

In an agrarian economy like India and confers personality to an individual or a group. It endows social respectability. It is a means of political empowerment.

It is the basic ingredient of a dignified life and living. Hence a just and fair distribution of land resources is of utmost importance for building an egalitarian and strife-free society. It is for the state to arrange for equitable redistribution of land and water resources and to restore the traditional livelihood rights of the tribal in the forest areas. Unmet just demands may provoke the sufferers to use force whether for occupation of land or for exercising rights over forestry resources. The ruling establishment cannot avoid taking responsibility for its failure to read the writing on the wall.

Another major cause of rural discontent is the trident of mall governance by the forests revenue and the police Administration. What we are witnessing in India, in the form of rural land movement of violent nature is basically the "third wave" of left politics.

Community Development Programme

The community development programme, first organised effort to undertake the tasks of rural development, was described as "Magna Carta" of hope and happiness of two thirds of India's population. Studies (See Taube, 1969; Mathur, 1972, Singhi, 1974, Jain 1978, Tiwary, 1994) reveal that from the very beginning the Indian model of development had a kind of built in tension; a strong accent to both earnest and determined exercise of power on the part of state to achieve development objective and on mass enthusiasm and the active interest and support of the people. Infect, rural development administration under C.D. dispensation was heavily weighted towards the Bureaucratic component in terms of its composition and hence it could not transform the traditional pattern of bureaucrat client relations.

Programmed evaluation organisation of the planning commission, in its reports (2004) also brought out certain shortcomings of CDP, which brought out certain shortcomings of CDP, which include institutional weaknesses, lack of proper co-ordination among agencies implementation community development programmes, financial stringency, little attention paid to agricultural improvement techniques, unsatisfactory progress of education, healthy, irrigation, animal husbandry, schemes, wide disparity accruing of benefits, failure in creating the spirit of self reliance among the rural masses. We accept that CDP programmes bring change in the rural society but could not bring prosperity to the rural masses up to the extended level.

Panchayati Raj

The attempts of democratic decentralisation under Panchayati-raj institutions have remained a partial denture for structural weakness in the system. For a long time these Institutions have remained moribund or non-existent. They have still remained as one of the most under developed segment of our political system and have failed to develop their full stature. It is only in West Bengal that a small beginning has been made to till the balance of power in rural society in favor of landless, the low middle class and the deprived sections through panchayats.

Moreover, the benefits of community development, gives benefit to rich peasants and capitalist farmers who also came to dominate the Panchayati Raj Institutions. Its Basic weakness was that they ignored the class division of the rural society. Where nearly half the population was landless or had marginal holding and was thus quite powerless. The village was dominated socially and economically by the capitalist farmers and the rich and middle peasantry; and neither the dominant rural classes nor the bureaucrats could become agents of social transformation or popular participation.

In the 1990's Government by 73rd amendment act (1993-94) provided 33 per cent reservation in PRI's for the weaker's section of society to bring social transformation at grass root level. In earlier phases it is successful, but in last decade, it is part of political lacunae where rural people divided on caste, religion, linguistic line and it is not as successful as considered. However recently central and state government provided 50 per cent reservation in P.R.I.'s to women, which is also for political gain, not for social change because most of the rural women are even today govern and guided by their husband, father as other male head. However, we hope that this bring rural transformation in the upcoming year and it brings drastic social change in all sphere of life social, economic, cultural and political and it fulfilled the dream of Mahatma Gandhi, who considered villages as back bone of Indian Society.

Special Programmes

Since 1990s a number of special schemes were launched by state under rural development measures. These schemes were oriented to wards target groups of different variety, in come generation, special area development employment generation, sectoral development, education and training, social welfare, etc. The major objective behind introducing these programmes was to raise the consumption level of the lowest rung of rural population substantially. As far as target group oriented programmes are concerned several evaluation studies brought out the evidence that the big farmers posed as small farmers and preempted the benefits meant for genuine small holders (Athavale, 1973) lack of proper supervision of loan and major diversion for consumption (Ali and Basthakur, 1972) inadequate extension support and lack of follow up (Planning Commission, 1995) wide gap between quantitative targets and achievement of various schemes (Khan, 1978) inadequate market support and lack of infrastructure for processing of output as major constraints (consultancy and applied research division, 1978) very little attention paid to identification of agricultural labourers (Planning commission, 1979), lack of coordination among various institution engaged under the schemes and inadequate monitoring and evaluation (Haragopal, 1980). Lowe participation of the poor in the asset and income generation programmes, and the poor benefited so little that it could not help them to crops the poverty (Programme evaluation org+, 1979).

In the context of area development programmes such as DPAP, DDP, HADP, TADP, etc. the evaluation studies reveal their weaknesses in many ways; maintenance of irrigation works had not received the desired attention, the actual irrigation works quite lower than indicated at the stage of sanction, extremely poor quality maintenance of soil conservation, disappearance of work which have been projected absence of clear and conscious efforts etc. Verma writes that most of the people hesitate to participate in the programme because of lack of knowledge about its operation and other objectives.

Integrated Rural Development Programme (IRDP)

IRDP differs from other rural development programmes mainly on ground that it is based on the assumption of creation of assets and sills which along with credit provided are expected to generate a permanent flow of income for the beneficiaries identified as poorest of the poor. Secondly, it covers a wide range of activities; minor irrigation, dairy developments animal husbandry, animal powered transport, petty industry, services and business. It has been observed that the cluster approach in the selection of villages, of the Antodaya approach in the selection of beneficiaries as envisaged under IRDP appears to be basically sound (Singh, 1986, 48).

It has been recognised that although IRDP with a total investment of Rs. 13,280 crores during sixth and seventh five year plans has provided benefits to more than 34 millions of the rural poor families in terms of poverty alleviation.

Promotion of self-employment was an important sector of IRDP but in reality, the activities of IRDP concentrated on much animals and the non-agricultural sector was not given priority. Various studies conducted in different states revealed that great many of the target groups have been wrongly identified misclassification i.e. the inclusion of non-target group persons into the pool of beneficiaries is quite high in many states. On top of this, there was the usual problem of leakage i.e. misuse of the loan funds at different levels, a general survey of the sponsoring government bank, NABARD, revealing this to be about 20 per cent, which should be taken as a minimum estimate NSSO's consumption expenditure survey in the middle of the eighties show no visible impact of the IRDP on the dimension of poverty in rural India (Rath, 1985).

Apart from the fact of wrong selection of beneficiaries and inadequacy of loan amount and subsidy, the studies conducted on IRDP have also revealed certain other drawbacks. Such as rigid and non cooperative attitudes of the officials corrupt practices in sanctioning of loans and passing of animals, lack of inter sectional linkages and infrastructural facilities, involvement of mediators, lack of adequate staff in the blocks, absence of effective supervision and follow up actions. This has not only deprived the weaker sections of getting intended benefits but also has resulted in diversion and misappropriation of funds.

Maheshwari (1985; 121): Points out that rural development programmes in India suffer from a high degree of centralisation as illustrated by IRDP. This programme has been formulated at central level with little flexibility permitted at implementation level.

Sociologically, the two major problems with the implementation of IRDP can be identified as under; (a) ensuring that the resources intended for the poor actually reach them, rather than leaking to the non-poor; and (b) ensuring that the ingestible resources which do reach the poor are effectively capitalised so as to ensure a lasting stream of benefits.

Training of Rural Youth for Self-Employment (TRYSEM)

The main thrust of TRYSEM Scheme which is an integral part of the IRDP is on equipping the rural youth from families below poverty line with necessary technical and entrepreneurial skills to enable them to take up self-employment in the fields of agriculture and allied activities, industries, service and business activities.

Programme evaluation organisation in its evaluation reports on IRDP (1985) notes some important deficiencies in the implementation of TRYSEM Programme, which include;

(a) Improper selection of Trainees.

(b) Undue concentration o a few vocations.

(c) Minimum involvement of district industries centers.

(d) Poor infrastructural support to enable the trainees to follow the pursuits.

(e) Lack of coordination among DIC, Banks and Training Institutes.

(f) Lack of follow up of the trained youth.

Problems like lack of finance and confidence among the trainees have also been observed by the evaluation studies undertake from time to time. Another major deficiency of this programme.

Development of Women and Children in Rural Areas (DWCRA)

Under the programme of DWCRA, income generating opportunities to women belonging to rural poor families are provided to enable them supplementing their family income. Since its inception up to Feb. 1990, over 31,000 groups benefiting over 5.18 lakhs women in 184 districts (covered till then) were formed.

Some weaknesses have been highlighted by the studies which show that individual choice of activity was superseded in the name of choice under group approach resulting in lack of interest among the group members and consequent adverse effects on the functioning of the Units, established. Another study found that there was considerable delay in grounding of schemes grounding of schemes (quoted Singh, 1992:19) Sivasan (1991:39) points out shortage of raw materials, lack of common work-shed, etc.

Moreover, delayed income generation leads to dampening of interest and undermines the very objectives of the schemes.

Novodaya Vidyalaya Yojana

To provide quality education free of cost to the promising children, especially of rural setting, govt. of India has evolved a scheme under new Education policy (1986), in which residential co-education Jawahar Navodaya Vidyalayas are being established in each districts. The objectives behind establishing JNV's are to provide equal opportunities to learn and to reach a better institution for excellence and for national integration.

No doubt, the objectives are sound enough. But practically, it has been observed that the location of many Navodaya vidyalayas has been shifted at times from remote villages to fringe semi-urban centers because of political pressures and bureaucratic maneuverings and there by the opportunities of other aligned developments in such remote villages have been lost. It has also been observed that many students belonging to urban middle class families, by manipulation have been successful enough in getting admissions to such vidyalayas. Obviously, the opportunities to promising children of rural poor families are restricted by these attempts.

Rural employment

Rural employment measures began with EREP (1980) which was followed by RLEGP (1983). Both NREP and RLEGP were merged into one programme called Jawahar Rozgar Yojana, introduced in April 1989.

The studies (Jain, 1987, Tiwari1990,) on NREP and RLEGP realised the phenomenal leakages at every stage of allocation of funds for these programmers from the Bureaucracy to the local contractor. The short comings of the programmers are Inadequate investment, insignificant for skilled labourers, implementation of the programme could cover only 55 per cent of the villages etc, it has been observed during the short period of implementation of JRY that many ingredients are missing in it, which seeks to create employment, as it were from New Delhi, albeit through the Panchayat (Singh,1991) practically it may not be possible for a gram panchayat to meet all worms instructed especially in a situation when the total allocation has been quite meager. There is another problem of prevailing oppressive power structure in village in which a few powerful villagers collude with local officials to corner a big share of the benefits of the schemes meant for weaker section of rural society.

The programmes of this variety, in fact help the landless beneficiaries on a one off-basis, since it does not generate any permanent capacity for generating higher incomes in other years. Ironically, on the other hand, the rural infrastructural investment provides sources of growth for the local land owners on a permanent basis. Frequently, roads allow for better marketing and profitable changes in cropping patterns and opportunities for commercialisation; minor irrigation schemes likewise, help the landed classes. No doubt these are some permanent benefits for poor through the impact of these changes on the demand for hired labor, but such effects are weak and account for a tiny fraction of the total net income stream generated.

Rural Unemployment and Poverty Alleviation Programme

According to a general survey done by the National sample survey organisation (NSSO) 62 per cent of total unemployment exists in rural areas. The ministry of rural development accords foremost priority to development in rural areas and eradication of poverty and hunger from the face of rural India. A number of initiative have been taken in the recent years for creation of social and economic infrastructure in rural areas to bridge the rural urban divide as well as to provide food security and fulfill other basic needs of the rural populace.

Addressing the challenge of unemployment in the rural areas of the country is central to the development of rural section for ameliorating the economic condition of the people. Wage employment is provided in rural areas under National Rural Employment Guarantee Act (NREGA) and Sampoorna Grameen Rozgar Yojana (SGRY) whereas self employment is provided under Swarnajanti Gram Swarozgar Yojana (SGSY). Besides generating employment these wage employment schemes also ensure creation of durable assets in rural areas. Initiatives are also taken by the ministry to build and upgrade the basic rural infrastructure through various schemes. Under Pradhan Mantri Gram Sadak Yojana (PMGSY) construction and repairing of rural roads are taken up to ensure rural connectivity. It is expected under the scheme that an expanded and renovated rural road network will lead to an increase in rural employment opportunities, better access to regulated and fair market, better access to health, education and other public services so as to accelerate the pace of economic growth in rural areas. Similarly basic amenities for housing, drinking water and toilets etc. are provided under Indira Awas Yojana (IAY), accelerated rural water supply programme (ARWSP) and Total Sanitation Campaign (TSC) to enhance the welfare and wellbeing of the vulnerable sections of rural population. Area Development is encouraged through water shed development programmes to check the diminishing productivity of waste-land and loss of natural resources.

The above programmes of rural development and poverty alleviation are not on marks, lack of coordination between centre-state governments, red tapism of bureaucracy. Due to lack of transparency, accountability in implementation not given fruitful result, these programmes are becoming medium of gaining more and more money through Nepotism, corruption and black marketing.

The government dream of rural transformation cannot be possible without solving the problem of above loop-hole in the programme implementation.

In recent year, Right to Information Act, (R.T.I.) and Role of Civil Society do there best and we hope in the coming year we saw rural transformation and prosperous India in upcoming decades.

Mahatma Gandhi National Rural Employment Guarantee Schemes (MGNREGS)

This programme was launched on Feb, 2, 2006. It is consider as one of the most successful scheme of Rural Development of Country. This scheme has been launched with following guidelines:

- An applicant not provided employment within fifteen days, to be entitled to a daily unemployment allowances as specified by the State Government subject to its economic capacity.
- Panchayat at the district level to constitute a standing committee of its members to supervise, monitor and oversee the implementation of the scheme within the district.
- For every block State Government to appoint a programme officer for implementing the scheme.

MNREGA, biggest draws back is transparency and accountability, recent year incidence in Rajasthan, Chhattisgarh, Jharkhand, U.P. and many states shows that it becomes a medium of gaining money, in the name of various schemes R.T.I's activist Aruna Roy, Arvind Kejriwal, in Rajasthan shows how this programme misused by the powerful bureaucracy and politician Nexus and it not reached to grass root level.

Gram Pradhan, and B.D.O. are the key player who involved in corruption, Pradhan issue card to those people who voted them in panchayat election, whether he comes under the provision of MNREGA or not.

There are the drawbacks, which can be solving as soon as possible, to fulfill the Mahatma Gandhi dream of 'Decentralisation Democracy (D.D.).

Mid Day Meal Scheme

Its biggest drawback, in its implementation village head master and teacher, sells the food grain to local market or providing bad or less calories to children in school, there is also need of transparency and accountability.

National Rural Health Scheme

In recent past killing of Chief Medical Officer in Uttar Pradesh and other States shows that, it is one of the biggest schemes which give benefit to bureaucrats, politician and criminal Nexus. Around 3,000 crores rupees alone come to Uttar Pradesh under this scheme, but it benefits not reaches to rural poor and downtrodden section of society.

Backward District Initiative (B.D.I.): Rashtriya Sam Vikas Yojana (RSVY)

Under this scheme central govt. allotted 15 crores rupees to backward and naxal affected district every year for infrastructural development, but this scheme is becoming medium of gaining more money for bureaucratic elite people, who misused money by various ways. In grass root level, even today this money not utilised properly and rural population still not get benefits of their schemes.

The foregoing analysis highlights that rural development in India has remained unsatisfactory both in substance and speed. The diverse programmes like IRDP, MNREGA, and others reduce capitalist exploitation by reducing the gap between poor people's assets and average per capital market and by raising poor people's reservation price in the labor market and they are not to be written off as bogus historical accident, concealed means of social control, etc. But the overall scenario reveals that state interventions have provided partial and temporary relief to the rural poor, at the best, they may be treated as mere patchwork, insufficient in generating a major shift in the rural formation. We feel that state's role as surplus manager/mediator, rent mediator as well as exploitation mediator has to be analyzed a fresh and theories of rural society and the state be improved by testing against the analytical case histories.

Major Initiatives Schemes in Social Sector at a Glance: Launced Especially in Rural Areas of Sonbhadra

Aam Admi Bima Yojana

Under a new scheme called "Aam Admi Bina Yojana" (AABY) launched on October 2, 2007. Insurance to the head of the family of rural landless households in the country is provided against natural death as well as accidental death and partial/permanent disability. This cover is Rs.75000 on death due to accident and permanent disability due to accident Rs 37,500 in case of partial permanent disability due to accident and Rs 30,000 in case of a member, prior to terminal date. The premium to be charged under the scheme is Rs 200-per annum per member, 50 per cent of which is to be contributed by the central government and remaining by state Government.

Midday Meal Scheme

This scheme, which was launched in August, 1995, is intended to give boost to universalisation of primary education by increasing enrolment retention and attendance while contributing to the nutrition of student in primary classes.

Rashtriya Swasthya Bima Yojana

The RSBY was formally lunched on October, 1, 2007. All workers in the unorganised sector who come in the category of below poverty line (BPL) and their families are covered under the scheme. The scheme also has a provision of smart card to be issued to the beneficiaries to enable cashless transaction for health care. Total sum insured would be Rs. 30,000 per family per annum with government of India contributing 75 per cent of the annual estimated premium amount of Rs.750 subject to a maximum of Rs.565 per family per annum, while state government are expected to contribute 25 per cent of the annual premium as well as any additional premium. The cost of smart card would also be borne by central government.

National Rural Health Mission

The National Rural Health Mission was launched on April 12, 2005, to provide accessible, affordable and accountable quality health services to the Poorest Household in the remotest rural regions.

Rajiv Gandhi National Drinking Water Mission

This programme was introduced as one of five social missions in 1986 and was called the national drinking water mission. It was renamed as Rajiv Gandhi National drinking water mission in 1991.

Backward Districts Initiative (BDI)

Rashtriya Sam Vikash Yojana (RSVY)

Government launched Rashtriya Sam Vikas Yojana on the backward district of country specially the naxal affected district. Since, the naxalite menace has to be addressed on the developmental front also, the Government has provided financial assistance of Rs 2,475 crores for 55 naxal affected district in 9 states of Andhra, Bihar, Chattisgarh, Orissa, Jharkhand, Maharashtra, Madhya Pradesh, Uttar Pradesh and West Bengal under the Backward District Initiative B.D.I.) Component of the Rashtriya Sam Vikas Yojana (RSVY) under this scheme, an amount of Rs.15 crore per year has been given to each of the district for five years so as fill in critical gaps in physical and social development in the naxal affected areas. Apart from these districts, other naxal affected areas/districts have also been included under the backward regions grant fund (BRGF) scheme which covers 250 backward districts in the country.

Scheduled Tribes (Recognition of Forest Rights) Bill, 2005

In order to address the areas of disaffection among the tribal, and marginalised section of society, the government has introduced the scheduled tribes (Recognition of Forest Rights) Bill, 2005 in parliament. Further, to facilitate social and physical infrastructure in the forest areas. Ministry of environment and forests has, as requested by the ministry of Home affairs issued general approval to such infrastructure by utilizing up to 1 hectare of forest for non-forest purposes. The ministry has also permitted up gradation of Kutcha recorded constructed into pucca roads.

Social Transformation Occurred in Sonbhadra District after the Emergence of Naxalite Movement especially in last two Decades

Sonbhadra is the one of the most backward district of India. It is earlier part of Mirzapur district since 1989, due to it backwardness and social economic condition and other factor attracted government attention and it declared as separate district. Sonbhadra is isolated from long time, it is rich in natural and mineral resources, and also called power capital became here many hydro project situated. Sonbhadra people social-economic condition is very worse, even today they are not getting proper benefit of government launched schemes and programme and it provided ground to naxalite in 1990's due to its geographical location and mostly marginalised section population presence in this district. It touches border with four states-Bihar, Jharkhand, M.P. and Chhattisgarh, and it is covered with dense forest and hilly terrains also.

Sonbhadra people after naxal emergence, become aware about their social, political and economic right, and presently they get benefited of many government schemes. Such as MNREGA, old age pension scheme, midday meal scheme, national rural health scheme etc. In their life, many changes occur, caste discrimination and exploitation reduced, women gets equal opportunity etc.

References

Asian Development Bank, Key Indicators for the Asia and the Pacific 39th Editions, Manila, 2008.

Banerjee Sumanta, *Ibid.*, p. 11.

Banerjee Sumanta, In the Wake of Naxalbari; A History of the Naxalite Movement in India, Subarnarekha, Calcutta, 1980, p. 99.

Banerjee, Sumanta, India's Simmering Revolution, The Naxalite uprising, Selected Service Syndicate, New Delhi,1984, p. 88.

Bipin Chandra, Mridula and Aditya Mukherjee: India since Independence Pengeun Book, India, 2008.

Chakravarti, S.: Red Sun, Penguin-Publication, New Delhi, (2006).

Chattopadhyaya, Sankar, Subrid, To Establish a Liberated Area (Interview with Koteswar Rao), Frontline, Vol. 26, No. 22 Octber 24, November 6, 2009, p. 22-23

Cropp, James, H. (1972), Rural Sociology and Rural Development, Rural Sociology, Vol. 87, No. 4, Dec., pp. 515-33

Dasgupta, Biplab, *Ibid.,* p. 11

Dasgupta, Biplab, *Ibid.,* p. 211.

Dasgupta, Biplab, The Naxalite Movement Bombay, Allied Publishers, New Delhi, 1975, p. 219.

Desai, A.R. (1985), A New Policy for Rural Development in South and South-East Asia, Its Sinister Significance (India a Case Study, Bombay, (G.S. Shah, Memorial Trust Publication)

Dhanagare, D.N. (1988), The Green Revolution and Social Inequalities in Rural India, Bulletin of Concerned Asian Scholars, 20 (2).

Dubey Abhay: Kranti Ka Atma Sangagharsh, Vinay Publication, 1991, p. 59.

G. Kotovsky: Agrarian Reformsd in India, New Delhi, 1964.

G.S. Bhalla and G.K. Chadha: "Green Revolution and the Small Peasdant : A Study of Income Distribution in Pubjab Agriculturi, EPW, 5 and 22 May, 1982.

Ganpathy Interview with various Foreign Journalists, Interview with Ganapathy, Generl Secretary, CPI (Maoist), April 24, 2007.

George, P.T. (1986), Land Reforms: Promises and Performances Kurukshetra, Vol. XXXVIII, No.4, January.

Gopal, S., The Naxalite Movement : Impact of External Networking Cited in Ramana.

Government of India: Report of 1979, 1985, 1988, 1990, 2002, 2007.

Haragopal, G. (1980), Administration of Anti Poverty Programme in Rural Andhra Pradesh, in Chaturvedi, T.N. and Chandra S.K. (eds.), Social Administration, Development and Change, New Delhi, IIPA.

Haris, John, (1986), Rural Development: Theories of Peasant Economy and Agrarian Change, Hutchinson, ELBS.

Harison, S. Selig: India, The Most Dangerous Decade, Madras, 1960, p. 338.

Johri, J.C., Political Ideas of Marxist Leninist Communist in India, Indian Journal of Political Sciences, Vol. XXXII, No.2, April-June 1971, p. 179-180.

K.P. Bagchi and Company, Kolkatta, 2007.

Kohli, Atul: Democracy and Discontent India's Growing Crisis of Govern ability, New Delhi, 1992.

Kohli, Atul: Parliamentary Commission and Agrarian Reforms.

Kujur, Rajat, Child Solders of the Naxal Movement,, Insdtitute of Peace and Conflict Studies Issue Brief, New Delhi, No. 2738, November 24, 2008.

Kujur, Rajat, From CRZ to SEZ: Naxal Reins of Terror, IPCS ISSUE Brief, New Delhi, No.2271, April 21, 2007.

Kujur, Rajat, Naxalite Violence : Hijacking Train the New face of Red-Terror, IPCS, ISSUE brief, New Delhi, No. 1967, March, 16, 2006.

Kurian, C.T. Poverty, Planning, and Social Transformation, Allied Publishersd, Bombay, 1978, p. 8

Liberation, Vol. 3, No.1, Nov. 1969.

Lipton, Michael: (1977), Why poor people stay poor; Urban Bias in World Development, London, Temple Smith.

Louisprakash, The Naxalite Movement in Central Bihar, New Delhi, Wosdvariths, 2002, p. 259.

Maheswari, S.R. (1985), Rural Development in India : A Public Policy Approach, New Delhi, sage publication.

Mankenkar, D.R., A Revolution of Rising Frustrationsd, Vikas Publication, New Delhi, 1975, p. 2

Mathur, Kuldeep, (1972), Bureaucratic Response to Development, New Delhi, National Publishing House.

Mehta, Ashok (1978), Report of the Committee on Panchayati Raj Institution, Govt. of India.

Morris Jones, W.H. : Politics mainly Indian, Bombay, 1978, pp. 131-32.

Mridula Mukherjee : Peasant Resistance and Pesant Consciousness in Colonial India, "Subhaltern" and Beyond EPW, 1988, Oct. 8 and 15.

Mukherjee, A.P. : Maoist Spring Thunder, The Naxalite Movement (1967-72)

P. Sundarayya : Telengana People's Struggle and its Lesson, Communist Party of India (Marxist), Calcutta, 1972, pp. 115-16, 239-40, 424.

Prasad, B.N. : Radicalism and Violence in Agrarian Structure. The Maoist Movement in Bihar, Manak Publication Pvt. Ltd., 2002, New Delhi.

Rai, Haridwar and Prasdad, K.M., Naxalism , A Challenge to the Proposition of Peaceful Transition to Socialism Indian Journal of Political Science cited in Nimbram, Amrik, Singh, Poverty, land and violence.(An analytical study of Naxalism in Bihar, Chandhary Printing Press, Patna, 1992, p. 2.

Ramani, R.Venkata, The Naxal Strategy in Urban Area, IPCS ISSUE brief, New Delhi, No. 3047, January, 21, 2010.

Rath, N. (1985), Garibi Hatao, Can IRDP DO it? E.P.W., Vol. 20, No. 6.

Reddy, K. Srinivas, Revolutionary and Counter Revolutionary Strategties of the Naxalite and the State, 2008, P.92, cited in P.V., Ramana, The Naxal Channenge (Cause linkages, and policy options), 2008.

Selected weorksd of Mao Tse-Tung, Peop0le's Publishing lHouse, Peking, Vol. II, p. 224.

Sen, A, Development as Freedom, New York, Randam House, 1999

Singh, Ayodhyaya : Bharata Ka Mukti Sangram, MacMillian, New Delhi, p. 162.

Singh, Kartar (1986), Rural Development Principle, Policies and Management, New Delhi, Sage Publications.

Singh, Mohinder (1992), Rural Development in India, Cultural Perspectives, New Delhi, Intellectual Publishing House.

Singh, N.K. (1974), Bureaucracy, Person and Position, New Delhi, Abhinav Publication.

Singh, Prakash, Ibid., p. 123.

Singh, Prakash, The Naxalite Movement in India, Rupa and Company, Newdelhi, 2006, p. 121-122.

Singharoj, Debojeet : Role of Women in Telengana and Naxalite Women, 1995, I.G.N.O.U., New Delhi.

The Evidences from India's Bengal, Asian Survey, Vol. 23, No.7 July, 1983, pp. 780-800.

Tiwari, Jaikant: Rural Development Administration, Chugh, Publication, Allahabad, 1984.

Tiwari, Jaikant : Rural Transformation in India, Reliance Publishing House, New Delhi, 1994.

Tiwari, R.K. (1990), Rural Employment Programme in India: The Implementation Process, New Delhi, IIPA.

Tiwary, J.K. (1984), Rural Development Administration, Perspectives and Prospects, Allahabad, Chugh Publication.

Tiwary, J.K. (1994), Rural Transformation in India, Reliance Publishing House, New Delhi

U.N.D.P. Report, 1999, Oxford University Press, Oxford, 1999.

Yojana, August, 2008, NREGA- Implementation.

2

Review of Literature

A Literature review is a body of text that aims to review the critical points of current knowledge including substantive finding as well as theoretical and methodological contributions to a particular topic. Literature reviews are secondly sources, and as such, do not report any new or original experimental work.

Simai Haji Mati was quoted saying that literature review should be referred to as reviewing and analyzing the work of literature in relation to the specified topic in research.

Most often associated with academic-oriented literature, such as thesis, a literature review usually precedes a research proposals and results section. Its ultimate goal is to bring the reader up to date with current literature on a topic and forms, the basis for another goal, such as future research that may be needed in the area. A well structured literature review is characterised by a logical flow of ideas, current and relevant references with consistent, appropriate referencing style; proper use of terminology and an unbiased and comprehensive view of the previous research on the topic.

Studies on naxal affected areas are of different varieties: sociological, political, economical, governmental as well as non-governmental, etc. These studies highlights the nature of Social transformation in a rural setting especially naxal affected areas. The process of social transformation is an out come of various factors such as state intervention measures, role of civil society, people's participation, NGO's, banking system, micro finance, SHG's etc.

Rout Ray, J.K and **Patnaik, M** (1982) mentions the path of rural transformation in various phases. Each Phase is characterised by its own distinctive complexity of phenomena and structure and functions. To him, the approaches to rural transformation are linked together in the following ways:-

A. Physical Transformation: (Structural arrangement change in shape and form) it is guided mainly by:-

(i) Transport networks

(ii) Irrigation networks

(iii) Power networks.

B. Economic Transformation: (shifting primary to secondary and Tertiary activities) it is guided by technology with respect to structural variation in resources endowment.

C. Socio Cultural Transformation: It is guided by the cross interaction of physical and economical factors with the degree of modernisation.

The phenomenon include

(i) Occupational mobility

(ii) Gradual replacement of caste system by class system

(iii) Religious mobility

(iv) Ascriptive to Achieved Society.

Kumar, Ravindra (1983): In his study, mention that the creation of physical infrastructure facilities in rural areas through the Industrialisation of the Area, buildings roads, schools, hospitals etc. creating growth centers with trickle down effect will serve the purpose, while others agree that creating organised employment in rural Areas with reasonable facilities will automatically lead to their transformation.

Tiwary, Jai Kant (1984): The book provides interesting insights into the nature of Bureaucrat client relationship that stands in the way of socio-economic development. He portrays a comprehensive picture of rural development administration, in which the government has launched the big programmes of economic development and trying to utilize the participation of people in completing these tasks.

Desai, A.R. (1985) In his study he define Rural development as "an approach which, by better utilisation of local resources and by creating infrastructural facilities for economic and social development aims at improving the quality of life of the rural population, especially the rural poor, by creation of expanded employment and Income opportunities for them.

He also mentions some of the measures taken by state machinery of rural transformation are:

1. More Zealous implementation of land reform and ceiling measures.
2. Concerned efforts to distribute the surplus land which was not adequately distributed.
3. Elimination of the loopholes in the land records to avoid malpractices perused by influential groups in rural Areas.
4. Efforts to place the financial allocation to the Middle and poor farmers to enable them to take profitable production.
5. Crash Scheme for rural Employment.
6. Small farmer development agencies to make them available the Inputs, including credit, for utilizing the technology and practicing Intensive agriculture.
7. Drought prone area programmes for chronically drought affected area.
8. Special schemes for Non-agricultural nature like afforestation, minor Irrigation Soil and water conservation, road building, drainage, embankments etc.
9. Welfare, Education, and Employment schemes in Rural Areas to bring change in all sphere of life.

Harris (1986: 37) Discusses three paths of Agrarian transformation:

(a) Through development of Capitalist farming, involving, the establishment of relatively large scale units of production and observing most of the peasant sector.

(b) Through the establishment under state initiative of large scale cooperative, collective or state farms and

(c) Through Capital intensive, small scale farming.

Yogendra Singh (1990: 35) argues that the pace of Social restructuration, the emergence of new classes and decline of traditional cultural institutions exemplify the phenomenon of contemporary transformation in rural India. Since the process of restructuration is closely associated with regionalisation, the pattern and syndrome of rural transformation varies region to region.

The foregoing analysis reveals that the term social transformation has multi-dimensional connotations. It comprehends enormous diversity in analysis among the various disciplines of social sciences. We feel that the concept can be grasped more vividly if it set in motion under specific historic context of social forces, ideology and national policy. The context leads us to Identification of social transformation in contemporary rural India.

Identifying Social Transformation in contemporary India

The scenario of transition in rural society, especially in Post-Independence era, suggests that the process of planned development has created diverse patterns of social transformation in its different regions. It is difficult to comprehend all such patterns in a limited manner. However, the major tends evolving out of the varied patterns may be summarised as under:-

1. The transition of agrarian society from subsistence base to market based agrarian sector;
2. The introduction of modern technology, techniques and devices to transform the existing loose, scattered and underdeveloped colonial agrarian economy into a well knit compact one and its organic integration into the total national economy.
3. The emergence of complex network of various associations and Institutions within the agrarian society having close links with and being shaped by external influences.

4. Emergence of power blocks which try to work within the constitutional frame using a combination of protests through mass action, appeals to bureaucracy and courts and even-lobbying in centers of power.
5. State intervention in adopting different measures to strengthen certain communities, groups or classes on the one hand and weaken others, on the contrary.
6. Emergence of dominant groups like neo-rich peasants, intermediary castes, etc. and their tightened hold over avenues of political power and the use of public resources.

Breman, Jan and Sudipto Mundle (eds.) 1991: He mentioned the changing nature of the relationship between landlords who usually belonged to the dominant castes and Agricultural workers (usually low caste) was described in their study.

Jan Breman: Described a shift from patronage to exploitation such change took place in many areas where agriculture was becoming more commercialised, that is, where crops were being grown primarily for sale in the market. The transformation in labor relations is regarded by some scholars as Indicative of a transition to capitalist agriculture, because the capitalist mode of production is based on the separation of the workers from the means of production (in this case, land) and the use of 'free' wage labor. In general, it is true that farmers in the more developed regions were becoming more oriented to the market. As cultivation became more commercialised these rural area were also becoming integrated into the wider economy. This process increased the flow of money into villages and expanding opportunities for business and Employment. This process of rural transformation starts in the 19th century during colonial period. In many regions in the 19th century large tracts of land in Maharashtra were given over to cotton cultivation and cotton farmers became directly linked to the world market. However, the Pace and Spread of change rapidly increased after independence, as the government promoted modern methods of cultivation and attempted to modernize the rural economy through other strategies. The state invested in the development of rural infrastructure, such as irrigation facilities, roads and electricity, and on the provision of agricultural inputs, including credit through banks and cooperatives. The overall outcome of these efforts at 'rural development' was not only to transform the rural economy and agriculture, but also the agrarian structure and rural society itself.

Bhardwaj (1991: 77) in his study suggest that the alternative paradigm, focusing centrally on class relations around the production, distribution and accumulation of surplus, is far more powerful as a theoretic device for understanding the dynamics of rural transformation. He explores the main features of these alternative paradigms and the kinds of perspectives which they bring to bear on the problematic of development in the context of the role of state in the dynamics of rural transformation.

Lipton (1991-93-124) in his study examines what insights and Implication in Economic theory may have to offer with regard to the state agriculture relationship, in particular the role of state in enlarging, transferring or extracting the surplus product. He tends to support the coalition theory on ground that it provides immense scope to state's active intervention in pre-empting the small group distributional coalition from monopolizing public goods.

Dhangare, D.N. (1992) in his studies reveals rural development programmes implemented by the State Serve the interests of some groups and class not others, and that their real effects may be very different from what is claimed for them or from the rhetoric surrounding them. It is in this contradictory context that an attempt is made here to evaluate the state interventions in rural development programmes in India. His objective is to analyses whether the state's measures of rural development programmes in India. Our objective is to analyze whether the state's measures of rural development have been successful enough to bring rural transformation? To what extent they have reduced Inequalities in Income, employment, access to public goods and service and how much potential are in alleviation of poverty in rural society.

Tiwary (1994) In his study entitled rural transformation in India defined the concept of rural transformation and analyzed how it is related to mode of production, political, economy and land reforms. He also explained the State Intervention measures and nature of rural development in India. In his study also includes the role of voluntary organisation and rural Industrialisation in bringing social transformation in rural Areas and its Impact on Social, political, economical, cultural life of rural people.

Gupta, Akhil 1998, Das, Raju. J 1999: In there studies, they saw that land reform have had only a limited impact on rural society and the Agrarian structure in most regions. In contrast the Green Revolution of the 1960's and 1970's brought about significant changes in the areas where it took place. Green Revolution is a government programme of Agricultural modernisation. It was largely funded by International agencies that was based on providing high yielding variety (HYV) or hybrid seeds along with pesticides, Fertilizers and other inputs, to farmers. Green Revolution Programmes were introduced only in Areas that had assured irrigation, because sufficient water was necessary for the new seeds and methods of cultivation. It was also targeted mainly at the wheat and rice growing areas. As a result, only certain regions such as Punjab, Western U.P., Coastal Andhra Pradesh, and parts of Tamil Nadu, received the first waves of the Green Revolution Package. The rapid Social and economic transformation that were seen in these areas stimulated a spate of studies by social scientist and vigorous debates about the Impact of the Green Revolution.

Agriculture productivity increased sharply because of the new technology. India was able to become self-sufficient in food grain production for the first time in decades. The green revolution has been considered a major achievement of the government and of the scientists who contributed to the effort. However, there were certain negative social effects that were pointed out by sociologists who studied the green revolution areas, as well as adverse environmental impacts.

In most of the green revolution areas, it was primarily the medium and large farmers who were able to benefit from the new technology. This was because inputs were expensive and small and marginal farmers could not afford to spend as much as large farmers to purchase these inputs. When agriculturists produce primarily for themselves and are unable to produce for the market, it is known as 'Subsistence agriculture' and they are usually termed 'peasants'. Agriculturists or farmers are those who are able to produce surplus, over and above the needs of the family, and so are linked to the market. It was the farmers who were able to produce a surplus for the market who were able to reap the most benefits from the green revolution and from the commercialisation of agriculture that followed.

Thus in the first phase of the green revolution, in the 1960's and 1970's the introduction of new technology seemed to be increasing inequalities in rural society. Green Revolution crops were highly profitable, mainly because they yielded more produce well-to-do farmers who had access to land, capital, technology and know how and those who could invest path new seeds and fertilizers could increase their introduction and earn more money. However in many cases it led to the displacement of tenant cultivators for land owners began to take back land from their tenant and cultivate it directly because cultivation was becoming more profitable. This made the rich farmers better off, and worsened the condition of the landless and marginal holders.

In addition, the introduction of machinery such as tillers; tractors threshers and harvesters (in area such as Punjab and parts of M.P.) led to the displacement of the service caste groups who used to Carry out this agriculture related activities. This process of displacement also increased the pace of rural-Urban migration.

Following the first phase of the green revolution, the second phase is currently being introduced in the day and semi arid regions of India. In these areas there has been a significant shift from dry to wet (irrigated) cultivation, along with changes in the cropping pattern and type of crops grown. Increasing commercialisation and dependence on the market in these areas (for instance, where cotton cultivation has been promoted) has increased rather than reduced livelihood insecurity, as Farmers who once grew food for consumption now depend on the market for the incomes. In market oriented cultivation especially where a single crop is grown, a fall in prices or a bad crop can spell financial ruin for farmers. In most of the green revolution areas, farmers have switched from a multi crop system, which allowed them to spread risks to a mono crop region, which means that there is nothing to fall back on in case of crop failure.

Another negative outcome of the green revolution strategy was the worsening of regional inequalities. The areas that underwent this technological transformation became more developed while other Areas stagnated. For instance, the green revolution was promoted more in western and Southern parts of the country, and in Punjab, Haryana and Western U.P., than in the eastern parts of the country (Das, 1999). As a result, we find agriculture in states such as Bihar and in eastern U.P. and in dry region such as Telengana, Bundelkhand to be relatively undeveloped. These are also the regions that continue to have an entrenched 'Feudal' Agrarian Structure, in which the landed castes and landlords maintain power over the lower castes, landless workers and small cultivators. The sharp caste and class inequalities, together with Exploitative labor relation in these regions has given rise to various kinds of violence (Including inter caste violence) in recent year.

Suri, K.C., 2006: In his studies of ' Farmer's suicide' and Government measures of Agrarian development measures, he mention the spate of Farmers' suicides that has been occurring in the different parts of the country since 1997-98 can be linked to the agrarian 'distress' caused by structural changes in agriculture and changes in economic and agricultural policies. These include the changed pattern of landholding' changing cropping patterns especially due to the shift to cash crops; liberalisation policies that have exposed Indian agriculture to the forces of globalisation; heavy dependence on high cost inputs; the withdrawal of the state from agricultural extension activities to be replaced by multinational seed and fertiliser companies; decline in state support for agriculture; and individualisation of agricultural operations. According to official estimates (statistics) there have been 8,900 suicides by farmers between 2001 and 2006 in Andhra Pradesh, Karnataka, Kerala and Maharashtra.

Bandyopadhyay, D. (2007): In this study of rural development and state measures, he shows the real picture of social transformation in rural areas. He says peasants did not disappear. Tribals could not be assimilated with the mainstream populace. Dalits continue to be the landless haves of wood and drawers of water for the upper classes and castes. The projected trajectories of the development paradigm of large scale withdrawal of surplus labor from the rural areas to be absorbed in the massive development of the secondary and tertiary sectors had gone away.

58 per cent of Indian labor force is still changed in agriculture an allied occupations. Tribals are being pushed up the hills because of illegal incursion of outsiders in their traditional domain. Poverty ratio among SC's and ST's continued to be much higher. Neo liberal development process totally by passed them. Not only that the invasion of the corporate sector into agriculture and forestry and enhancement of ceiling limits on land in some states has exacerbated the incidence of landlessness with the consequential rise in the free floating mass of rural poor moving around in search of employment.

This lead to rural unrest in society, poor and marginalised joins the naxal movement.

Jain, L.C. (2007): Noted economist and former member of planning commission in his study, consider Panchayati Raj System is not a panacea but they can ply our boat to a wholesome life.

Mr Jain gives the reference of former Panchayati Raj Minister, Mani Shankar Aiyer message which he delivered on three day conference on Panchayat at Vigyan Bhawan (June, 2006) that there is a non police way of halting the spread pf Naxalism. Aiyar said that he had heard that in tribal areas, where the Panchayat extension to Scheduled area Act (PESA) is effective and where there is respect for traditional institutions, customs and usages as stipulated in PESA; there is an absence of Naxalism. Hence implementation of PESA and the holding of meeting of the tribal advisory council as stipulated in the Fifth Schedule of the Constitution, he added, are "critical to ending the naxalite menace that threatens our unity, stability and democracy."

The participants under scored that gram sabha activism and social audit are the only way of securing better and cleaner government at the grass roots. It has been brought out that in states where, there is better governance in terms of law and order, there is better Panchayati Raj.

Chaudhari, Arindam (2011): In his book 'he mention the day is not far when they (Maoist) will rule a grand majority of India. These 200 districts will become 400 districts in no time and inch towards. No government in India will be able to stop their growth through police Salwa Judum or Army. India's crony capitalism is responsible for the naxalite Massacre. Only development is the way, with bilateral talk is method to tackle naxal menace in India.

Some of the Studies based on Naxalite Movement in India

Banerjee, Sumanta (1980): S. Banerjee, joined the naxalite movement and was arrested in 1975, released from Jail, started career as Journalist but soon become academician becoming part of many universities in later year of life.

He talks about cultural perspective of naxalite movement in early decades. He says that every political rebellion is Iconoclastic. In its belief in the need for destroying the old-order, it rejected the culture of that regime lock, stock and barrel and break out into assaults on even the best artistic products of the past.

He mentioned that in 1960-70's naxalite movement have base in rural areas mostly but also popular in urban youth also. The naxalite youth upsurge in Calcutta and other urban centre of west Bengal during that period was marked by iconoclastic acts in the cultural scene like destruction of educational institution burning of literature of the past and vandalsing the statutes of 19th century Bengali social reformation.

In Andhra, story is just opposite; naxalite was not assaults on icons of Telugu culture. They even used Telugu literature, dramas to mobilize the people for movement.

Bengal naxalite movement of 1960-70 periods should be located first, in the domestic urban context of rising youth discontent against the moth eaten legacy of colonial education system; Bengali youth attack the statues and pictures of Indian political leaders and social reformers.

Bengali youth, under the leadership of Charu Mazumdar and CPI (ML) hailed it as "a war against Gandhi and Bourgeoisie leaders. CPI (ML) leadership also considers Rabindranath Tagore and other Bengali authors as bourgeoisie reactionaries who did not show enough interest in the light of the rural poor and working class.

This movement gives many historian, thinker and social reformer who even today give their valuable contribution in the society.

Ray Rabindra (1988): He explained, Charu Mazumdar in his life as in his Ideas was more a leader of the revolutionary than of peasants. His opinions of intellectual-erstwhile communist party cadres and student - youth deserve more attention than his reading of working people. Charu mazumdar has far sighted view, he understanding the mentality of peasants. He mobilised the people in 1970's (of the last century) the decades of liberation, which saw with his following and the Motivated Maoist leadership in China in the minuscule confrontation of naxalbari. The spring thunder of revolution in India, which proclaimed in the snatching of a rifle from a policemen by a peasant the founding of a people's Army; on his mystic faith in the Intense class hatred of the peasants for their superiors, which he believed was on the very point of exploding into action on a Mass scale.

Mao-Zedong, the avowed inspiration of the naxalites and Charu Mazumdar, has nothing explicitly to say about the psychology classes and class relations, but many of his works presume the psychological outburst of revolution and revolutionary situations and out breaks, and try to express in the way they are they written in the spirit of this psychology.

At the time of the leadership of Charu Mazumdar, there was a revolutionary crisis in Bengal and indeed in the country as a whole. This crisis mobilised rural masses. The naxalites themselves, urban intellectuals and communist activists, had rather first to foment such hatred and then give in murderous intent and organize it to begin to constitute the people's army that would liberate Bengal and the whole of the country, in Charu Mazumdar own explicit strategy. The crisis was rather a matter of the breakdown of trust, confidence and consensus necessary for governance and maintenance of order-a situation that characterised almost the whole of the country at the time and particularly Bengal. The central government suppressed the revolutionary movement and after the death and arrests of naxalite leaders this movement gets weaker in country and especially in Bengal. Congress government formed in the state and taken many steps to solve the problem and suppressed the people and leaders who support the people and leaders who support the movement.

Abhay, K. Dubey (1997): He mentioned the causes and factor responsible for origin of naxalite movement in India. In his book, he mentioned how naxal problem emerged in North Bengal in 1967 and spread to other part of country. In this movement student, peasant and Intellectual played important role Charu Mazumdar, Kanu Sanyal and Jangal Santhal are the prominent leaders of this movement. He also mention the state Intervention measures to solve the naxalite problem in 1970's He also explained how earlier movements like Tebhaga and Telengana provides grounds to naxalite movement.

Ajit Kumar (2002): He explains the factor responsible for emergence of naxalite Movement in Bihar. He also identified the naxal affected districts in Bihar and what are the factors responsible for emergence of naxalite Movements. He also discusses the organisational structure of naxalite organisation and private armies in Bihar.

In his studies he find out that mostly people worked as bonded agricultural labor, in rural areas. Poverty and unemployment is the biggest problem of Bihar, it leads to migration of people from Bihar to other states for Job opportunities.

In Bihar, mostly people depend on agriculture for their survival, they work on land of master for their livelihood and they are exploited by one or other ways, which leads to dissatisfaction among labour class and lastly they revolted against their feudal landlords.

Rao, M.S.A. (2002): In the book, he discuss that social movements have emerged throughout the history of Indian society and culture their study in a sociological framework is recent. Earlier social movement is considers as the issue related to history and its study starts after 1975 in sociology discipline in India.

In his book, he divided into two parts, part I, 6 chapter devoted mainly to peasant, backward classes, sectarian, tribal and women's Movement. He discusses the three peasant movements. Naxalbari, movement in Bengal Nijai Bol (declare ownership of land) and land grab movement in U.P. and the peasant movement of Telengana unfold the object conditions of the Indian peasant the way they organised around revolutionary ideologies of class struggle and the changes these movement has produced in agrarian relation.

Part II, six chapters discuss six types of movement and concept. It also covers three others types of movement student, trade union and naxalite which are not included in the volume.

Rao, focus is what are factors responsible for emergence of movement, what are role played by leadership, ideology on social movement, he also discuss the social movement and change occur in society, due to that movement.

Prasad, B.N. (2002): In his book, B.N. Prasad analyses the change in agrarian social transformation in the post-colonial era. The traditional agrarian social formation has undergone a sea change due to democratic value system, modernisation rising level of literacy, disintegration of feudal mode of production and emergence of capitalist mode of production, etc. However, traditionally disadvantageous castes/classes find themselves alienated from democratic institutions which are beyond their reach. Their discontent got interwoven with a Marxist-Leninist and Maoist Ideology. For their emancipation they followed the path of radical agrarian movement-leaving a trail of violence and challenged the very basis of feudal domination. On the other hand, traditionally influential castes/classes are finding it increasingly difficult to maintain their dominant positions, because democratic institutions have their own mode of functioning and logic of articulation. These two contradictory trends encourage various power groups to launch their 'caste senas' in order to consolidate their hegemony. These senas are mainly based on violence and derive their strength through extra-constitutional and extra parliamentary means. This syndrome further takes democratic institution to turn creates a vicious cycle in the agrarian social system. This study intends to explain the problems and prospects of agrarian social formation due to the emergence of capitalist mode of production within the structural, Marxist, frame work of social change.

Mukherjee, Arun Prasad (2007): A.K. Mukherjee, is district's superintendent of police in July 1965 and is posted in 1967 at Darjeeling district when a new brand of radical politics in India giving birth to a series of militant agitations and activities now known as the naxalite movement or naxalism.

He divided whole book into 5 chapters

CHAPTER-I	:	Discuss the Naxalbari Movement.
CHAPTER-II	:	Lesson to Naxalbari Movement.
CHAPTER-III	:	Naxalite activities in West Bengal and other parts of India.
CHAPTER-IV	:	Discuss the critiques of Charu Mazumdar, especially some if his writings and the CPI (ML) Policies and programmes by leader of the Chinese communist party and other fraternal parties.
CHAPTER-V	:	Then axalite leader view on this movement

He discusses his experience and his views and recent changes occur in this movement.

Bhonsle, R.K. (2007): He focuses on 2nd phase of Naxalism, after 1990, how it spread to 160 district of country land become biggest internal security problem.

He mentioned contrast between the forces of globalisation and naxalism in India, explains the prosperity poverty dyad that co-exists. The reality is that both these trends are significant for national development India cannot acquire the resources to develop its, "other" in which the naxals operate and without developing the, others" We cannot call ourselves citizens of a developed world, an aspiration of every Indian. Naxalism thus needs to be understood as a phenomenon of nation building, as its failed dimension, needing urgent palliatives essentially at the grass root level.

He also mention factor and causes responsible for second phase of naxal movement in India, he also discuss the contours of naxalite movement and explain how this movement becomes popular in India. Today 55 districts are worst affected where the naxalite are reportedly running a parallel government. He divided naxal affected areas into three categories.

Tier 1 : **Abujmadh Area** : Under total control of the naxals, needs to establish state Authority.

Tier 2 : 55 worst affected district-reestablish state authorities, neutralise parallel influence of naxals.

Tier 3 : Balance of 100 plus districts contain naxal influence, enhances effectiveness of state authority.

He also discusses the counter naxal strategies to deal naxal menance in India.

He also discuss the grass root governance importance to deal this problem, he focus on state action of socio-economic and infrastructural development of naxal affected areas and changes or transformation occur in last two decades in India.

Singh Prakash (2006): P. Singh is former DG BSF and DGP of Uttar Pradesh. He has spent most of his life on security of country, he is expert on India Internal Security Problem, in his book, and he mentions the emergence of naxalite movement in West Bengal of 1967, at the tri-junction of India, Nepal and Bangladesh. He mention what are the factor responsible for it spread from one part to other part of country. This movement is against the feudal landlord and their exploitative nature. Santhal tribes of Naxalbari village under the leadership of Charu Mazumdar and Kanu Sanyal take violent action against this oppressor class of West Bengal.

He also mentions the role of CPI (ML) and its cadres in this movement. This movement is drawing inspiration from Maoist ideology. This violent movement was at a peak from about the middle of 1970 to the middle of 1971.

The political parties realised the emergence of new force. The government became conscious of a new threat not only to law and order but to very democratic structure of the country. He also mentions the state role to suppress this movement in country in 1974. But this movement again enters into second phase in 1980's, with the formation of people's war group in Andhra Pradesh under the leadership of Kondapalli Seetharamaih. This phase movement is stronger and attracts the poor and marginalised section of society because of P.W.G. policy and programmes.

This movement is more violent in Bihar, Andhra, Chhattisgarh, Jharkhand, W. Bengal, Orissa, Maharashtra, M.P. and Uttar Pradesh specially.

The movement got a tremendous boost when its two major components, the people's wear (PWG) and the Maoist Communist Centre of India (MCCI) decided to merge on March, 21, 2004. They form a Red corridor from Tirupati to Pashupati (Nepal). They seem parallel Government in 55 districts of country and having strong hold.

He also mentions the Government comprehensive 14 point plan to deal with the problem. There is special emphasis on Socio-Economic Development and Land Reform in naxal affected areas.

S. Chakravarti (2008): In this book, he discuss the emergence of naxal movement and it path of four decades in which many changes occur in this movement he mainly focus the changes occur after 1991, and government policy of liberalisation, privatisation and globalisation and its impact on society.

He discuss, Maoism today is something vaguely alarming, to do with shifting lines on the country's map that they see every once in a while in the mainstream media.

The danger lies in increasing the degree of denial. By all accounts, half a billion people will remain a long way away from the country's high-growth party in the foreseeable future. They won't like it one bit, and many even a modest one percent of this amounts to five millions people could do anything to crash the party, to destroy the framework, if they cannot join in the merry making. There is already enough ill will and resentment about for generation. Here's just one example; by the government's own reports, of the 40 million people displaced since independence by various projects like dams and big industries, less than a quarter have been rehabilitated. For the rest, policy is as you go, or none at all. There was the incident of the chief engineer for a dam on the Narmada river in Madhya Pradesh simply painting '162' over the 'approved' figure of '101' when the number of villages sub-merged by the dam project exceeded the latter amount. *A/c to a report by Amrita Patwardhan, 'Dams and Tribal people in India, more than 1.7 million tribals have been displaced by major dam projects*. The areas for which these members are highest match the naxalite-affected areas of Orissa, Bihar, West Bengal, Andhra Pradesh, Madhya Pradesh, Maharashtra and Uttrakhand.

He also discusses the new strategies adopted by naxalite and their urban base in the city, and government measure taken to solve this problem in his book.

Ramana, P.V. (2008): This book is the out come of a two day national workshop on the naxalite movement, hosted by observer research foundation (ORF) at Chennai on 28th and 29th January 2005. Academician, Journalist with grass root knowledge, experienced policy makers, bureaucrats and police officers with hands on experience in dealing with the naxalite issue.

These people express their view on social and economic causes of the naxalite movement; its political bases; the viability of a political approach to solve the problem; the revolutionary and counter revolutionary strategies of the naxalites and the state, respectively and the external linkages of the naxalites additionally, there is an insightful discussion on the Maoist people's war in Nepal.

He also discuss naxalite movement is essentially an ideological movement and not an ethnic or religious one. It gets its sustenance from social evils such as poverty, unemployment, exploitation of the poor classes etc. It is also a movement which has drawer into its fold a large number of poor people across the tribal belt of India.

It cannot be tackled through an exclusively law and order approach. It has to be tackled through a judicious mix of incentives, disincentives and political initiatives incentives for the large sections of the population in the affected areas who have kept away from the movement despite intimidation; disincentives for those who have taken to violence in the form of vigorous application of the law against them and political initiatives to counter the ideological attraction of the movement and to wean away from violence those who cannot be described as die hard. Disincentives and political initiatives are not alternatives. They have to go together.

The review of literature reveal theoretical as well as practical aspects of naxalism-its ideology, genesis, patterns of structural in equality in rural India, the history of naxal movement, state intervention and measures of rural development in naxal effected areas, etc. In the background of these studies, the present study attempts to investigate the patterns of socio-economic development in contemporary context, nature of satisfaction/dissatisfaction with developmental measures and suggest strategies of rural development in naxal affected areas.

Chattopadhyaya, Kunal (2010): He discussed about the emergence of naxalite movement in 1960's and its relationship with classical Marxism.

He discuss the early history of communism in India went through a rupture Meerut conspiracy case dealt the emerging communist party a sharp blow. He talks about the role of International communist and Stalin role. How Indian communist leaders influence by Mao-Zedong and his ideologies how these leaders rejected the parliamentary model of government. He also mention the political drift between the communist party on the issue of political system i.e. parliamentary Democracy in India. Parties like CPI (ML) consider in democracy state run by bourgeoisie leaders and democratic system not gives fruitful result to all section of society, it is good for elite class only.

Pradeep Basu (2010): The Book seeks to present Insightful analysis of various aspects of the naxalite movement, especially in relation to different broader aspects such as social, political, economic and cultural issues.

In the 'cultural' section, we have opinion and view on naxalite politics as related to various topics like Bengali culture, the subaltern post colonial theory, Bourgeois rewriting and representation in the press.

In the 'Ideology' section there are different view on class-hatred; Ideological causes of disaster, Marxist-theoretical criticism and dialogue with post structuralism.

In the 'Social Issue' section researchers addressed issues of gender, environmental degradation and naxalites in Orissa; land, caste and tribal question of poverty, Tribals and Dalits, etc.

In the Socio-Economic Issues, section contribution are on alternative model of development in Dandakaranaya, the issue of poverty, landlessness, caste and feudal exploitation etc.

In the 'organisation section' articles have discussed new theoretical concept of party organisation, democracy, problem of fragmentation.

In the legal-administrative issues section, scholars presented Ideological issues from an administrator's point of view, the perspectives of constitutional Jurisprudence, police response and critiques by an experienced administrator.

In the 'Political section' we have researcher view on civil society, also democracy and revolution, evolution of Naxalism in Kerala; analysis of political factors, Urban violence in Kolkata and evolution in other parts.

Sahni, Ajay (2010): He explains internal security problem in India emerged due to state's response to critical security challenges. Centre launched operation 'Green Hunt' in the Maoist affected areas specially centre India, in reaction to this operation naxalite started targeting poorly trained police and central Para-military force (CPMF) personnel naxalite are more trained, and master in Guerilla warfare.

The government policies and programs are not sufficient. The effort to construct monolithic national internal security architecture is enormously misdirected as a response to conflict that demands the widest possible decentralisation of response capabilities and decision making.

In the age of liberalisation, globalisation and rapid growth, the Indian reality remains polarised between great and at least occasionally obscene-wealth and Abysmal poverty. One side rich people number increased in country, on the other side, there has been a deepening of poverty among the countries poorest over precisely the period of its great development the past decade and a half.

The National commission for enterprises in the unorganised sector thus noted, in 2008, that 77 per cent of the populations (836 million) were living on less than INR 20 per day.

The Suresh Tendulkar Committee has determined that those living in 'Absolute-Poverty' with a consumption of less than INR 12 per day constitute 37 percent of the population.

He mentioned the state measures, in this direction, government focus on the basic problems of people and developed infrastructure in remote areas of country. Awareness generation by both government and NGO's in rural areas, so that they get benefit of various government policies and programme. Corrupt Bureaucrat and police officer, forest officer punished and the naxalite people who are willingly surrender provide them relaxation in Imprisonment and after there released to Jail provide them some money and provided them some self-employed programme to their future needs naxalites children learn and educated and provide them basic necessary facilities to naxalite family member one or the other ways so that they also come into mainstream of the society and given their valuable contribution.

Anuradha M. Chenoy and Kamal A. Mitra Chenoy (2010)

In this book, they mention that one-sixth (1/6) of India's citizen live in area of armed conflicts. People used weapon to resolve disputes or fulfill demands that have a political, social, cultural, economic origin.

The goals or social transformation that armed conflicts seek to achieve may originate from contesting claims. Terrorism or violence may be used as a tactic or sometimes as a statement of communication. Conflicts can be between groups or between groups and the state, over control of political power and resources. It often originates because of and sustains itself on the deprivation of rights and is aggravated by conditions of poor human security. Armed conflict is different from war, since it can be of lower intensity and sustained over longer periods of time, armed conflicts can encompass insurgency. Violent political struggles, violent liberation movement and violent movement for social change.

He also mention the political or economic grievances and disagreement or belief in certain rights like the right to self determination or the struggle for a change in the structure of power may acts as a trigger. These demands could be interpreted as being for more autonomy or even Independence and thus be met with force by the state.

They explain conflict model and their relevance low intensity armed conflict between extreme left wing. Maoist cadres and the Indian state forces have been going on for over four decades in various regions. They explain their origin and factors responsible for it.

Priyedarshi, Vinita (2010): He explained the origin of naxalite movement in West Bengal (1967). She also explains the factor responsible for rise of naxalite movement and also explains and witnessed the method adopted by Andhra Pradesh Government to check the threat of Naxalism. She also discusses why the same strategy does not seem to yield similar results in other naxal-affected states. This is because each prong has a number of Imperative attached. These form an intrinsic part of the overall strategy which the Government has failed to knit into a comprehensive whole. Until each of these imperatives are addressed and interlinked to formulate a comprehensive and coordinated counter naxalite strategy, success will continue to elude the security forces. The counter naxal experience of the state shows that whenever these strategies imperatives have been considered, the strategy has paid dividends. There is therefore, an urgency to make the agencies dealing with naxalism aware of these strategic imperatives and incorporate these at the tactical and operational levels.

Rana, Subir (2010): He is talking about the emergence of naxalite movement in eastern Uttar Pradesh district namely

Sonbhadra, Mirzapur and Chandauli. In these areas, naxalite activities started taking roots since the last part of 1990's and the early decades of the 21st century. Naxalism in South Eastern Uttar Pradesh owes it genesis to Issues like deprivation, poverty, caste oppression and the lopsided, inequitable and conked out models of development.

In his case study, he explain that these areas are rich in natural resources, and having Industrialisation also at some extent but yet district witnessed number of starvation death especially of women and children in the past few years. It has high incidence of Malaria cases and the maximum numbers of victims of floursis in India are from the nine village of Sonbhadra.

Poverty and Backwardness of eastern Uttar Pradesh get further contextualised by taking a look at the internal disparities within U.P. and between U.P. and rest of India. In these districts nearly 40 per cent of total population constituted by the scheduled caste literacy ratio is also very poor;

He is also mentioning the emergence of naxalite movement in 1970's but that time naxal activities were more frequent in the hilly districts which are now part of Uttarakhand.

He also discusses the naxal violence occur in last two decades in Eastern Uttar Pradesh. In his study he discusses what are the factors responsible for emergence of Naxalism in Eastern Uttar Pradesh.

Samanta, K. Amiya (2010) for more than forty year the naxalite movement has been an essential part of India's police security scenario. Apparently political in nature the movement has deep roots in various types of deprivation, economic exploitation and discrimination in the rural society. During long course of the movement a variety of strategies have been experimented by a multitude of groups, but its core ideology has undergone little change. The reckless violence resorted to by the Maoist revolutionaries and the counter revolutionary forces as also by the state has often stirred the nation to its depth drawing criticism from all and sundry. But still the magnitude of violence and number of deaths, show hardly any sign of diminishing, over a vast area of jungle and hilly terrain they have established some kind of fluctuating Authority through terror; yet they are far away from capturing state power which is their declared objective.

Pattanaik, Sarmistha (2010): In her study of 'Environmental Movement' is quite exploratory and new in the area of naxalite movement and secondly the study of social movement is very sensitive and so also naxalite movement particularly, any observation and generalisation on an inadequate or incomplete understanding of the issues and events are academically unethical and may be unjustified. She also explains the current and contemporary linkage and relevance to Ecology-Maoist movement.

For the last several years the state of Orissa has become a centre of many militant mass struggles against displacement and land grabbing.

The struggle of Adivasis (Scheduled Tribes) in Orissa and its violent reprisal highlight how conflicts over land and related natural resources viz. water, forest and minerals remain central to the challenge of India's development.

The heroic sacrifice of 13 Tribals in Kalinga Nagar in 2006 and the subsequent resistance which is still going on against Vedanta and Posco as well as Tata is a pointer to this fact. Equally the most crucial issue is the case of naxalite's struggle vis-a-vis the use of their violent means in many part of India and in Orissa has created havoc for our democracy since they claim to represent a single party with the sole aim of over throwing the Bourgeoisie state and seizing political power.

According to Planning Commission Report 2006 development challenges in extremist affected areas like Land alienation, poverty amongst scheduled Tribes and Dalits and lack of access to basic forest resources have contributed to the growth of Naxalism.

(Down to Earth; 2008)

The report also critiques SEZs and the complete failure of Instruments like the Panchayat (Extension to scheduled area) Act 1996 (PESA) and the Forest (Conservation) Act 1980. The Question today is poised as whether the role of Environments degradation does escalate Maoist violence n India.

Rani Midatala (2010): She explain the emergence of naxalite movement and role played by Radical communist party CPI (ML) and its leaders Charu Mazumdar she explain how movement start in small pocket of north Bengal and emerged as one of the biggest movement in the history of India. In 1969 Movement people used violent means against their oppressor and state machinery. Intellectual, student, media also supported the movement.

Today naxalite are active across 220 districts in 20 state accounting for 40 per cent of India's geographical areas known as the 'Red corridor', where they control 92,000 square kilometers. According to the Research and Analysis wing, 20,000 armed cadres' naxalites were operating apart from 50,000 regular cadres working in various mass organisations.

Manivannan, Ramu (2010): In his study, he mentioned the Red corridor phenomenon is beginning to haunt the Indian party/political system and our ruling elites. It is failure of our political democracy that has created a situation like the present due to marginalisation and exploitation of the tribal population. They have not been included in the discourse of democracy and development in Post Independence India. The core Issues are those of development and empowerment. India's electoral democracy cannot be sustained with the conduct of elections as a political function but with the more open and Inclusive process of the marginalised communities and poor people being brought in as part of our world view real challenge that cannot be dismissed as the problem of political violence that can only be resolved through another form of violence state violence. In either way, India awaits a revolution-Democratic Revolution through dialogue or Revolutionary democracy saturated in violence. The choice is before us.

Mishra, S.K., Naxalwad (2010): Surendra K. Mishra as a defense analyst explains the factors and causes responsible for emergence of naxalite movement in India. He discusses the naxalite issue in his book, and discussed separately naxal terror in different states.

He differentiates between naxalism and maoism in his book. He also discuss, how naxalite ideology change in recent years, and their main objective is totally change-they want only political power in their hand, they also attack the government property and collecting extortion money to government agencies and private companies in recent year.

References

Bandyopadhyay. D (2007): Rural Unrest, Yojana, February issues on Naxalism.

Banerjee, Sumanta (2008): Mapping a Rugged Terrain : Naxalite politics and Bengali culture in the 1970.

Basu, Pradeep (2010): Naxalite Movement (1967-2009) Insight into Radical left Politics, Setuprakashani, Kolkatta, 2010.

Bhardwaj, K. (1991), Alternative Analytical Paradigms in theories of Development, "Breen rah Jan and Mundle, S. (Edited) : Rural Transformation in Asia, Delhi, Oxford University Press.

Bhonsle, R.K. (2007): An Integrated strategy, Yojana, Feb. 2007, Issue on Naxalism.

Breman, Jan and Sudipto Mundle (Eds) (1991): Rural Transformation in Asia, Oxford University Press, Delhi.

Chakravorti, Sudeep (2006): Redsun, Penguin Indian Publication, New Delhi.

Chattopadyaya, Kunal (2010): The Path of Naxalbari.

Chaudhary Arindham (2011): Long live the Naxalite Movement.

Chenoy, M. Anuradha and Kamal A. Mitra Chenoy (2010): Maoist and other Armed Conflict Penguin Book India, 2010, New Delhi.

Dak, T. M (ed) Social Transformation in India Ajanta Publications, Delhi.

Das, Rajput (1999): Geographical Unevenness of India's. Green Revolutionary Journal of Contemporary Asia, 2a (2).

Desai, A.R. (1985), A New Policy for Rural Development in South and South East Asia's, C.G. Shah Memorial Trust Publication, Mumbai.

Dhanagare, D.N. (1980), The Green Revolution and Social Inequalities in Rural India, Bulletin of Concerned Asian Scholars, 20(2).

Gupta, Akhil (1998): Post Colonial Development: Agriculture in the making of Modern India, Oxford University Press, Delhi.

Harris, John (ed.) (1986), Rural Development: Theories of Peasant Economy and Agrarian, Change Hutchinson; ELBS.

In the wake of Naxalbari: A History of Naxalite Movement in India, Subarnarekha, Calcutta, 1980, 2008.

Jain, L.C. (2007) Panacea could lie in Panchayats, Yojana, February Issue on Naxalism.

Kumar, Ajit (2004): History of Naxalite Movement in Bihar, Samkaleen Publication.

Kumar, Ravindra (1983), Need of bring about Rural Transformation, Kurukshetra, March, 16-31.

Lipton, Michael (1991): "Agriculture, Rural people, The State and the Surplus in some Asian countries. Thoughts on some Implications of three recent approaches in social sciences." Bremean and Mundle (ed), op.cit.

Manivannan, Ramu (2010): Democratic Revolution or Revolutionary Democratic.

Mishra, S.K (2010) Naxalwad K.W Publishers, New Delhi.

Mukherjee, Arun Prasad (2007): Maoist Spring Thunder: The Naxalite Movement (1967-1972), K.P. Bagchi and Company, Kolkatta.

Prasad, B.N. (2002): Radicalism and Violence in Agrarian Structure The Maoist Movement in Bihar, Manak Publications Pvt. Ltd., New Delhi.

Priyedarshi, Vinita (2010): Drafting a counter Naxalite strategy Journal of U.S.I. of India, Vol CXL, No 580, April-June 2010.

Ramana, P.V. (2008): The Naxal Challenge Causes, linkages and policy options. Pearson long man, India.

Rana, Subir (2010): Land, Caste and Tribal Imbroglio. A Case study on Naxalite movement of Uttar Pradesh, Published in Naxalite Movement (1967-2009) edited by Pradip Basu, Setu Prakashani, Kolkatta,

Rani, Midatala (2009): Analyzing political Dimension of the Naxalite Movement.

Rao, M.S.A. (2002): Social Movement in India, Manohar Publishers and Distributors, New Delhi.

Ray, Rabindra (1988) Naxalism and Class Hatred The Naxalite and their Ideology, Oxford University Press, New Delhi, 1988.

Routray, J.K. and Patnaik,M. (1982), "Transformation of Rural Habitat: Concept and Approach", Kurukshetra, Vol. XXX, No. 8, Jan.16-31.

Sahni, Ajay (December, 2010): The Threat within strengthening Internal security Mechanism, U.S.I. Defense Journal, Vol. CXL, No 58, New Delhi.

Samanta, K. Amiya (2010): Ideological Issues in the Naxalite Movement Left Extremist Movement: An Experiment in Armed Agrarian Struggle, FIRMA, KLM Pvt. Ltd. Calcutta.

Samistha, Pattanaik (2009): Does Environmental Degradation Escalate Naxalist Violence.

Singh, Prakash (2006): The Naxalite Movement in India, Rupa and Company, New Delhi, 2006.

Singh, Yogendra (1990): Contemporary Social Transformation in India. Processes and contradictions."

Suri, K.C. (2006): Political Economy of Agrarian Distress: Economic and Political Weekly 41;15;23-29.

Tiwary, Jai Kant (1984), Rural Development Administration, Chugh Publication, Allahabad.

Tiwary, Jai Kant (1994), Rural Transformation in India Reliance India Publication, New Delhi.

3

Design of Research

Statement of the Problem

The present study is an attempt to analyze the nature and process of social transformation in a rural setting especially in naxal affected areas. The process of social transformation is an outcome of various factors such as State Intervention Measures, role of civil society, people's participation, role of NGO's, banking system, micro finance, SHG's etc.

After Independence India attempted to eliminate the colonial legacy of underdevelopment and social backwardness by adopting various measures to reshape the economy, social structure and cultural life. The newly emerged Independent State has been trying to follow a path of rural development. Under the rubric of this path of rural development, various types of measures have been adopted by state in India.

Some of the significant measures of States Interventions include:

1. Legislative efforts: Laws in the form of land reforms viz. Zamindari abolition, ceilings tenancy reforms, Land redistribution, cooperatives, scale down of debts; consolidation and reconstitution of extremely fragmented and subdivided units of land.
2. Agricultural Innovations like green revolution generating irrigation and power facilities, standardisation of weight and

measures, building up a network of transport and communication facilities.

3. Establishment of Research Institute in Agriculture Sector to improve the productivity of Agriculture and augment Production.
4. Poverty Alleviation Programmes
5. Distribution of fertilizers, seeds, agriculture equipment etc.
6. Minimum Price support by government.
7. Marketing.

It was assumed that these programmes of Social transformation would provide the initial stimulus and the people will actively and willingly cooperate in these programmes. It was assumed that the benefits of these programmes will percolate down to the rural poor, all these assumption proved to be wrong in the coming years. The programmes were also ambitious both in terms of financial outlays and targets and expectation of the people because of these, all over hopes were belied and its generated general apathy, resistance and unrest among the rural poor and this lead to anti-state movement in different part of country in 1967 and famously called naxalite movement, because this movement originated in naxalbari village of Darjeeling district of West Bengal, hence it is name (Naxalite Movement) but soon spread to other part of country.

In the context of these problems, present study is based on Sonbhadra district of Uttar Pradesh to find out the Social transformation in naxal affected areas, especially after the emergence of naxalite movement. In this study, we attempt to find out the result of various state intervention measures and how this programme brings Social transformation in rural areas especially in last two decades.

Objective of the study:

1. To conceptualize the process of social transformation.
2. To analyze the emergence of naxalism in the Sonbhadra region.
3. To evaluate the measures of State intervention and Social transformation

4. To observe the nature of Social transformation in Sonbhadra district in a socio-historical perspective.
5. To observe government programmes implemented in Sonbhadra district after Independence and particularly in last two decades.

Hypothesis:

- Greater the level of poverty and unemployment, higher the chances of involvement in naxal activities.
- Greater the political socialisation, higher the participation in naxal activity.
- Greater the state interventions in poverty alleviation and employment generation programmes greater the decrease in violent activities in the naxal region.
- Greater the police suppression and restrictions, higher the naxal activities in region.

Historical Background:

Sonbhadra district have a historical cultural heritage since ancient time it is famous centre of Buddhism and Hinduism, many Stupas, Vihars and Archaeological importance, evidences found in recent year, this shows that it centre of ancient cultural importance in Asoka reign it is also famous for its natural beauty and part of Magadha kingdom, Chinese traveler, in their literature they mention this area as a importance centre of Buddhist Religion. This area is also centre of Hindu Religion, it covered with dense forest, hilly terrain where many Rishi, established their Ashram in recent times.

In this region, there is many famous Kingdom in Ancient and Medieval period, such as Kol, Kingdom, Bhara, Kharwar, Shivery, Cherro Kingdom who ruled thousand of year but soon power struggle begin and this area come under the Rajput ruler of Ghardwal and Chandelle Ruler in Ancient period.

In medieval period, this region come under the dominance of Mughal Ruler, Sonbhadra is famous for red sand stone, which is used in Agra Fort, Red Fort, and many historical monument of the Mughal period. Many evidences found in this region shows that, in this region, Aurangzeb, destroyed 150 Hindu Temples.

In modern time, this region comes under British Empire till 1947.

Administrative Structure:

Sonbhadra district is second largest district (Area-wise) of Uttar Pradesh. It headquarter is situated in Robertsganj.

Sonbhadra is divided into three tehsils- Robertsganj, Duddhi and Ghorawal Tehsils; District having 8 Blocks-Duddhi, Ghorawal, Robertsganj, Chatra, Nagwa,Chopan, Myorpur and Bhabhani district having 67 Nyaya Panchayat and 501 Gram Panchayat, which is backbone for local administration. At grass root level district having total 1443 village in which 1382 village population lived rest 61 with no population lived and 12 declared as forest village. District has one Nagar Palika and seven Nagar Panchyat.

District having total 16 police stations 8 in Rural Areas and Rest 8 in urban areas, which is responsible for maintaining law and order condition in the region.

Development Blocks

1. **Duddhi:** This block having total population of 1225515 (According to 2001 census) total village in this block is 102. In this block mostly people involved in agricultural activities.
2. **Ghorawal:** Ghorawal block having 354 villages, with rural population of about 218825, mostly people involved in agricultural activities for their livelihood.
3. **Robertsganj:** The district headquarters is in this town. It is more developed compared to other blocks. Mostly administrative office hospitals, located are in this block. In these block total 359 villages comes with a population of about 232562, in which 121561 Male and 111001 female populations. Most people involved in non-agricultural activities.
4. **Chatra:** Chatra is located between Nagwa block and Robertsganj, this block is naxal affected block where mostly

people involved in agricultural activities or worked as labor under various government schemes such as MNREGA. In this block total population is bout 88267, in which 40 per cent population belongs to scheduled caste and scheduled tribes' category. This block having 103 primary school, 32 middle and 5 high school, which are mostly a recently constructed by government.

5. **Chopan:** In this block total population is about 2, 27022, in which male population is 119020, and 108002 female. Most people involved in agricultural activities.
6. **Myorpur:** In this block, total village is 118, with a population of 1,79,332, in which block also more than 50 per cent population belongs to scheduled caste and scheduled tribes category, mostly areas covered with forest, and people dependent on forest and forest product for their livelihood. In this block there are only 9 middle schools and 55 primary schools. Infrastructure development is also very less.
7. **Bhabhani:** This block is also very less developed situated near to Chhattisgarh state. So it is also naxal affected areas, where recent year many naxal activities reported. In these block only 72 villages comes, with total population of 79870 in which more than 60 per cent population belongs to scheduled caste and tribes' category. Most of the people involved in agricultural and labor works.
8. **Nagwa Block:** This is the mostly backward and less developed block compare to other 7 blocks. This block covered with forest and hilly terrain and boundary touches with Kaimur district of Bihar, which is part of red corridor and one of the worst naxal affected district of country, Nagwa block is also worst affected by left extremism and declared as naxal block and many villages comes under this villages are declared as naxal villages an special fund allotted to these villages for infrastructure development. This block have 153 villages, with population of 73922 in which more than 50 per cent people belonged to schedule caste and scheduled tribes. In this block more than

70 per cent area come under forest development and remaining are as comes under villages. Mostly people worked as labor in this block under various government programmes. This block also received major part of backward district initiative and Samvikas Yojana of central government schemes.

In last decade between1998 to 2010 some of the major naxal activities in this region are-

10th August, 1998: In Siyariya Chalaka village, naxalite attack superintendent of police, Radheshyam Tripathi vehicle.

25th February, 2003: Naxalite attack Vijaygarh King Shri Sharat Chandra Padma Shah Vehicle, killed king and his two associate in this attack.

26th February, 2004: Naxalite attack the stone industry and burns the machines, tractor, Dumpher etc.

2nd August, 2005: Naxalite killed Indra Kumar Gujjar, as police suspect and informer.

April, 2007: Naxal leaders Sanjay Kol killed in police counter.

February, 2008: Top naxal leader Satendra Kushwaha of Sonebhadra district was arrested by intelligence inputs.

March, 17, 2009: Three C.P.I. Maoist cadres, identified as Vinod Yadav, Vinod Thakur and Shyamlal were arrested by the police during a search operation near the bank of Sone River, under Kone police station in the Sonbhadra, the three hail, by police also recovered some gelatin rods and detonators from their possession.

September 6, 2009: A suspected naxalite identified as Raju alias Raj Mohan, who was operating in state and in adjoining Bihar, was arrested near Bewdar village in Sonbhadra district with 20 gelatin sticks, 10 detonators, revolver and cartridge.

October 1, 2009: Sonbhadra police arrested an Area Commander of C.P.I. Maoist Identified as Anil Thakur alias Baikunth in Maikaha area under Kone police station after a brief gun battle.

Novermber 9, 2009: A naxalite, identified as Kamlesh Chowdhary, was killed in an encounter with the police in Kanach village under Chopan police circle in Sonbhadra District, a senior government officer said in state capital, Lucknow, Chowdhary was wanted in 32 different cases including that of murder in Bihar and Uttar Pradesh, he was carrying a reward of INR 1,50,000.

December, 3, 2009: Ram Krishna Kol, a cadre of the CPI Maoist carrying a head money of INR 50,000 was found dead in Kone forest area of Sonbhadra, after police encounter, two other Rakesh Mishra and Amarnath Kushwaha were arrested.

December 11, 2009.: CPI Maoist cadres be headed a 25 year old man after branding him a police informer.

Universe of Study

The present study is based on 3 blocks of Sonbhadra district namely Robertsganj, Chatra and Nagwa block.

In these three blocks, the following twelve villages have been selected for empirical investigation work.

In Robertsganj	: Dewari, Bahuara and Bhavanauli
In Chatra	: Alkar, Rakki and Harthan
In Nagwa block	: Suarsoat, Kamhariya, Benni, Padri, Khadra and Kuran village.

The selection of these villages is based on the criterion that these villages are recognised by the Government as naxal affected.

Sonbhadra is the 2nd largest district of Uttar Pradesh. The district has an area of 6788 km sq having a population of 1,463,468 (2001 census) with a population density of 216 persons per km. sq. It lies in the extreme southeast of the state, and is bounded by Mirzapur District to northwest, Chandauli districts of Bihar state to the Northeast, Garhwa district of Jharkhand state to the east, Koriya and Surguja districts of Chhattisgarh state to the south and Singrauli district of Madhya Pradesh state to the west. The district headquarter is in the town of Robertsganj. It is the only district in India which borders four states namely Madhya Pradesh, Chhattisgarh, Jharkhand and Bihar. It is currently a part of Red Corridor Movement.

The Red Corridor is a term used to describe an impoverished region in the east of India that experiences considerable naxalite Communist Insurgency, these are also areas that suffer from the greatest illiteracy, poverty and over population in modern India and span parts of Andhra Pradesh, Bihar, Chhattisgarh, Jharkhand, Madhya Pradesh, Orissa, Uttar Pradesh and West Bengal states.

Naxalites have been declared as a terrorist organisation under the unlawful activities prevention act of India (1967). According to Govt. of India, as of July 2011, 83 districts have worst affected district across nine states.

The Sone river flows through the district from east to west and its tributary the Rihand River, while rises to the South in the highlands of Surguja district of Chhattisgarh, flows north to join the son in the center of the district.

Sonbhadra is located in the South-Eastern ranges of the Vindhyachal Mountain. The Govind Ballabh Pant Sagar, a reservoir on the Rihand, lies partly in the district and partly in M.P. The district has historic cultural and ecological affinities with the Bagelkhand region. Obra and NTPC Rihand are the power projects located in this city.

The Southern region of Sonbhadra district is referred as the Energy Capital of India. This region has many electrical Power stations.

This region became an Industrial heaven from an area of forest and hills. Some of the hills were having limestone while most of them were having coal.

Owing to the limestone hills, initially one cement factory was established at Churk in 1956. Later another cement factory started at Dala in 1971 and ancillary unit of Dala got started at Chunar in 1980. The Cement industry became the foundation on which other Industries were built. A big dam constructed at Pipari in 1961, named Rihand Dam. The dam produced 300 MW of Electricity.

The Birla group set-up an aluminum plant at Renukoot, which is one of the largest aluminum plant of Hindalco.

Demographic Structure

The total geographical area of Sonbhadra district in 6788 Km^2- and population of 18,62,612 (2011 census) with a population density of 268 person per Km. (Approx.) Literary rate is 66.18 (2011 census) earlier it was only 34.40 per cent (2001 census) this shows that there is improvement in literacy comparison to 2001. Male literacy is 77.19/ (2011) earlier (2001) it was only 47.56 per cent same to female also. 54.11 per cent (2011) earlier, it was only 18.65 (2001).

In Sonbhadra district, due to Government welfare programme and measures, there is improvement in sex ratio 913/1000 male 2011, earlier it was only 898 (2001 census). In this region many tribal's are also found such as Kol, Kharwar, Ghasia etc. but till 2005-2006, there are included in scheduled caste population only 493 tribal population counted in 2001 census, which is increased to 600 in 2011 census data, but due political mobilisation among these tribes, they recently included in Tribal at national level census at presently there population is about 3 lakhs (approximately).

Demographic Feature of Sonbhadra (2011)

Person	:	18,62,612
Sex Ratio (F/1000M)	:	913
Sex Ratio (0-6 Years)	:	920
Growth (2001-2011)	:	23.77 per cent
Rural	:	15 Lacs (approx.)
Urban	:	3 lacs 80 thousand (approx.)
Literacy	:	66.18 per cent
(a) Male	:	77.19
(b) Female	:	54.11

Source: Census of India-2011.

The present study is based on 3 blocks of Sonbhadra district namely Robertsganj, Chatra and Nagwa block.

In these three blocks, the following twelve villages have been selected for empirical investigation work.

In Robertsganj	: Dewari, Bahuara and Bhavanauli
In Chatra	: Alkar, Rakki and Harthan
In Nagwa block	: Suarsoat, Kamhariya, Benni, Padri, Khadra and Kuran village.

The selection of these villages is based on the criterion that these villages are recognised by the Government as naxal affected.

In my study, I am choosing 12 villages for my study, in my study Nagwa is worst affected. So I am choosing 6 villages, and Robertsganj and Chatra having less Naxal violence, therefore 3-3 village from both block has been chosen for study.

Sample: The total member of households in 12 villages of Robertsganj, Chatra and Nagwa blocks is 3334 households of these households we have selected 10 per cent as sample households for the present purpose. Numerically, the ten percent of the total households comes 333. But despite our repeated efforts, no contact could have established by the 13 householders. Hence, the present study consists of 320 samples. These samples represent one member from each household selected randomly. Both male and female members according to their availability during field survey have been incorporated in the sample. Altogether the study consists of males and females as a sample that represents their households.

Statistical Method Used in Study:

Social statistics is the use of statistical measurement systems to study human behavior in a social environment. This can be accomplished through polling a particular group of people evaluating a particular subset of data obtained about a group of people, or by observation and statistical analysis of a set of data that relates to people and their behaviors. Statistical analysis of present data is done by using SPSS 16.0 software package.

Social scientists use social statistics for many purposes, including (but not limited to)

1. The evaluation of the quality of services available to a particular group or organisation.
2. Analyzing behaviors of groups of people in their environment and special situations, and
3. Determining the wants or needs of people through statistical sampling.

A number of methods, techniques and concepts have been developed or extensively used in various branches of quantitative social sciences some of the statistical method used in my Research work are mention below:

1. **Percentage:** Percentage is a way of expressing a number as a fraction of 100 (per cent) meaning per hundred in Latin. It is often denoted using the percent Sign %"

   Percentages are used to express how large/small one quantity is relative to another quantity. The first quantity usually represents a part of, or a change in, the second quantity, which should be greater than zero.

2. **Arithmetic mean:** The most popular and widely used measure of representing the entire data by one value is what most laymen call an 'average' and what the statisticians call the arithmetic mean. Its value is obtained by adding together all the items and by dividing this total by the number of items.

$$X = \frac{\Sigma X}{N}$$

   Here:

   $\overline{X}$ = Arithmetic means

   Σ X = Sum of all the values of the variable X

   N = Number of observations

3. **T-Test:** In social statistics, an effect size is a measure of the strength of the relationship between two variables in a

statistical population, or a sample based estimate of the quantity.

$$t = \frac{X_1 - X_2}{S.E}, SE = \sqrt{SE_{1^2} + SE_{2^2}}$$

4. x^2 **Defined-Chi square:** The x^2 test (pronounced as chi-square) test is one of the simplest and most widely used non-parametric tests in statistical work. The symbol x^2 is the Greek letter Chi. The x^2 test was first used by Karl Pearson in the year 1900. The quantity x^2 describes the magnitude of the discrepancy between theory and observation. It is defined as:

$$\chi^2 = \Sigma \frac{(0-E)^2}{E}$$

Where O, refers to the observed frequencies and E refers to the expected frequencies.

5. **Degree of Freedoms:** Comparing the calculated value of with the table value we have to determine the degrees of freedom. By degrees of freedom we mean the number of classes to which the values can be assigned arbitrarily or at will without violating the restrictions or limitations placed.

   df = (r-1). (C-1)

   Where r = no. of rows

   c = no. of columns

6. **Level of Significance:** In final decision, level of significance is that point where we accept or rejected the statistical Result. Mostly two level of significance is mainly important: (1) 0.05 levels and 0.01 levels.

   In above two levels, researcher can choose any one of the level in social science research.

7. **Standard Deviation:** The standard deviation concept was introduced by Karl Pearson in 1823. It is by far the most important and widely used measure of studying dispersion.

Standard deviation is also called Root-means square deviation.

$$SD = \frac{\sqrt{\Sigma\chi^2}}{N}$$

Where $\chi = (\chi - \chi)^N$

S.D. = Standard Deviation:

Step-I : Calculate the actual mean of the series, i.e. X

Step-II : Take the deviations of the items from the mean, i.e. find (X-X). Denote these deviations by X.

Step-III : Square these deviations and obtain the Total

Step-IV : Divide by the total number of observations i.e., N, and Take the square root. This gives us the value of standard deviation.

In the present study, data have been obtained both from the primary sources as well as secondary sources. The primary sources include observation, interview schedule and case studies.

The secondary sources consist of earlier studies on naxal movement and social transformation of rural areas, Published sources of government institution and organisation, published article, reports and book by non-government organisation. Book and articles related to National Movement, Peasant Movement and naxalite Movement Communist Manifesto of CPI (ML), Agenda and published article by left extremist organisation, Articles written by Intellectual and Newspapers, Reports of Planning commission, finance commission and ministries of defense and internal securities.

Experience from Field work:

While collecting primary data from the field the present researcher faced many problems. The first problem was building a confidence among the respondents as I was viewed as an agent of bureaucracy, police and they were not ready to accept; me for responding. However, I came in contact with few active workers, who not merely provided me security but helped in rapport building and creating an environment of confidence among the respondents.

The second challenge was to visit the village which was in remote areas not linked with public transportation. However, I managed to reach the destination through my personal vehicles and some times barefooted as well.

The researcher had to face difficulties in obtaining data from local level of government agencies-police records, bureaucratic official records, etc. At times, I had to file RTI to get some in formations about the field reports.

The challenges of the field study were two fold from the public/ clients as well as on the one hand and from the bureaucracy police and forest official, on the other.

Limitation of the Study:

The study has certain limitations. The findings of the study are confined to 3 blocks of Sonbhadra district. The limited field data not may be enough to provide sufficient basis to analyses the nature and patterns of relationship between, social transformation and naxalism in the wider contexts. Nevertheless, the findings reveal the trends of developmental measures and patterns of reactions to them in a limited frame.

4

Socio-economic and Demograpic Profile of Respondents

The socio-economic conditions play an important role in characterizing the social life and behavior of an individual.

The socio-economic status of an individual affects the patterns of interaction in the society. It is, therefore, essential to analyze the socio-economic background of the respondent to understand the patterns of social transformation in the naxal affected areas. In a backward district like Sonbhadra were forces of caste, and kinship influences the social life and acute disparity in the standard of living, among various groups of the region.

In the study area 320 heads of the households were selected for the intensive study. The socio-economic and family background of these respondent are presented in this chapter to serve as a frame of reference for the opinions and attitudes expressed by them to certain aspects of the present situation and also to serve as a reflection of the socio-economic situation of the naxal affected people of Sonebhadra.

The study of Mittal and KetKar (1970) reveals that the socio-economic status such as age, education, religion, place of resident and standard of living are capable of an exerting and independent influence on individual personality. Thus we can say that that socio-economic factor play and important role in the assessment of once/ individual personality. Considering the importance of the socio-economic and demographic characteristics and analysis of data in present study is done on the basis of age, gender, caste and ethnic categories and occupational status household structure, income status and religious status and presented in the following tables.

Age and Gender profile of Respondent:

Biologically age structure defined on physical structure and development process. When age increases people learn and experience new things which lead to changing behavior, motives, thought and decision making power in life. Experience of ageing provided power to individual to take right direction in life.

Table 4.1: Age-wise Distribution of the Respondents

Age Group	*Frequency*	*Percentage*
20 - 34	99	30.9
35 - 49	154	48.2
50+	67	20.9
Total	**320**	**100.0**

Average ± SD = 40.40 ± 12.14, Range (20-80)

The above table shows that majority 48.2 per cent of respondents were in age group of 35-49 years. While it was 30.9 per cent and 20.9 per cent respondent in the age group of (20-34) years and more than 49 years respectively. It is also observed that the average age of the respondent with standard deviation is calculated (40.40 $\pm$ 12.14) years in the range of (20-80) year respectively.

Table 4.2: Sex-wise Distribution of the Respondents

Sex	*Frequency*	*Percentage*
Male	160	50.0
Female	160	50.0
Total	**320**	**100.0**

The above table reveals that 50.0 per cent male respondent and 50.0 per cent female respondent were purposively selected for the interview of the selected areas in the present study.

Sex:

Women are biological different from men. Though there is disagreement about the exact nature and consequences of this difference. Basic sexual difference is division of labor in all societies.

Table 4.3: Age and Sex Wise Distribution of Respondents

Age Group	*Sex*				*Total*	
	Male		*Female*		*Frequency*	*Percentage*
	No.	Per cent	No.	Per cent	No.	Per cent
20-34	51	31.9	48	30.0	99	30.9
35-49	76	47.5	78	48.8	154	48.1
50^{+}	33	20.6	34	21.2	67	20.9
Total	160	100.0	160	100.0	320	100.0
Mean age±S.D.	39.66±	12.88	41.15±	11.35	40.40±	12.14

$t = 1.10$, d.f. $=318$, $P>0.05$

The distribution of interviewed subject according to their age and sex is presented in table 4.3, which depicts that the respondents selected in the age group 35-49 years maximum were 48.8 per cent females and 47.5 per cent were males were as in the early age group (20-34) years maximum were male (31.9 per cent) in comparison to female respondent (30.0 per cent). In older age group that is 50 and above the proportion of female respondent were slightly more in comparison to male respondents. The average age of male respondents was (39.66±12.88) years while it was (41.15±11.35) years in female respondents.

The difference in average age between male and female is not found to be statistically significant. ($t = 1.10$, $df = 318$, $p>0.05$).

It may be concluded that higher age group of females were selected more in comparison to the male respondents which may be more useful for getting the needful and required correct information.

Caste and Ethnic Structure

The Indian society is highly stratified into the age old division of castes and sub-castes. The Indian caste system manifests itself as a vertical structure in which individual castes are hierarchically graded and kept permanently apart, and at the same time, are linked by well defined expectations and obligations which integrate them into the village social system, after independence, government initiative and measures, there is upliftment in weaker section and lower castes people status in society. During 1990's when we open our economy, these is lot of social change occur in all sphere of life. Caste system weaken and its place class system is the basis of stratification, which included wealth, power, education, occupation as base. But it does not mean that caste loose it identity, even today in rural areas as well as in urban areas. Caste is closed group and decided by birth (ascribed basis). Bailey, 1958, 107-124 Louis Dumont and Pocock defined caste stratification on basis of purity and pollution basis, decided on religious-cultural basis (Dumont 1961;34).

Table 4.4: Caste and Sex Wise Distribution of Respondents

	Sex					
Caste	***Male (M)***		***Female (F)***		***Total***	
	No.	*Per cent*	*No.*	*Per cent*	*No.*	*Per cent*
SC/ST	65	40.6	80	50.0	145	45.3
OBC	56	35.0	57	35.6	113	35.3
General	39	24.4	23	14.4	62	19.4
Total	**160**	**100.0**	**160**	**100.0**	**320**	**100.0**

χ^2 **= 5.69, df =2, P>0.05**

The above table shows the distribution of study subject according to their caste and gender. It is found that out of total respondents majority 45.3 per cent belonged to SC/ST's in which 50.0 per cent were female and 40.6 per cent were male, remaining 35.3 per cent and 19.4 per cent respondents belongs to O.B.C's category and general caste category respectively. In O.B.C's the female respondents were slightly more as compare to the male respondents. While in general caste category it was just a reverse that is 20.4 per cent were male and only 14.4 per cent were female respondents. The difference in the proportion between male and female respondents in connection to caste category is not found to be statistically significant.

The result clearly shows that the female respondent were more interviewed in O.B.C's and SC/ST's than general castes category, might be due to easily availability in out side the home and involved in one or other economic activities where general caste women less participation in economic activity and more in domestic house hold works inside the home.

Educational Qualification

Education, in fact, helps in social and occupational mobility for the members in social hierarchy. Educational attainments, to a large extent, determine the nature and type of job opportunities. Hobble, rightly argues that there is a broad tendency for people with higher education to have higher ranking occupations.

According to Linton in their study based on Education and Household structure, explain that increased in education level in society decreased in household structure.

He also finds out that in rural areas expansion of education leads to nuclear family structure. Desai (1973) Kalhari (1973) and Adams (1973) in their study based on relationship between education and family planning methods; find out that with increase in education level decreased in population growth. It gives positive result in social transformation in society.

Table 4.5:Educational and Sex Wise Distribution of Respondents

	Sex					
Education	*Male (M)*		*Female (F)*		*Total*	
	No.	*Per cent*	*No.*	*Per cent*	*No.*	*Per cent*
Illiterate	94	28.1	106	66.2	151	47.2
Up to High School	94	58.8	45	28.1	139	43.4
Inter+	21	13.1	09	05.6	30	09.4
Total	**160**	**100.0**	**160**	**100.0**	**320**	**100.0**

χ^2 = 46.72, df = 2, P<0.001

Khan (1980) consider education as the main agents of political socialisation in society for bringing change in all sphere of life social, political, economic and cultural education act as main agent of social transformation. Education not only responsible to individual personality development but it is also related to social status, prestige, and our role performed in the society. Education is one of the major factors of social stratification in modern society.

Demographer Arun Mahapatra (1990), in his study of development, he found that tribal have worst condition comparison to scheduled castes and other communities in the field of education.

The educational status of the respondents is distributed according to their sex and noted in the table no.4.5. It reflects that about half (47.2 per cent) of the respondent were illiterate in which females (66.2 per cent) were found to be more as compare to male respondents (28.1 per cent). The respondents who were qualified at primary to high School level were observed to be (43.4 per cent) and higher secondary and more than this were (9.4 per cent) respectively. The respondents literate at primary to higher level, male respondent were more in comparison to the female respondents. The statistical chi-square (χ^2) test prove the fact that there is highly significant difference between male and female respondents regarding educational status in the study area (χ^2=46.72, df=2, P<0.001).

The result clearly shows that the educational status is very low in the present study area especially in female population. It may be due to non-availability of infrastructure development, road connectivity and low socio-economic status.

Occupational Structure

Occupation constitutes the important elements of the socio-economic and demographic status. For practical empirical purposes, a classification of the population into the class groups based on occupation has been found to be most generally useful occupation is an index of person's social standing and although this is not identical with class, it is closely related.

The various occupation have emerged and a result of the process of urbanisation, industrialisation, educational advancement and the development of technology etc. There may be various categories of occupation, e.g. administrative, agricultural, business, teaching, judicial and health services, etc.

Table 4.6A: Occupation Wise Distribution of Respondents

6(A)

Sl.No.	*Occupation*	*Frequency*	*Percentage*
1.	Agriculture	122	38.1
2.	Service	20	06.2
3-	Business/S.S.I	61	14.1
4.	Labor	106	33.1
5.	Others	11	03.4
	Total	**320**	**100.0**

Table 4.6A: Occupation Wise Distribution of Respondents

6(B)

Sl.No.	*Occupation*	*Frequency*	*Percentage*
1.	Agriculture	122	38.1
2.	Labour	106	33.1
3.	Other	92	28.8
	Total	**320**	**100.0**

The occupational status of the respondents is categorised to five groups as agriculture, service, business/SSI, labour and engaged in other types of activities and again it is summed up into three categories-like as agriculturist, labourers groups and others for the comparison purposes and regarded in table 6(A)(B) respectively. It reflects that more than one third (38.1 per cent) of respondent were agriculturist whereas remaining 33.1 per cent and 28.8 per cent of respondents were and labourers and engaged in different types of activities like as service, business, small scale industries, shopkeepers etc.

It clearly indicates that maximum number of the respondents are either agriculturists or working as labour due to which may fall in lower socio-economic and educational status.

Income source status

Income decided the social status in society, Income fulfilled the basic necessity of life. Income decided the class in society, stratified people on income basis which also affect the lifestyles, values, mores ethics, customs, tradition and religious belief in society. In society people divided into high class, middle class and lower class income group in society. Lower income people lived a marginalised life and unable to fulfilled the dream and desire of his/her life whereas rich income people easily fulfilled their dream and desire and lived a luxurious life, having power, privilege and prestige in society, comparison to lower and middle income class person in society.

Table 4.7: Income Wise Distribution Of Respondents

Monthly Income (in Rs.)	*Frequency*	*Percentage*
Less than 1500	140	43.8
1500-3000	119	37.2
3000 and above	61	19.0
Total	**320**	**100.0**

Average Income ± S.D.=2411.56±1727.53 Range (500-10,000).

The above table shows the distribution of respondents according to their monthly income of the family. It reveals that maximum (43.8 per cent) of respondents has monthly income less than Rs 1500 while rest 37.2 per cent and 19.0 per cent of respondent had their monthly income in the range of Rupees (1500-3000) and more than Rs 3000 respectively. The average monthly income of family is observed to be Rs (2411.56 ± 1727.53) in the range of minimum Rs.500 to maximum to Rs.10,000 in the study area.

It also clearly shows the lower socio-economic status of the individual in rural community of the study area.

Religious Status

Religion is the belief in the supernatural.

Roland Robertson: States that religion refers to the existence of supernatural being which have a governing effect on life.

In terms of religion, two main theories developed animism and naturism, were advanced to account for its origin.

Animism means the belief in spirits. Edward. B. Tylor believes this to be the earliest form of religion. Naturism means the belief that the forces of nature have supernatural power. F. Max Mueller believes this to be the earliest form of religion. Emile Durkheim, Max Weber, Karl Marx also given their functional and conflict view on religion in society. In Indian society, religion play both functional and dysfunctional role according to situation and condition.

Table-4.8: Religion Wise Distribution Of Respondents

Religion	*Frequency*	*Percentage*
Hindu	287	89.7
Muslim	33	10.3
Total	**320**	**100.0**

The above table show the distribution of respondent according to their religion which indicates that majority of the respondent (89.7 per cent) was belongs to Hindus family while remaining 10.3 per cent were Muslims. It clearly shows that in the study area the dominant communities were Hindus and thickly populated in the selected area. So, Hindus respondents were selected more comparison to Muslim respondents.

Marital Status

Marriage is an institution which admitted men and women to family life. It is a stable relationship in which a man and a woman are socially permitted to have children implying the right to sexual relations (Green, 1957; 127-30 and Singh, 1958).

In Indian society, marriage played important role, specially, in Hindu Society it is a sacrament, because of some important factors like-

1. Hindu marriage is performed mainly to carry out Dharma.
2. Hindu marriage cannot be dissolved easily.

3. Concept of Mehar, dowry and wali is not there in Hindu marriage.
4. Various ritual aspect related to Dharma are attached to Hindu marriage like 'Kanyadan', Panigrahana, Sapta-padi. Agniparinaya, Vivaha home etc.

The table No.4.9 shows the distribution of respondents according to their marital status. It is apparent from the above table that majority (88.8 per cent) of respondent were married whereas rest 7.2 per cent and 4.0 per cent respondents were unmarried and widow/widowers respectively.

Table 4.9: Marital Status of Respondents

Marital Status	*Frequency*	*Percentage*
1. Married	248	88.8
2. Unmarried	23	07.2
3. Widow/Widower	13	04.0
Total	**320**	**100.0**

The unmarried individuals are selected for getting the correct and valuable information because they were highly educated and had better knowledge regarding various government programmes and planning for welfare of naxal affected areas.

Summary

On the basis of different dimensions of Socio-economic and demographic characteristics, the trend and pattern is summarised as follows:

- It is found that majority 48.2 per cent of the respondents belongs to middle age group followed by equal number of male and female respondents were interviewed in the present study. The average age of male respondent was (39.66 $\pm$ 12.88) years and it was (41.15 $\pm$ 11.35) years in female respondents.
- Majority 45.3 per cent of respondents were from SC/ST caste category followed by 35.3 per cent O.B.C. Castes and minimum 19.4 per cent of respondents were from general

caste category, significantly similar type of pattern in the proportion was observed between male and female respondents.

- Out of total respondents, 47.2 per cent were illiterate in which female proportion 66.2 per cent was significantly more than male subjects 28.1 per cent.
- The main occupation in the study subject was accounted to be agriculturists and laborer group i.e. (38.1 per cent and 33.1 per cent) respectively.
- About almost half (43.8 per cent) of respondents had their monthly income less than Rupees 1500/- followed by 37.2 per cent between the range of Rupees (1500-3000) respectively. Average monthly income of the family is estimated Rupees (2411.56 $\pm$ 1727.53).
- Majority of the respondents (89.7) belongs to Hindu community while remaining 10.3 per cent were belongs to Muslim community.
- Majority of the respondents (88.8 per cent) were married whereas remaining 7.2 per cent and 4.0 per cent of respondents were unmarried and Widow/Widower respectively.

References

Bailey, F.G, : Caste and the Economic Frontier, Oxford University Press, 1959.

Beteille, A: Castes: Old and New; Asia Publishing House, Bombay, 1969.

Bongleystin: Essays on Caste system, Cambridge University Press, Cambridge, 1971.

D'souza, V., Educational Inequalities among Scheduled Castes, Punjab University Press, Chandigarh, 1974.

Desai, A.R.: Urban Family and Planning Family in India, Popular Prakashan, Bombay,1980.

Dumont, Louis: Homo Hierarchicus, Vikas Publication, Bangalore, 1966,

Ghurye, G.S.: Caste, Class and Occupation, Popular Prakashan, Bombay, 1961.

Hobel, E.A.: Man in the Primitive World, Macgraw Hill Book, Co. Inc, New York, 1958.

Johnson, H.M.: Sociology: A Systematic Introduction, Allied Publishers Pvt. Ltd., Bombay, 1967.

Kuppuswamy, B.: A Scale to Measures Socio-economic Status. The Indian Journal of Psychology, Vol.34, 1959.

Linton, Ralf : Cultural Background of Personality, New York, App Lentan Century Crafts. 1945.

Maciver, R.M. and Page, C.H. : Society ! An Introductory Analysis, London. 1962.

Maharatna, Arun, : Demographic Perspective on India's Tribes, Oxford University Press, New Delhi, 2005.

Murphy and Morris: Occupational Status, Subjective Social Class Identification and Political Affiliation, American Sociological Review, 1961.

Sharma, K.N.: Occupational Mobility of Castes in a North Indian Villages, Southern Journal of Anthropology, Vol. 17, 1967.

Singh, D.R. : "Rural Leadership Among Scheduled Castes" Chugh Publication, Allahabad, 1985, Rural Youth, Chugh Publication Allahabad, 1981.

Tiwary, Jai Kant: Rural Development Administration: Perspective and Prospects, Chugh Publication, Allahabad, 1984.

5

Rise of Naxalism and Social Transformation in Naxal Affected Areas

The naxalite movement, starting from a small village 'Naxalbari' on the tri-junction of India, Nepal and Bangaladesh in 1967, spread like wildfire to different parts of the country. The movement had a meteoric phase for about two years from the formation of the CPI (ML) in 1969 till the end of 1971. These early stirrings were however easily crushed by the Government of India through police action following Charu Mazumdar's death in 1972, there were divisions and fragmentations in the movement. This is the end of the first phase of naxal movement.

The formation of people's war group in Andhra Pradesh in 1980 under the leadership of Kondapalli Seetaramaiah gave a new lease of life to the movement for about ten years, the PWG remained strident. The Andhra Pradesh government banned the PWG and its front organisation in 1992, and the state police undertook well organised counter insurgency, operations. The arrest of Kondapally Seetharamaiah and other important leaders marked the end of this phase.

The current, phase which commenced in 2001 is marked by a conscious attempt to militaries the armed component of the party, the people's Guerilla army with a view to launching attacks on the state apparatus.

The nine party Congress, held in early 2007 "reaffirmed the general line of new democratic revolution with agrarian revolution as its axis and protracted peoples war as the path of the Indian revolution", and resolved to advance the peoples war throughout the country, Further strengthen the people's army deepen the mass, base of the party and wage a broad-based militant mass movement against the neo-liberal policies of globalisation, liberalisation and privatisation."

The Government of India has already expressed concern over the spread of the naxalite movement over a huge geographical area. According to the Institute for Conflict Management, the movement has actually spread to 194 districts in 18 states.

The movement got a tremendous boost when its two major components, the people's war (PW) and the Maoist Communist Centre of India (MCCI) decided to merge on March 21, 2004 The Unified Party was called the Communist Party of India (Maoist). The merger, a part from augmenting the support base of the movement, has given it the character of a pan-Indian revolutionary group. The naxals plan to have a compact revolutionary zone stretching from Indo-Nepal border to the Dandakaranya region is likely to get a fillip with the unification of their ranks.

The naxalite group nexus with the other extremist organisations has added to the complexity of the problem. There are indications that the PWG cadres received training in the handling of weapons and IEDs from some ex-LTTE cadres. They have also some understanding with the National Socialist Councils of Nagaland (I-M) to support each others cause. Some batches of CPM-L Party unity also appear to have received arms training under the guidance of ULFA. The communist party of India (Maoist) has close fraternal relations with the communist party of Nepal (Maoist) also. The nature of Naxal Violence has undergone a subtle change in the recent years. Small scale isolated attacks have been replaced by large scale, well organised attacks on the government apparatus.

The naxalite movement emerged in late 1990's in the Sonbhadra district of Uttar Pradesh because of it geographical location and demographic structure. Sonbhadra district touches border with four major naxal affected states of country, Madhya Pradesh, Chattisgarh, Jharkhand and Bihar. This district is rich in mineral resources, having hilly terrains and almost 50 per cent of area is covered with dense forest, here mostly people belongs to scheduled castes and scheduled tribes all this factor provide ground in late 1990's for emergence of naxalism. In this area tribals like Kols, Kharwar, Ghasasiya are maximum in number and they totally depend on forest goods for their livelihood, but forest department exploitative policies are other factor for this socio-economic problem emergence in this area.

In the study area, mostly people belong to poor, illiterate, unemployed section of society. The government plans to combat the naxal problem appear generally sound on paper there is a huge gap between the formulation of policies and their implementation at the ground level. According to my finding, the number of people lived below poverty line (BPL) is more than double the national level (26.6 per cent). This situation is compounded by the mismatch between growth and its distribution resulting in accumulation of economic disparities. This uneven growth leads to social unrest. Latest report on news paper, on 2003, the extent of chronic hunger and Malnutrition is also critical in sonebhadra on several counts. It says that even though we have enough food to feed but hunger death is common here, 18 Ghasasiya Tribes death in 2003 shows how much government public distribution system works in backward areas. Water scarcity, flourination is other common problem of people in this district.

Land reform unfortunately remain a romantic theme for the intellectual, a populist slogan for the politician and a persistent source of hope for the landless, but in this district there is unequal distribution of land among various castes groups specially neo-landlord castes, Yadav and Patel, have big landholding in the study area.

The land belonging to the tribals, were alienated in this area, despite the existence of an umbrella of protective legislation.

It would thus appear that the factors which gave rise to naxalism, the extent of poverty, uneven development, poor governance, neglect of land reforms, rising unemployment and tribals getting a raw deal are, unfortunately very much present today also.

Table 5.1: Profile of Respondents and their Awareness Towards Naxalism

Awareness	*Frequency*	*Percentage*
Yes	307	95.9
No	13	04.1
Total	**320**	**100.0**

We attempted to know whether the respondents were aware towards naxalism or not? It is found that majority 95.9 per cent of the respondent were aware about naxalism while 4.1 per cent were unaware of it. It is clear from the result that in the naxalite area more than 95 per cent of individuals had some knowledge about naxalism.

Table 5.2: Opinion Towards Factors of Naxalism

Factors	*Yes*		*No*		*Total*	
	No.	*Per cent*	*No.*	*Per cent*	*No.*	*Per cent*
Socio-Economic	184	59.9	123	40.1	307	100.0
Ideological	58	18.9	249	81.1	307	100.0
Labour/Land	149	48.5	158	51.5	307	100.0
Caste Conflict	99	32.2	208	67.8	307	100.0

It is from above table further more information is gathered from those respondents who had some knowledge about naxalism about the factors of naxalism. The analyzed data is presented in table 5.2, it is found that majority 18.9 per cent of the respondents reported that ideological attitudes is the most important factors of naxalism and 32.2 per cent of respondent reported the factors of naxalism to the caste conflict. Socio-economic disparity as well as labour/land issues were also the factors of naxalism, which was reported by 59.9 per cent and 48.5 per cent respondents respectively. Thus it may be concluded that labour/land disparity caste conflict as well as Socio-economic disparity are the most powerful factors for emergences of naxalism.

The various factors of naxalism is also distributed according to the sex of respondents and given in table No.5.3; it is evident from the above table that the respondents reported the various factors in which Socio-economic and land disparity maximum (66.7 per cent and 50.3 per cent) were females as compared to the male

(53.8 per cent and 46.9 per cent) respondents respectively. It is seeing that ideological attitudes and caste conflict were considered in higher proportion by male respondents in comparison to the female respondents. The statistical chi square (χ^2) test signifies the fact that the difference in proportion between male and female regarding consideration of various root cause of naxalism is found to be significant except the ideological attitudes and land disparity.

Table 5.3: Factors of Naxalism and Sex Status of Respondents

Factors of Naxalism	*Sexd*						*f=1*
	Male(160)		*Female(147)*		*Total(307)*		χ^2 P
	No.	*Per cent*	*No.*	*Per cent*	*No.*	*Per cent*	
Socio-Economic	86	53.8	98	66.7	184	59.9	5.32,<0.05
Ideological	35	21.9	23	15.6	58	18.9	1.94, >0.05
Land/Labour	75	46.9	74	50.3	149	48.5	0.37, >0.05
Caste Conflict	68	42.5	31	21.1	99	32.2	16.08 ,<0.001

Table 5.4: Factors of Naxalism and Caste Status of the Respondents

Factors of Naxalism	*Caste*								
	SC/ST(136)		*OBC (109)*		*General(62)*		*Total(307)*		*df =2*
	No.	*Per cent*	*No.*	*Per cent*	*No.*	*Per cent*	*No.*	*Per cent*	*X^2 P*
Socio-Economic	67	49.3	72	66.1	45	72.6	184	59.9	12.28,<0.01
Ideology	03	02.2	27	24.8	28	45.2	58	18.9	55.09,<0.001
Land/ Labour	68	50.0	48	44.0	33	53.2	149	48.5	1.55, >0.05
Caste Conflict	48	35.3	34	31.2	17	27.4	99	32.2	1.29, >0.05

The opinion regarding the factors of naxalism of the study subject is classified according to their caste basis and recorded in table No.5.4. It is evident from the above table that the opinion regarding Socio-economic disparity and ideology was produced by general caste in (72.6 per cent and 45.2 per cent) while it was minimum (49.3 per cent and 2.2 per cent) in the respondent of SC/ST's and this difference in proportion is found to be statistically highly significant. The opinion as the caste conflict had been reported by maximum (35.3 per cent) SC and ST's castes and land disparity by the general caste followed by SC/ST's and O.B.C. respectively, but statistically the difference in the proportion among the various caste groups is not observed to be significant.

It shows that majority of general caste individual are of the opinion that socio-economic and land/labour disparity and ideological attitudes are the main factors of naxalism whereas SC/ST's caste consider to the caste conflict respectively.

Table 5.5: Education Wise Distribution

Factors of Naxalism	*Education*								
	Illiterate(140)		*Upto High School(137)*		*Inter+(30)*		*Total(307)*		*df=2*
	No.	*Per cent*	*No.*	*Per cent*	*No.*	*Per cent*	*No.*	*Per cent*	χ^2 *P*
Socio-Economic	84	60.0	77	56.2	23	76.7	184	59.9	4.29,>0.05
Ideology	14	10.0	21	15.3	23	76.7	58	18.9	73.71<,0.001
Land/ Labour	78	55.7	61	44.5	10	33.3	149	48.5	6.55, <0.05
Caste Conflict	37	26.4	49	35.8	13	43.3	99	32.2	4.63, >0.05

The opinion of the respondents regarding factors of naxalism according to the educational status is also distributed in table No.5.5; which reveals that majority of the respondents qualified at intermediate and higher level of education were of the opinion that ideological attitudes, socio-economic disparity and caste conflict are the most important factors for emergence/rise of naxalism. Whereas maximum 55.7 per cent respondents who were illiterate proposed the factors to land/labour disparity, statistically, the difference in the proportion of opinion regarding factors of naxalism among various educational status group of respondents is found to be statistically significant with the exception of factors of socio-economic disparities and caste conflict respectively. It may be concluded that the highly educated respondents were considering socio-economic disparity caste conflict and ideological attitudes are the main factors for rise of naxalism.

Table 5.6: Emergence of Naxalism and Sex Status of Respondents

Emergence of Naxalism	*Sex*					
	Male		*Female*		*Total*	
	No.	*Per cent*	*No.*	*Per cent*	*No.*	*Per cent*
1970	4	2.5	24	15.0	28	8,8
1980	30	18.8	10	6.2	40	12.5
1990	38	23.8	63	39.4	101	31.6
After 1990	88	55.0	45	28.1	133	41.6
Don't known	0	0.0	18	11.2	18	5.6
Total	160	100.0	160	100.0	320	100.0

χ^2=62.38, df = 4, P<0.001.

The knowledge of respondents regarding emergence of naxalism is assists according to their sex and noted in the above table. It is apparent from the table that majority 41.6 per cent of respondents had the correct knowledge about the emergence of naxalism in the study area. In which male respondents were 55.0 per cent and 28.1 per cent were female respondents. Only 5.6 per cent of respondents had no knowledge about emergence of naxalism in which 100 per cent were females. About one third (31.6 per cent) of respondents, in which females were more than males, considered the year 1990 for the beginning of naxalism. The difference in proportion regarding correct knowledge about the commencement of naxalism in the study area is found to be statistically highly significant. The results clearly shows that majority of the respondents had the correct knowledge about the emergence of naxalism may be because of facing problem due to naxal menaces in their area during last two decades.

Table shows the distribution of respondent's knowledge regarding different naxal organisation active in their area. Gender wise classification is presented in table 5.7. It reveals that out of total respondents more than one third (34.7 per cent) had no knowledge about active naxal organisation whereas 37.2 per cent of respondent's were known about other type of organisation. (Ganga-Son-Vindyachal Frontal Organisation) out of total respondents, 11.9 per cent; 8.4 per cent and 7.8 per cent of respondent's named party unity, M.C.C. and CPI (ML) respectively. The proportion of male respondents was having more knowledge regarding different organisation than the female respondents. Chi square (χ^2) test proved the fact that the difference in the proportion of knowledge about various naxal organisation is highly significant.

($\chi^2 = 45.51$, df = 4, P<0.001)

Table 5.7: Profile of Respondnets and their Awareness Towards Naxal Organisation

Naxal org.		*Sex*					
		Male		*Female*		*Total*	
		No.	*Per cent*	*No*	*Per cent*	*No*	*Per cent*
1	M.C.C.	14	8.8	13	8.1	27	8.4
2	CPI (ML)	19	11.9	6	3.8	25	7.8
3	Party unity	28	17.5	10	6.2	38	11.9
4	Others	32	20.0	87	54.4	119	37.2
5	Don't know	67	41.9	44	27.5	111	34.7
	Total	**160**	**100.0**	**160**	**100.0**	**320**	**100.0**

$\chi^2 = 45.51$, df = 4, P<0.001

We may conclude from the above results that male individual had more knowledge than female. This might be because of higher education, participation in various outer activities or being part of naxal movement.

Table 5.8: Awareness About Type of Social Transformation and Sex Status of Respondents

Opinion of Respondent about Naxalism		*Sex*					
		Male		*Female*		*Total*	
		No.	*Per cent*	*No.*	*Per cent*	*No.*	*Per cent*
1	Y	58	36.2	72	45.0	130	40.6
2	N	85	53.1	52	32.5	137	42.8
3	Can not. Say	17	10.6	36	22.5	53	16.6
	Total	**160**	**100.0**	**160**	**100.0**	**320**	**100.0**

$\chi^2 = 16.27$; df = 2; P<0.001

The above table shows the distribution of respondent opinion about social transformation due to naxalism in their area. It reflects that majority 42.8 per cent of respondents did not accept any type of social changes due to naxalism. While 40.6 per cent of respondents had the positive opinion about the social transformation and only 16.6 per cent did not provide their opinion regarding this matter. The proportion of females who had positive opinion was more in comparison to the male respondents. Statistically this difference is observed to be highly significant.

The high proportion of positive response by the female respondents regarding social transformation due to naxalism may be because rise of women status and empowerment and well as decreased of exploitation and domestic violence due to naxalism.

Table 5.9: Type of Transformation due to Naxalism with Sex Status of Respondents

Opinion of S.T. by Naxalism		*Sex*							
		M (58)		*F (72)*		*T(130)*		*df = 1*	
		No.	*Per cent*	*No.*	*Per cent*	*No.*	*Per cent*	χ	*P*
1	Social	56	96.6	58	80.6	114	87.7	7.62	<0.01
2	Pol.	46	79.6	65	90.9	111	85.4	3.10	>0.05
3	Eco.	54	93.1	61	84.7	115	88.5	2.21	>0.05

The study subjects who were of the opinion of social transformation in any manner due to naxalism, further, classified according to types of social transformation with their sex and presented in table 5.9, it depicts that majority 87.7 per cent of total respondents accepted for the social changes in which maximum were males than females' respondents. Whereas 85.4 per cent and 88.5 per cent of respondents reported for political and economical change due to Naxalism higher percentage of female respondents were reported for political transformation while in case of Economical changes it was found to be more from male respondents. Statistically, there is no significant difference in the proportion of opinion between males and females respondents regarding political and economic transformation while in social transformation it is highly significant again the result clearly elaborates the empowerment of women in the field of social and political as well as advancement in educational status.

Table 5.10: Types of Transformation due to Naxalism with Caste Status of the Respondents

Social Transfor-mation	*Caste*								*df = 2*	
	SC ST(58)		*OBC (51)*		*General (21)*		*Total (130)*			
	No.	Per cent	No.	Per cent	No.	Per cent	No.	Per cent	χ^2	P
1. Social	47	81.0	47	92.2	20	95.2	114	87.7	4.43	>0.05
2. Political	58	100.0	37	725	16	76.2	111	85.4	18.08	<0.001
3. Economical	46	79.3	49	96.1	20	95.2	115	88.5	8.61	<0.05

It is perceptible from the above table that for social changes the pattern of proportion was found to be in increasing order as caste status was increasing. While in political change maximum were SC/ ST's followed by general and minimum proportion was of O.B.C's. respectively. Economical changes due to naxalism were accepted by general and O.B.C.'s in equal proportion and the minimum were reported by the respondents of SC/ST's caste. The statistical chi square (χ^2) test signifies the fact that the difference in proportion of having opinion regarding different types of transformation due to naxalism among various caste groups is found to be significant except social transformation.

Higher proportion of SC/ST's respondents regarding political transformation might be because of active participation in different political parties and party related to naxalism as well as empowerment regarding vote casting.

Table 5.11: Types of Transformation due to Naxalism and Educational Status of the Respondents

Educational Status	*Educational status*								*df=2*	
	Illiterate(67)		*Upto High School (40)*		*Inter+ (23)*		*Total (130)*			
	No.	*Per cent*	*No.*	*Per cent*	*No.*	*Per cent*	*No.*	*Per cent*	χ^2	*P*
1	55	82.1	37	92.5	22	95.7	114	87.7	4.16	>0.05
2	64	95.5	34	85.0	13	56.5	111	85.4	20.88	<0.001
3	55	82.1	37	92.5	23	100.0	115	88.5	6.30	<0.05

The association between educational status of the respondents and their opinion regarding types of transformation due to naxalism is presented in table no.5.11 which shows that the respondents who were of the opinion regarding social and economical changes due to naxalism were found to be in increasing order as educational status advanced while a just reversed trend was observed in case of political transformation. Statistically, the difference in proportion regarding different types of transformation due to naxalism among the respondents of various educational status levels is highly significant with the exception of social transformation.

The result also signified that the illiterate individual had the opinion in more proportion in comparison to the other literate population regarding political transformation, may be due to active participation in politics and freedom for vote casting in ;different elections.

Table 5.12: Monthly Family Income wise Distribution of Respondent's Opinion Regarding types of Transformation due to Naxalism

Sl.No.	*Monthly Income (in Rupees)*									
	<-1500 (55)		*1500-300(49)*		*3000+ (26)*		*Total (130)*		*df=2*	
	No.	*Per cent*	*No.*	*Per cent*	*No.*	*Per cent*	*No.*	*Per cent*	χ^2	*P*
1	44	80.0	49	100.0	21	80.8	114	87.7	11.5	<0.01
2	54	98.2	42	85.7	15	57.7	111	85.4	23.2	<0.001
3	44	80.0	47	95.9	24	92.3	115	88.5	6.9	<0.05

The association of monthly family income of respondent's is also assessed with their opinion regarding different types of social transformation due to naxalism and presented in Table 5.12, it is found that the respondents who accepted the social changes due to naxalism majority were in monthly income group of Rupees (1500-3000) group. while for the political and economical transformation, it was maximum in the monthly income group of (Rs.<1500) and (Rs.>3000) respectively it is also observed that the difference in the proportion of respondents having opinion for different types of transformation due to naxalism among different monthly income group is found to be statistically highly significant. The above result clearly shows that the political transformation due to naxalism was reported maximum by female respondents, SC/ST's caste groups, illiterate and lower socio-economic status group of respondents. It may be due to women participation in political activities reservation in different field's as well as various government programmes and policies implemented for low socio-economic status group in the naxal affected area.

Table 5-13: Ways of Social Transformation and age Status of Respondents

	Age	*Age Structure*							
		Less then<35 (37)		*35-49(51)*		*50+ (42)*		*Total (130)*	
		No.	*Per cent*	*No.*	*Per cent*	*No.*	*Per cent*	*No.*	*Per cent*
1.	By Gun	09	24.3	06	11.8	01	2.4	16	12.3
2.	Awareness	02	05.4	04	7.8	11	26.2	17	13.1
3	Both	23	62.2	39	76.5	26	61.9	88	67.7
4	None of these	03	08.1	02	3.9	04	9.5	09	6.9
	Total	**37**	**100.0**	**51**	**100.0**	**42**	**100.0**	**130**	**100.0**

$\chi^2 = 18.08$; df = 6 ; $P<0.01$

It is apparent from the above table that out of total respondents who were in favour of social transformation due to naxalism, majority 67.7 per cent reported the changes by Gun and to aware the people altogether in which maximum were in the age group of (35-49 Years) followed by less than 35 years and greater than 49 years of age group respectively. The respondents believe the social transformation by gun only were 12.3 per cent, 13.1 per cent by awareness method, while rest 6.9 per cent of respondents refused the stated ways respectively. It is also observed that the difference in proportion among various age group of respondent regarding the perception of way of getting social transformation due to naxalism is found to be statistically highly significant.

We may concludes from the results that the younger's of the study area were believing more in naxalism or naxalite ideas for social or any types of changes.

Table 5.14: Sympathy Towards Naxalites and Naxal Organisation and Sex wise Distribution of Respondents

Sex wise sympathy to Naxalite		*Sex*					
		Male		*Female*		*Total*	
		No.	Per cent	No.	Per cent	No.	Per cent
1.	Yes	17	10.6	20	12.5	37	11.6
2.	No	118	73.8	91	56.9	209	65.3
3.	Can not say	25	15.6	49	30.6	74	23.1
	Total	**160**	**100.0**	**160**	**100.0**	**320**	**100.0**

$\chi^2 = 11.52$; df = 2; $P<0.01$

The above table reveals that about two third (65.3) per cent of respondents had no sympathy, with naxalites connected with naxal movement whereas remaining 23.1 per cent and 11.6 per cent of respondents had no opinion and had full sympathy with naxalites respectively. Sex wise distribution shows that the female respondents were found to be more as compared to male respondents who had no opinion or had full sympathy with naxalites and this difference is found to be highly statistically significant (χ^2= 11.52; df = 2; P<0.01).

Table 5.15: Solution of Problem by Naxalite Sex, Caste and Education wise Distribution of Respontents

Sex		*Yes*		*No*		*Total*	
		No.	Per cent	No	Per cent	No	Per cent
1.	Male	61	38.1	99	61.9	160	100.0
2.	Female	103	64.4	57	35.6	160	100.0
	Total	**164**	**51.2**	**156**	**48.8**	**320**	**100.0**

χ^2 = 22.06; df = 1; P<0.001

Caste Structure

SC/ST	83	57.2	62	42.8	145	100.0
OBC	59	52.2	54	47.8	113	100.0
General	22	35.5	40	64.5	62	100.0
Total	**164**	**51.2**	**156**	**48.8**	**320**	**100.0**

χ^2= 8.29; df = 2; P<0.05

Educational Status

Illiterate	95	62.9	56	37.1	151	100.0
Upto High Schoo	150	36.0	89	64.0	139	100.0
Inter+	19	63.3	11	36.7	30	100.0
Total	**164**	**51.2**	**156**	**48.8**	**320**	**100.0**

χ^2= 22.96; df = 2; P<0.001

The table no.5.15, describes that more than half 51.2 per cent of respondents reported for taking interest to solve the problems, out of which maximum where females than male respondents. Caste wise distribution shows that majority of SC/ST's respondents accepted to solve the problems by naxalites followed by O.B.C's and general castes respectively. The respondents who were qualified at intermediate level and above, had of the opinion that naxalite take interest to solve their problems, much more proportion than qualified at primary to high school level and illiterate respondents respectively. Statistical (χ^2) chi square test proves the fact that the difference in proportion between male and female, among various caste and educational group regarding the interest of naxalites for solving different types of problems in their area is found to be highly significant.

Table 5.16: Problem Solving by Naxalite and Sex Status of Respondents

	Sex wise Respondent view on punish on Naxalite	*Sex*							
		M (61)		*F (103)*		*T(164)*		*df = 1*	
		No.	Per cent	No.	Per cent	No.	Per cent	χ^2	P
1.	Moral, emotional and economic support	9	14.8	24	23.3	33	20.1	1.74;	>0.05
2.	Killed the exploiter	38	62.3	60	58.3	98	59.8	0.26	>0.5
3.	Running parallel government	30	49.2	41	39.8	71	43.3	1.37	>0.5

The present table 5.16 shows the distribution of respondents opinion with reference to the type of activities done for solving the problem according to their sex which elaborates that out of total respondents 20.1 per cent reported that the naxalite solve the problem by moral, emotional and economical support. In which females respondents were more as compared to the male respondents more than half (59.8 per cent) of respondents were of the opinion that the naxalite either killed or suppressed the exploiters. In which in significantly the proportion of male respondents were more than female respondents. While (43.3 per cent) accepted to solve the problem by running the parallel government and by taking quick action for social justice. It is also observed that there is decrease or increased in the proportion male and female respondents for providing various types of activities done by the naxalite for helping the rural people is not statistically significant at any level of significance.

Thus the results shows that the opinion of male and female population regarding the ways of solving the problem is more or less similar.

Table 5.17: Awareness About Different Problems Solving by Naxalite and Caste Status of Respondents

Caste wise Distribution		*Caste*								*df* = 2	
		SC/ ST's(83)		*OBC(59)*		*General(22)*		*Total(164)*			
		No.	Per cent	No.	Per cent	No.	Per cent	No.	Per cent	χ^2	P
1.	Moral, emotional and economic support	19	22.9	10	16.9	4	18.2	33	20.1	0.82	>0.05
2.	Killed the exploiter	40	48.2	41	69.5	17	77.3	98	59.8	9.75	>0.01
3.	Running parallel government	47	56.6	13	22.0	11	50.0	71	43.3	17.28	<0.001

The above table 5.17 reveals that moral, emotional and economic support by naxalite to solve the people problem in the area was reported maximum by SC/ST's (22.9 per cent) caste group, and minimum by O.B.C.'s (16.9 per cent). The majority 77.3 per cent of respondent of general caste were of the opinion that the naxalite killed or suppressed the exploiters and this proportion significantly lowered down to the respondents of O.B.C.'s and SC/ST's respectively. The respondent who reported for quick justice after running the parallel government majority were of SC/ST's caste group followed by General and O.B.C.'s castes respectively. It is also seen that the difference in proportion regarding different opinion about naxalite activities for solving the problems among various caste categories is found to be statistically significant with the exception of moral, emotional and economic support.

Thus it may be concluded that the respondent belongs to SC/ ST's castes were more supporter for social, moral, economical support and right justice in any ways.

Education status also may plays significant role for giving correct opinion regarding the way of activity for helping people. The collected information is analyzed and produced in table no. 5.18, it indicates that the respondent qualified up to the level of high school, majority were of the opinion that naxalites provides moral, emotional, economical support as well as took correct and right decision for the justice, whereas the respondents had the qualification at intermediate level or above reported in maximum percentage to the activities of suppression or killings of exploiters. Statistically, in all types of activities done by the naxalites, the difference in proportion among various educational status, is observed to be highly significant.

Table 5.18: Education wise Distribution of Respondent

Education wise Distribution		*Education*									
		Illiterate (95)		*Upto High School.(50)*		*Inter(99)*		*Total(164)*		*df = 2*	
		No.	Per cent	No.	Per cent	No.	Per cent	No.	Per cent	χ^2	P
1.	Moral, emotional and economic support	15	15.8	16	32.0	2	10.5	33	20.1	6.59	<0.05
2.	Killed the exploiter	62	65.3	21	42.0	15	78.9	98	59.8	10.66	<0.01
3.	Running parallel government	32	33.7	34	68.0	5	26.3	71	43.3	18.24	<0.001

It clearly shows that the males respondents belong to SC/ST's and minimum educationally qualified were supported to the quick justice by any way and social, moral, emotional and economic support for solving the problems in the selected area.

Table 5.19: Sex wise Distribution of Respondent 's Knowledge about the Female Naxalite in Study Area

Knowledge about Female Naxalite		*Sex*					
		Male		*Female*		*Total*	
		No.	Per cent	No.	Per cent	No.	Per cent
1.	Yes	52	32.5	53	33.1	105	32.8
2.	No.	86	53.8	74	46.2	160	50.0
3.	Can not say	22	13.8	33	20.6	55	17.2
	Total	**160**	**100**	**160**	**100.0**	**320**	**100.0**

$\chi^2 = 3.11$; df=2; P>0.05

The above table, represents that about one third (32.8 per cent) of respondents had knowledge about the female naxalites in their area in which female proportion was 33.1 per cent and proportion of male was 32.5 per cent majority 50.0 per cent of respondents did not accept the presence of female naxalites and 17.2 per cent of respondents did not know about the presence of females. in naxal organisation. The difference in the proportion of knowledge between male and females respondent about the participation of females in naxal organisation or movement is not statistically significant.

Table 5-20: Awareness about Distance of Police Station from Respondents Villages

Sl. No.	*Distance*	*Frequency*	*Percentage*
1.	0 - 5 Km.	127	39.7
2.	5 - 15 Km.	172	53.8
3.	More than 15 Km.	21	06.6
	Total	**320**	**100.0**

It is evident from the above table that more than one-third (39.7 per cent) of respondents reported that the police station is situated for away in the range of 1 to 5 Km. whereas remaining 53.8 per cent and 6.6 per cent of respondents reported the location

Table 5.21: Knowledge About Police Behaviour with Caste and Sex Status of the Respondents

	Sex Status Of The Respondents							
Sex-wise	*Yes*		*No*		*Can not say*		*Total*	
	No.	*Per cent*	*No.*	*Per cent*	*No.*	*Per cent*	*No.*	*Per cent*
Male	17	10.6	122	76.2	21	13.1	160	100.0
Female	35	21.9	102	63.8	23	14.4	160	100.0
Total	**52**	**16.2**	**224**	**70.0**	**44**	**13.8**	**320**	**100.0**

= 8.11; df=2;P<0.05

Caste wise	*Yes*		*No*		*Can not say*		*Total*	
	No.	*Per cent*	*No.*	*Per cent*	*No.*	*Per cent*	*No.*	*Per cent*
SC/ST	34	23.4	89	61.4	22	15.2	145	100.0
OBC	11	09.7	91	80.5	11	09.7	113	100.0
General	07	11.3	44	71.0	11	17.7	62	100.0
Total	**52**	**16.2**	**224**	**70.0**	**44**	**13.8**	**320**	**100.0**

= 14.11; df=4;P<0.01

of police station at a distance of between 5 to 15 Km. and more than 15 Km. respectively. The result shows that the distance of police station was far away from the locality of the study area. So help by the government personal is not at reasonable and approachable from safety point of view.

The present table shows the distribution of respondent's knowledge regarding police behaviour for rural people according to sex and their castes. It reveals that only 16.2% of respondents were of the views that the police administration creates problems and exploited the people on the name of naxalites in which 21.9% were female respondent and 10.6% were male respondents and this difference is statistically significant.

The caste wise distribution shows that the respondents belongs to SC/ST 's castes were reported in more proportion for creating problem and exploitation by the police administration in comparison to the respondents of general and O.B.C.'s respectively. we may conclude that the SC/ST's individual were facing more problems while the police administration on the name of naxalites, might because of more active participation in naxal related activities by these people

Table 5.22: Caste Wise Distribution of Respondent's Knowledge About the Pressure on Rural People for Joining the Naxal Movement

For Joining the Naxal Movement	*Caste Wise*							
	SC/ST		*OBC*		*General*		*Total*	
	No.	*Per cent*	*No.*	*Per cent*	*No.*	*Per cent*	*No.*	*Per cent*
Yes	1	0.7	6	5.3	03	4.8	10	3.1
No.	122	84.1	80	70.8	51	82.3	253	79.1
Can't say	22	15.2	27	23.9	08	12.9	57	17.8
Total	**145**	**100.0**	**113**	**100.0**	**62**	**100.0**	**320**	**100.0**

= 10.34; df=4;P<0.05

It is evident from the above table that only 3.1 per cent of respondent of selected area accepted for exploitation and pressured for participation in naxalite movement in which the proportion of general and O.B.C.'s caste category was 4.8 per cent and 5.3 per cent respectively. While the proportion of SC/ST's caste group was very less (0.7 per cent) and this difference is found to be significant. Thus we may conclude that naxalites pressurised to only general and O.B.C.'s caste for participation in Naxal movement and naxal organisation.

Table 5.23: Behaviour of Government Officer and Sex Status of Respondents

Knowledge about People view		*SEX WISE*					
		M		*F*		*T*	
		No.	*Per cent*	*No.*	*Per cent*	*No.*	*Per cent*
1.	Cooperation	58	36.2	34	21.3	92	28.8
2.	Exploitation	17	10.6	12	07.6	29	09.1
3.	Neutral	49	30.6	89	56.3	138	43.4
4.	Can not say	36	22.5	25	15.8	61	19.2
	Total	**160**	**100.0**	**160**	**100.0**	**320**	**100.0**

X2 = 20.70; df=3; P<0.001

It is analysed from the above table that majority 43.4 per cent of respondents reported that the behaviour of government officers/ employees, was neutral followed by 28.8 per cent of respondents for cooperative behaviour and remaining 9.1 per cent and 19.2 per cent of respondents agreed for the fact that the government officer/ employees exploited the rural people and not answered in any favour of fact. The sex wise distribution shows that the proportion of male respondents was observed to be significantly more in comparison to the female respondents regarding various type of behaviour of government officers with the exception of exploitation.

Table 5.24: Profile of Respondents and Awareness Towards Behaviour of Government Officer in the Area

	Caste Wise							
	SC/ST		*OBC*		*General*		*Total*	
	No.	*Per cent*	*No.*	*Per cent*	*No.*	*Per cent*	*No.*	*Per cent*
1. Cooperation	43	29.7	29	25.7	20	32.3	92	28.8
2. Exploitation	05	03.4	15	13.3	09	14.5	29	09.1
3. Neutral	78	53.8	46	40.7	14	22.6	138	43.1
4. Can not say	19	13.1	23	20.4	19	30.6	61	19.1
Total	**145**	**100.0**	**113**	**100.0**	**62**	**100.0**	**320**	**100.0**

= 27.18; df=6;P<0.001

The result shows that the females of the naxalite areas were more sufferer than males; it may be due to easy availability in the home or in the villages for facing to various persons whether they are government officers/employees or selected people in Gramsabha elections.

Caste wise distribution shows that majority of general caste and OBC's castes respondents were reported for cooperative behavior or not answering about the behavior of government officers/employees, where majority of SC/ST's caste respondent accepted that the government officers or employees behaviors was neither cooperative nor exploitative. The difference in the proportion of opinion regarding behavior of government officers/employees among various caste groups is found to be statistically significant.

The results clearly shows that the SC/ST's respondents always afraid from the government officers/employees due to which they did not answered correctly regarding the behavior of government employees.

Table 5.25: Caste Wise Distribution of Respondent's According to the Quantity of Distribution of Agricultural Land

Caste Wise

Agricultural Land	*SC/ST*		*OBC*		*General*		*Total*	
	No.	*Per cent*	*No.*	*Per cent*	*No.*	*Per cent*	*No.*	*Per cent*
1. Yes	74	51.0	92	81.4	53	85.5	219	68.4
2. No.	71	49.0	21	18.6	09	14.5	101	31.6
Total	**145**	**100.0**	**113**	**100.0**	**62**	**100.0**	**320**	**100.0**

$\chi^2 = 37.48$; df=2; P<0.001

The respondents are distributed according to their castes and availability of agricultural land is recorded in table no. 5.25. It is found that in the study area majority 68.4 per cent of respondents had the agricultural land in which the proportion of general caste was 85.5 per cent followed by O.B.C.'s , 81.4 per cent and minimum 51.0 per cent was in SC/ST's respondents and this difference of proportion is observed to be the statistically significant.

$\chi^2 = 37.48$; df=2;P<0.001

Table 5.26: Availibility of Agriculture Land and Caste Status Of Respondents

Caste Wise

Agricultural Land	*SC/ST*		*OBC*		*General*		*Total*	
	No.	*Per cent*	*No.*	*Per cent*	*No.*	*Per cent*	*No.*	*Per cent*
1. Upto 5 Acre	70	94.6	70	76.1	36	67.9	176	80.4
2. 5 - 10 Acre	4	5.4	12	13.0	12	22.6	28	12.8
3. 10 - 20Acre	0	0.0	10	10.9	3	5.7	13	5.9
4. 20+ Acre	0	0.0	0	0.0	2	3.8	2	0.9
Total	**74**	**100.0**	**92**	**100.0**	**53**	**100.0**	**219**	**100.0**

The area of agricultural land was found to be in range of 1-5 acre, in majority 80.4 per cent of respondent in which proportion of SC/ST caste was more followed by O.B.C.'s and general caste categories respectively. Remaining 12.8 per cent and 6.8 per cent of respondents had the agriculture land between 5 to 10 acres and more than 10 acres respectively. In which maximum were the respondents of general caste followed by O.B.C.'s and SC/ST's castes respectively. It clearly shows that maximum agriculture land area was occupied by general castes and O.B.C.'s castes families in the selected area. Small agricultural land holding by SC/ST's may be one cause of poor economic status, lower educational status and increased in participation in naxal movement and organisations by SC/ST's caste.

Table 5.27: Caste Wise Distribution of Respondent's According to their Source of Livelihood in the Absence of Agricultural Land

Caste Wise

Source of Livelihood	*SC/ST*		*OBC*		*General*		*Total*	
	No.	*Per cent*	*No.*	*Per cent*	*No.*	*Per cent*	*No.*	*Per cent*
1. Labour	56	78.9	11	52.4	1	11.1	68	67.3
2. Self Employment/Service also	2	2.8	1	4.8	2	22.2	5	5.0
3. Both	13	18.3	9	42.9	6	66.7	28	27.7
Total	**71**	**100.0**	**21**	**100.0**	**9**	**100.0**	**101**	**100.0**

$\chi^2 = 21.33$; df=4; $P<0.001$.

It is evident from the above tables that more than two-third (67.3 per cent) were doing labour work and only 5.0 per cent were self employed and remaining 27.7 per cent were doing both types of work that is labour, service and self employed work. Out of total

SC/ST's respondents maximum 78.9 per cent were labourer, while 52.4 per cent and 42.9 per cent of O.B.C.'s respondent engaged in labour work and both labour with self employment. While in general caste maximum 66.7 per cent were self employed or doing labour work at their own home or in private sector. The difference in proportion of doing different types of work among the respondents of various caste category is highly significant.

Table 5.28: Distribution of Respondent's Knowledge about Naxalism Due to Geographical Location with their Educational Status

Educational Status

Geographical Location	*Illiterate*		*Upto High School*		*Inter and above*		*Total*	
	No.	*Per cent*	*No.*	*Per cent*	*No.*	*Per cent*	*No.*	*Per cent*
1. Yes	45	29.8	65	46.8	21	70.0	131	40.9
2. No.	36	23.8	24	17.3	7	23.3	67	20.9
3. Can not say	70	46.4	50	36.0	2	6.7	122	38.1
Total	**151**	**100.0**	**139**	**100.0**	**30**	**100.0**	**320**	**100.0**

$\chi^2 = 24.14$; df=4; $P<0.001$.

It is evident from the above table that majority 40.9 per cent of respondents agreed with fact that geographical location and topography is the main reason for the emergence of naxalism in Sonbhadra area. Whereas 38.1 per cent and 20.9 per cent of respondents did not answered and did not agree with geographical location and topography for emergence of naxalism. The proportion of illiterate respondents was found to be significantly lower in comparison to the literate respondents in connection to considering to the geographical location and topography as main reason for emergence of naxalism.

The above table reveals that only 13.1 per cent of respondents accepted for exploitation done by the forest officer and employees in which SC/ST's proportion was more than comparison to OBC's and general castes respectively. The respondents not answered at all about the exploitation maximum were from SC/ST's caste groups. The difference in the proportion for the opinion about the exploitation done by the forest officers and employees among the different caste group is observed to be the statistically highly significant. The data clearly shows that the lower castes afraid from various government officers and employees regarding their behavior.

Table 5.29: Awareness About Exploitation Done By The Forest Officer And Employees And Caste Status Of The Respondents

Caste Wise

Caste wise view in exploitation done by forest officers	*SC/ST*		*OBC*		*General*		*Total*	
	No.	*Per cent*	*No.*	*Per cent*	*No.*	*Per cent*	*No.*	*Per cent*
1. Yes	22	15.2	13	11.5	7	11.3	42	13.1
2. No.	75	51.7	97	85.8	54	87.1	226	70.6
3. Can not say	48	33.1	3	2.7	1	1.6	52	16.2
Total	**145**	**100.0**	**113**	**100.0**	**62**	**100.0**	**320**	**100.0**

$\chi^2 = 60.64$; df=4; P<0.001.

Table 5.30: Profile of Respondents and their Awareness Towards Imprisonment

Break down of Forest Law	*Frequency*	*Percentage*
Yes	13	04.1
No.	307	95.9
Total	320	100.0

The above table reflects that out of total respondents only 4.1 per cent of respondents were accepted for the punishment due to creating hindrance in the rules and regulation of forest department and remaining 95.9 per cent were accepting for not having such type of incidents.

Table 5.31: Dependency on Forest Good and Caste Status of Respondents

Caste Wise

Caste wise view on forest goods	*SC/ST*		*OBC*		*General*		*Total*	
	No.	*Per cent*	*No.*	*Per cent*	*No.*	*Per cent*	*No.*	*Per cent*
1. Yes	47	32.4	20	17.7	4	6.5	71	22.2
2. No.	98	67.6	93	82.3	58	93.5	249	77.8
Total	**145**	**100.0**	**113**	**100.0**	**62**	**100.0**	**320**	**100.0**

$\chi^2 = 18.99$; df=2; P<0.001

The distribution of the selected respondents according to their caste and dependency on forest goods for their daily requirement which clearly shows that only 22.2 per cent of respondents were dependent on forest good. In which the proportion of SC/ST's were observed to be more (32.4 per cent) in comparison to the O.B.C.'s (17.7 per cent) and general caste group (6.5 per cent) respectively and this difference is found to be the statistically highly significant.

The results shows that majority of SC/ST's caste who were residing near the forest and had low Socio-economic status may be totally dependent on forest goods for their daily requirement.

Table 5-32: Caste Wise Distribution of Respondent's about Utilisation of Forest Goods

Caste Wise

Utilisation of Forest Food	*SC/ST*		*OBC*		*General*		*Total*	
	No.	*Per cent*	*No.*	*Per cent*	*No.*	*Per cent*	*No.*	*Per cent*
1. Livelihood only	95	65.5	53	46.9	16	25.8	164	51.2
2. Livelihood + Trade	27	18.6	46	40.7	24	38.7	97	30.3
3. Others	23	15.9	14	12.4	22	35.5	59	18.4
Total	**145**	**100.0**	**113**	**100.0**	**62**	**100.0**	**320**	**100.0**

χ^2 = 38.55; df=4; P>0.001

Further an analysis has also been made for the utilisation of forest goods which is presented in table 5.32, it reveals that more than half (51.2 per cent) of respondents were accepted to utilised forest goods for their livelihood while remaining 30.3 per cent and 18.4 per cent of respondents for trade along with livelihood and for others purposes respectively. Again the respondents who were utilising forest goods for their livelihood majority were from SC/ST's caste groups which signify also the low socio-economic condition of the particular caste category. The utilisation pattern of forest goods is observed to be significant different by different caste groups.

The above table reflects that about 50.0 per cemt of respondents had knowledge about the implementation of land reform programmes in their areas in which the respondents qualified at intermediate level and more than this, were 90.0 per cent followed by illiterate 47.0 per cent and primary to high school 43.9 per cent respectively remaining 28.4 per cent and 21.9 per cent of respondents either had no knowledge or did not answer correctly. Statistically, the difference in proportion among various educational groups of respondents regarding the knowledge for the implementation of land reform in their respective area is highly significant.

Table 5.33: Educational Profile of Respondents and their Awareness Towards Implementation of Land Reform Programmes

Educational Status

Knowledge of Land Reform Programmes	*Illiterate*		*Upto High School*		*Inter and above*		*Total*	
	No.	*Per cent*	*No.*	*Per cent*	*No.*	*Per cent*	*No.*	*Per cent*
1. Yes	71	47.0	61	43.9	27	90.0	159	49.7
2. No.	23	15.2	45	32.4	2	6.7	70	21.9
3. Can not say	57	37.7	33	23.7	1	3.3	91	28.4
Total	**151**	**100.0**	**139**	**100.0**	**30**	**100.0**	**320**	**100.0**

$\chi^2 = 36.52$; df=4; $P<0.001$

It clearly shows that the knowledge about the land reforms programmes is increasing order as educational level is increasing.

Table 5.34: Knowledge about Getting Benefit of Land Reform Programmes and with Caste Status of Respondents

Caste Wise

Benefit of Land Reform Programmes	*SC/ST*		*OBC*		*General*		*Total*	
	No.	*Per cent*	*No.*	*Per cent*	*No.*	*Per cent*	*No.*	*Per cent*
1. Yes	23	39.0	44	73.3	21	52.5	88	55.3
2. No.	36	61.0	16	26.5	19	47.5	71	44.7
Total	**59**	**100.0**	**60**	**100.0**	**40**	**100.0**	**159**	**100.0**

$\chi^2 = 14.38$; df=2; $P<0.001$

The table 5.34 depicts that more than half (55.3 per cent) of respondents were accepted for getting benefit of land reform programmes out of which maximum were of O.B.C.'s caste, followed by general castes and minimum were SC/ST's castes. and statistically this difference is highly significant.

We may conclude that the beneficiaries are more from O.B.C.'s and less from SC/ST's might be because of dominating nature of O.B.C.'s community as well as active participation in administration.

Table 5.35: Profile of Respondents and their Awareness Towards Problem of Untouchability and Caste Conflict

Caste Wise

Problem of Village	*SC/ST*		*OBC*		*General*		*Total*	
	No.	*Per cent*	*No.*	*Per cent*	*No.*	*Per cent*	*No.*	*Per cent*
1. Yes	66	45.5	27	23.9	18	29.0	111	34.7
2. No.	79	54.5	86	76.1	44	71.0	209	65.3
Total	**145**	**100.0**	**113**	**100.0**	**62**	**100.0**	**320**	**100.0**

χ^2 = 14.19; df=2;P<0.001

Caste wise distribution of respondents' opinion regarding the problem of caste conflict and untouchability in their respective villages is analysed and presented in table No.5.35. It is found that 34.7 per cent of respondents were accepted the fact of caste conflict and untouchability problem in their villages in which maximum were of the respondents of SC/ST's caste, followed by O.B.C.'s and general caste groups. This difference is statistically found to be highly significant.

The caste conflict and untouchability problem were stated by the respondents of SC/ST's caste group may be due to maximum mishappening and exploitation were with SC/ST's caste group by other dominant caste group of their respective villages.

Table 5.36: Knowledge about Naxalite Fight for Social Justice With Respondents Caste And Sex Status

Caste Wise	*SC/ST*		*OBC*		*General*		*Total*	
	No.	*Per cent*	*No.*	*Per cent*	*No.*	*Per cent*	*No.*	*Per cent*
1. SC/ST	33	22.5	34	23.4	78	53.8	145	100.0
2. OBC	18	15.9	53	46.9	42	37.2	113	100.0
3. General	05	08.1	35	56.5	22	35.5	62	100.0
Total	**56**	**17.5**	**122**	**38.1**	**142**	**44.4**	**320**	**100.0**

χ^2 = 26.87; df=4; P<0.001

Sex Wise	*Yes*		*No.*		*Can not say*		*Total*	
	No.	*Per cent*	*No.*	*Per cent*	*No.*	*Per cent*	*No.*	*Per cent*
1. Male	19	11.9	64	40.0	77	48.1	160	100.0
2. Female	37	23.1	58	36.2	65	40.6	160	100.0
Total	**56**	**17.5**	**122**	**38.1**	**142**	**44.4**	**320**	**100.0**

$\chi^2 = 7.10$; df=2; $P<0.01$

It is evident from the above table that out of total respondent only 17.5 per cent of respondents were of the views that the naxalites are struggling for social justice for the rural people. Whereas remaining 38.1 per cent and 44.4 per cent of respondents' opinion was negative and did not open their views regarding this matter. The respondents who had positive opinion regarding fight for social justice by naxalites maximum were from SC/ST's caste groups and minimum from general caste groups. Sex wise distribution shows that the proportion of female respondents were 23.1 per cent and male respondents 11.9 per cent who opinion that naxalite fight for social justice. Statistically, the difference in the proportion among various caste groups and between male and female regarding opinion for struggling of naxalite for social justice as well as solving the general problems of rural people.

We may conclude from the result that the scheduled caste/scheduled tribes as well as female were more suppressed by the dominant groups and these dominant groups afraid some how from the naxalite.

Table 5.37: Profile of Respondents and their Awareness Towards Facilities Provided By The Government

Availability of Different Facilities

Type of Facilities provided by Government	*Yes*		*No*		*Total*	
	No.	*per cent*	*No.*	*per cent*	*No.*	*per cent*
1. Sanitation(Toilet)	126	39.4	194	60.0	320	100.0
2. Road Connectivity to Village	232 (Kacha)	72.5 (Pakka)	88	27.5	320	100.0
3. Electricity connection in Village	249	77.8	71	22.2	320	100.0
4. Drinking water	194	60.6	126	39.4	320	100.0
5. Health facility nearby the Village	129	40.3	191	59.7	320	100.0
6. School facility nearby village	266	83.1	54	16.9	320	100.0
1. Primary School	169	63.5				

(Contd...)

2. High School	39	14.7	
3. Degree College	01	00.5	
4. Both (1+2)	57	21.4	
Total	**266**	**100.0**	

It is perceptible from the above table that 39.4 per cent of respondents were aware regarding sanitation facility (Toilet), 72.5 per cent for road connecting to the villages, 77.8 per cent for electrification in their respective villages, and 60.6 per cent of respondents were accepted to facilitates drinking water supply, for rural area, it is also observed that the awareness regarding health facility near by the villages as well as school for educating the children were in 40.3 per cent and 83.1 per cent of the respondents awareness.

The respondent who had awareness regarding the school facility provided by the government, majority 63.5 per cent reported for primary schooling, 14.7 per cent for high school, 0.5 per cent for degree colleges were as 21.4 per cent of respondents had knowledge about primary and high school colleges both. It clearly shows that the government provided many types of facilities like sanitation, sources of communication for convenience, electricity and education as well as drinking water at maximum level in different programmes and planning in the study area.

Table 5.38: Profile of Respondents and their Awareness Towards Various Government Run Programmes and Compensation Given in the Case of Displacement

Displacement of People Compensation

Sl. No.		*No.*	*Per cent*		*No.*	*Per cent*
1.	Yes	31	9.7	Yes	7	22.6
2.	No	209	65.3	No	24	77.4
3.	Can not say	80	25.0			
	Total	**320**	**100.0**	**Total**	**31**	**100.0**

It is apparent from the above table that only 9.7 per cent of respondents were accepted for displacement due to various government programmes or industrialisation and rest 65.3 per cent and 25.0 per cent of respondents had no knowledge and did not remember of such type of incidents respectively.

The respondents who were of the opinion for displacement about one fourth (22.6 per cent) also accepted for getting compensation by the government and private companies.

Table 5.39: Awareness about Various Set up by Government/ Private Industries

Sex wise knowledge about Industrial Benefits.	*Male*		*Female*		*Total*	
	No.	*per cent*	*No.*	*per cent*	*No.*	*per cent*
1. Yes	2	01.2	37	23.1	39	12.2
2. No	102	63.8	54	33.8	156	48.8
3. Can not say	56	35.0	69	43.1	125	39.0
Total	**160**	**100.0**	**160**	**100.0**	**320**	**100.0**

$\chi^2 = 47.53$; df=2; $P<0.001$

The above table reflects that only 12.2 per cent of respondents were accepted the fact that the local people of the area were benefited by the establishment of government or private industries, while 48.8 per cent denied for any type of benefit and rest 39.0 per cent of respondent neither accepted any type of benefit nor denied about the fact. The individual who were in favour of getting benefits from industries maximum were female respondents and this difference is statistically highly significant. It may be due to employment of rural women in nearby the government/private industry.

Table 5.40: Profile of Respondents and their Awareness Towards Exploitation Done by Money Lender and Contractors

Distribution of Respondent view on	*Male*		*Female*		*Total*	
	No.	*per cent*	*No.*	*per cent*	*No.*	*per cent*
1. Exploitation by moneylenders and Contractors	186	58.1	134	41.9	320	100.0
2. on name of naxalite any family members arrested	23	7.2	297	92.8	320	100.0
Total	**160**	**100.0**	**160**	**100.0**	**320**	**100.0**

The above table predicts that out of total respondents more than half (58.1 per cent) of respondents were reported for any type of exploitation by money lenders and contractors and rest 41.9 per cent were not suffered from such type of exploitation. It is also observed that only 7.2 per cent (23) of respondents' were accepted that the male members of the family were arrested on the name of naxalites.

Table 5.41: Profile of Respondents and their Aweareness Towards Exploitation Done by Money Lenders and Contractors

Caste Wise Distribution

Exploitation by money lender and Contractors	*SC/ST*		*OBC*		*General*		*Total*	
	No.	*Per cent*	*No.*	*Per cent*	*No.*	*Per cent*	*No.*	*Per cent*
1. Yes	98	67.6	57	50.5	31	50.0	186	58.1
2. No	47	32.4	56	49.6	31	50.0	134	41.9
Total	**145**	**100.0**	**113**	**100.0**	**62**	**100.0**	**320**	**100.0**

$\chi^2 = 9.75$; df=2; $P<0.01$

Further, the distribution of respondents regarding exploitation by money lender and contractors is also analyzed according to their caste and presented in table 5.41, it reveals that the respondents (58.1 per cent) who reported for the exploitation by money lenders maximum (67.6 per cent) were from SC/ST's caste category followed by O.B.C.'s (50.5 per cent) and general (50.0) respectively. This difference is statistically significant.

The results shows that the majority of the respondents are in either below poverty line or just above the poverty line, who take the money for different purposes on interest from money lenders and contractors.

Table 5.42: Problem Faced by the Respondents's in Case of Arresting Male Member as Naxalite

Sl. No.	*Problem Faced*	*Frequency*	*Percentage*
1	Economical	05	21.7
2	Social	03	13.0
3	Both	15	65.3
	Total	**23**	**100.0**

The above table depicts that the respondents family members (23) were arrested on the name of naxalites maximum 65.3 per cent were facing economical and social problem both, whereas remaining 21.7 per cent and 13.0 per cent of respondents were reported for facing economical problems and social problems respectively.

The results clearly shows that the respondents family male members, if arrested on the name of naxalite economically morally as well as socially suppressed in the rural areas and again their socio-economic status goes lower and lower.

Table 5.43: Profile of Respondent's Opinion about Help at the time of any Problems

Sl.No.	*Help in Problem*	*Frequency*	*Percentage*
1.	Same Caste	74	23.1
2.	Naxalites	0	0.0
3.	Gram Panchayat	112	35.0
4.	Administration	66	20.6
5.	NGO	6	1.9
6.	Same Caste + Gram Panchayat (1+3)	5	1.6
7.	Same Caste + Administration(1+4)	24	7.5
8.	3+4(G.P.+Administration)	5	1.6
9.	1+3+4(Caste+G.P.+Admn.)	28	8.8
	Total	**320**	**100.0**

It is evident from the above table that majority 35.0 per cent, 23.1 per cent and 20.6 per cent of respondents, responded to help at the time of any problem by representatives of Gram Panchayats, same caste group members and government administration respectively. Only 8.8 per cent, 7.5 per cent and (1.61 to 1.9 per cent) of respondent accepted to get help from same caste, Grampanchayat and government administration along with non-government organisation respectively. Surprisingly, it is observed that no respondent were accepted to get help from the naxalites in situation of any problem.

The results clearly shows that the respondents are not ready to say any thing about matter regarding naxalite in the present study area.

Table 5.44: Profile of Respondent's According to the Emotional, Mental , Physical and Social Exploitation on the Name Of Naxalism

Sl. No.	*Exploitation (Naxalite)*	*Frequency*	*Percentage*
1.	Yes	53	16.6
2.	No	218	68.1
3.	Can not say	49	15.3
	Total	**320**	**100.0**

The above table depicts that regarding emotional, mental, physical and social exploitation by govt. or NGO's administration or by public dominant people on the name of naxalite, only 16.6 per cent of respondents reported correctly about these true facts. Whereas 68.1 per cent were reported negative response and 15.3 per cent did not answer about such type of exploitation.

Summary

An attempt has been made to analysed the nature and process of social transformation in a rural setting specially in Naxal affected areas. In this context the gathered information analysed and summarised as follows:-

- Analysis regarding the knowledge and factors of naxalism, shows that about 96 per cent of respondents had knowledge about naxalism. The main factors of naxalism were found to be Ideological attitudes, followed by caste conflicts, land/ labour disparity and lower socio-economic status respectively.
- Socio-economic status and land disparity causes of naxalism were reported by females in maximum proportions were as Ideological attitudes and caste conflicts by male respondents respectively.
- It is also found that majority of respondents belongs to general castes consider socio-economic status land/labour disparity and Ideology as a major root cause of naxalism whereas respondents of SC/ST"s caste category opined to the caste conflicts as major factor.
- Land / labour disparity was reported by majority of Illiterate respondents while other responsible factors were accepted by those respondents who were qualified either at intermediate or more than these qualifications.
- Analysing the fact, it is found that majority 73.2 per cent of respondents had correct knowledge about the emergence of naxalism. Out of which male respondents were significantly more than the female respondents.

- It is observed that out of total respondents majority 65.3 per cent of respondents had knowledge about different naxal organisations, out of which the proportion of male respondents were significantly more than the female respondents in the study area.
- Majority of respondents 40.6 per cent opinion about social transformation whereas 16.6 per cent of respondent did not project any views regarding this matter. In both the cases female respondents were observed to be significantly higher in proportion than the male respondents.
- It is also tried to know about the types of social transformation in the selected study area which shows that out of total respondents 88.5 per cent and 87.7 per cent of respondents reported to economic and social transformation out of which male respondents were observed to be significantly more in comparison to the female respondents. About 86 per cent of respondents credited to political transformation in which females were more as compared to male respondents.
- The views of the respondents according to their castes is also categorised regarding types of social transformation in naxal affected areas which projects that the respondents of general were give to social transformation in maximum proportion whereas SC/ST's and respondents of OBC's were of views of political and economic transformation respectively.
- The Association between educational status of respondents and their opinion regarding types of transformation due to naxalism, projects that the respondents who were of the views about socio-economic transformation were found to be an increasing order as educational status advanced while, just a reversed trend is observed in political transformation.
- By analysing the opinion of respondents regarding types of social transformation due to naxalism, we found that those respondents who were opinion to political and economic transformation maximum were in the monthly income group

of Rs 1500 (less than) and greater that Rs 3000(more) than respectively, while, in case of social transformation it was maximum in middle economic group i.e. 1500-3000.

- It is apparent from the analysis that out of total respondents, who were in favour of social transformation due to naxalism, majority 67.7 per cent reported the change by gun and to aware the people in which maximum were younger group of respondents.
- It is observed that the majority 65.3 per cent of respondents did not having any type of sympathy with naxalite or individual related with naxal movement whereas, remaining 23.1 per cent and 11.6 per cent had no opinion and had full sympathy respectively female respondents were found to be significantly more as compared to male respondents who had full sympathy with naxalite.
- Analyzing the fact, it is found that 51.2 per cent of respondents reported for taking interest to solve their problem by naxalites. Out of which female proportion was found to be significantly more than male respondents respectively.
- Caste wise distribution shows that majority of SC/ST's respondents was of the views that the problems generally solved by the naxalites followed by OBC's and general caste respectively.
- The respondents who were qualified at Intermediate level or above had of the perception that naxalite take interest to solve their problems in more proportion followed by illiterate and qualified at primary to high school level respectively.
- It is found that about 60.0 per cent and 43.3 per cent of respondent were of the views that naxalite solved their problems by killing the exploiter and by running parallel government out of which male respondents were more as compared to female respondents. Only 20.1 per cent reported that naxalites solves the problem by moral, emotional and economic support in which females were more than male respondents.

- Majority of respondents belongs to SC/ST's caste group were accepted moral, emotional and economic support as well as by running parallel, government while maximum general caste group said that generally killed the exploiter for solving the problems in the study area.
- Education wise distribution shows that the respondents qualified upto the level of high school, majority were of the views that naxalite provides moral, emotional and economical support and running parallel government whereas maximum qualified respondent were reported that naxalite killed the exploiters for solving their problems.
- Analysis regarding the knowledge about participation of female in naxal organisation or female naxalites shows that only 32.8 per cent of respondents had some knowledge about the female naxalites in their area. Out of which proportion of female were more than male respondents.
- More than half of the respondents (53.8 per cent) reported the location of police station between the distance (5-15km) while 39.7 per cent and 6.6 per cent within the range of 5km and more than 15km respectively.
- The analysis regarding police behavior in the study area shows that only 16.2 per cent of the respondents were of the views that the police administration creates problems and exploited the people on the name of naxalites, in which maximum proportion was female respondents and respondents of SC/ST's caste category respectively.
- It is also observed that only 3.1 per cent of respondents of selected area accepted for exploitation, misbehaving and pressure for participation in naxalite in which respondents of OBC's and general castes category were more in comparison to SC/ST's caste category.
- It is observed from the analysis that majority 43.4 per cent of respondents reported that the behaviour of government officer/employees was neutral and common. While 28.8 per cent, 9.1 per cent and 19.2 per cent of respondent agreed for

the fact that their behaviour are cooperative, exploitative and were unaware regarding the fact.

- Majority 68.4 per cent of respondents had the agricultural land out of which the proportion of general caste was significantly more as compared to OBC's and SC/ST's respondent respectively.
- The distribution of agricultural land area shows that 80.4 per cent of respondent had agricultural land within 5 acres remaining 19.6 per cent having more than 5 acres respectively. The respondents belongs to SC/ST's had less area of agriculture land in comparison to respondents of OBC's and general respectively.
- It is found that out of total respondents who had no agricultural land, majority 67.3 per cent were doing labour work and only 5.0 per cent were self employed, while remaining 27.7 per cent were doing labour work along with the self employment.

References

Mohan, Rakesh : Maoism in India, Vikas Publication, New Delhi,1971.

Oommen, T.K. : Social Transformation in Rural India, Vikas Publication House, New Delhi, 1984.

Joshi, P.C.: Marxism and Social Revolution in India and other Essays, Vikash Publication, New Delhi, 1980

Dubey, Abhay : Kranti Ka Atma Sangharsh, Vanni Publicatin (S.D.S.) Daryaganj, New Delhi, 1997.

Singharoy, Debal K.: Women in Peasant Movement : Tebhaga, Telengana, Naxalite and after; : A Cross Cultual Analysis, IGNOU, New Delhi, 1995.

Prakash, Louis : People Power : The Naxalite Movement in Central Bihar, Wordsmiths, Delhi, 2002.

Dreze, J. : Starving the Poor, The Hindu, Feb.26, Economics Times, 2001.

Sankaran, S.R. : Welfare of Scheduled Castes and Scheduled Tribes in Independent India on Overview of State Policies and Programmes, Journal of Rural Development, Vol. 19, No.4, PP.507-584.

6

State Intervention Measures and Rural Development in Naxal Affected Areas of Sonbhadra District

Rural transformation has been one of the major objectives of development planning in India. The concept of rural transformation has been interpreted in two ways. In a narrow sense, it refers to social change occur in rural areas through the development of activities based mainly in the rural areas such as agriculture, animal husbandry, village crafts and Industries, rural infrastructure, technology, communications and innovations etc. The broader view of rural transformation is not only large in scope and coverage but also with respect to its approach to the problem. Its focus is directly on the well being of the people in rural areas. In broader sense it includes changes in social, political, economic cultural, technological and structural aspects with a view to improving the quality of life of the rural people rural transformation is a multi-dimensional concept involving a multi-disciplinary approach. The concept is defined in various ways (Mehta A.K.; Shepherd, A) ed. 2006.

Desai (1988) defined it as "an approach which, by better utilisation of local resources and by creating infrastructural facilities for economic and social development aims at improving the quality of life of the rural population, especially the rural poor, by creation of expanded employment and income opportunities for them".

Maheshwari (1985) considers rural transformation as "interminable process to bring about improvement in the economic and social life of the rural poor".

It reveals that rural development programmes implemented by the state serve the interest of some groups and class and not others and that their real effects may be very different from what is claimed for them or from the rhetoric surrounding them. It is in this contradictory context that an attempt is made here to evaluate the state interventions in rural development programmes, in the naxal affected areas of Sonbhadra district of Eastern Uttar Pradesh. Our objective is to analyses whether the state's measures have been successful enough to bring about rural transformation. To what extent they have reduced inequalities in income and services and how much potential they are in alleviation of poverty in rural society and bring social transformation in Naxal affected areas, especially in the Sonbhadra district of Eastern Uttar Pradesh. The various programmes of rural development launched by the state from time to time, broadly can be categorised into four main groups on the basis of-

(a) Income Generation.
(b) Employment Orientation.
(c) Education and welfare, and
(d) Area Development.

Some of the major rural development programmes undertaken so far in different plan since Independence are the community development programme (C.D.P.) in 1952, Panchayati Raj Institution (PRI) in 1959, Green Revolution, 1966-67, Rural Electrification corporation, 1969, Twenty point programme in 1975, food for Work programmes, 1977-78, Jawahar Rozgar Yojana, 1989 etc.

Recently launched some of the major schemes in the rural development are Bharat Nirman, MNREGA, Aam Admi Bima Yojana, Midday meal Schemes, Rashtriya Swasthya Bima Yojana, National Rural Health Mission, Rajiv Gandhi National Drinking Water mission, Rashtriya Sam Vikash Yojana etc. These launched schemes bring social social-economic, cultural and political transformation in the backward area of Sonbhadra especially in last two decades. In the last two decades, with the expansion of education and telecommunication in the rural areas, many non-government organisations also played active role and creates awareness in the rural people about their social, political and economic rights of the people and various programmes and policies launched by the government in the concerned study area.

In this chapter we have attempted to discuss the various programmes and policies launched by government in Sonbhadra district. It also covers the type of changes occurred in the life of people due to rise of naxalism in the study area.

Table 6.1: Profile of Respondents and their Awareness Towards Vote Casting In Election

Caste	*Vote in Election*					
	Yes		*No*		*Total*	
	No.	*per cent*	*No.*	*per cent*	*No.*	*per cent*
SC/ST	123	84.8	22	15.2	145	100.0
OBC	86	76.1	27	23.9	113	100.0
General	62	100.0	00	00.0	62	100.0
Total	271	84.7	49	15.3	320	100.0

χ^2 = 17.63; df=2; P<0.001

Sex	*Yes*		*No*		*Total*	
No.	%	No.	%	No.	%	
Male	147	91.9	13	08.1	160	100.0
Female	124	77.5	36	22.5	160	100.0
Total	271	84.7	49	15.3	320	100.0

χ^2 = 12.75; df=1; P<0.001

Age	*Yes*		*No*		*Total*	
No.	%	No.	%	No.	%	
20 - 34	89	89.9	10	10.1	99	100.0
35 - 49	132	85.7	22	14.3	154	100.0
50+	50	74.6	17	25.4	67	100.0
Total	271	84.7	49	15.3	320	100.0

χ^2 = 7.43; df=2; P<0.05

The above table describes the profile of respondents and their awareness towards vote casting in election in which 84.7 per cent were accepted for vote casting during election period in which

100 per cent were belongs to general castes, 76.1 per cent and 84.8 per cent were from OBC's and SC/ST's caste groups respectively. Majority 91.9 per cent of male respondents were used their vote in different election while in females the proportion was 77.5 per cent. The trend of vote castings was observed to be in increasing order with increasing of the age structure of the respondents. Statistically, the difference in proportion of vote casting among various caste categories, between male and female respondents as well as among various age groups is found to be statistically highly significant.

We may conclude that the respondents of general castes and younger group of male respondents were taking more interest and active participation regarding vote casting during elections in the study area.

Table-6.2: Profile of Respondents and their Awareness Towards not Vote Casting in Election

Reason for not casting vote in election	*Yes*		*No*		*Total*	
	No.	*per cent*	*No.*	*per cent*	*No.*	*per cent*
1. To check by dominant caste	39	79.6	10	20.4	49	100.0
2. To check by naxalites pressure for	6	12.2	43	87.8	49	100.0
3. Pressure for Vote Casting for Special party by naxalite	5	10.2	44	89.8	49	100.0
4 Not believe in present political activity	31	63.3	18	36.7	49	100.0

The above table reveals that those respondents who did not cast their vote during election period, majority 79.6 per cent said that they checked by dominant caste for not casting their vote. The other important reason was the unbeliever in the present political activity which is reported by 63.3 per cent of respondents. Only 12.2 per cent and 10.2 per cent of respondents reported that they did not cast their vote due to naxalite pressure or pressurised by naxalite for vote casting to special parties who favoured or support naxalism in the study area.

It may be concluded that there are two main reasons for not vote casting in election are checked by the dominant caste and unbelief in present political activities. It means fear of dominant caste and naxalites as well as inactiveness of leaders are the major reasons for the people in the study area not to cast their vote freely.

Table 6.3: Profile of Respondents and their Awareness Towards Problems Solving In Gram Panchayat

Problem Recognition	*SC/ST*		*OBC*		*General*		*Total*	
	No.	*Per cent*	*No.*	*Per cent*	*No.*	*Per cent*	*No.*	*Per cent*
1. Yes	91	62.8	96	85.0	5.1	82.3	238	74.4
2. No	54	37.2	17	15.0	1.1	17.7	82	25.6
Total	**145**	**100.0**	**113**	**100.0**	**62**	**100.0**	**320**	**100.0**

χ^2 = 18.93; df=2; P<0.001

It is apparent from the above table 6.3 that about three-fourth (74.4 per cent) of respondents were of the opinion that the representative of grampanchayat recognised their problems in the meeting in which maximum 85.0 per cent were belongs to OBC's followed by 82.3 per cent of general caste and minimum 62.8 per cent were SC/ST's caste group respectively. Statistically, this difference is observed to be highly significant.

The recognition reported by OBC's in high proportion may be due to presence of maximum grampanchayat representatives from the same caste in the study area.

Table 6.4: Profile of Respondents and their Awareness Towards Solution of Problem by Bureaucrats

Problem Solution by Bureaucrats	*SC/ST*		*OBC*		*General*		*Total*	
	No.	*Per cent*	*No.*	*Per cent*	*No.*	*Per cent*	*No.*	*Per cent*
1. Yes	66	45.5	86	76.1	53	85.5	205	64.1
2. No	79	54.5	27	23.9	9	14.5	115	35.9
Total	**145**	**100.0**	**113**	**100.0**	**62**	**100.0**	**320**	**100.0**

χ^2 = 41.14; df=2;P<0.001

It is reveals from the above table that majority 64.1 per cent of respondents were accepted to solve their problem by bureaucrats, out of which maximum (85.5 per cent) were from general caste, 76.1 per cent from OBC's and minimum only 45.5 per cent were from SC/ST's respectively. Statistical chi square (X^2) also proved the fact that the difference in proportion of respondents opinion regarding the solution of problem by bureaucrats among various caste category is found to be highly significant.

Thus, the suppression of SC/ST's castes regarding solution of their problem is maximum in the present study area. It may be due to unawareness and illiteracy among the SC/ST's castes.

Table 6.5: Profile of Respondents and their Awareness Towards Solving the Problem at Thana Diwas or Tehsil Diwas

Sex	*Awareness*					
	Yes		*No*		*Total*	
	No.	***Per cent age***	***No***	***Per cent age***	***No.***	***Per cent***
Male	92	57.5	68	42.5	160	100.0
Female	69	43.1	91	56.9	160	100.0
Total	**161**	**50.3**	**159**	**49.7**	**320**	**100.0**
χ^2 = 6.61; df=1; P<0.01						
Caste						
SC/ST	42	29.0	103	71.0	145	100.0
OBC	70	61.9	43	38.1	113	100.0
General	49	79.0	13	21.0	62	100.0
χ^2 = 53.01; df=2; P<0.001						
Educational						
illiterate	59	39.1	92	60.9	151	100.0
upto high school	80	57.6	59	42.4	139	100.0
Inter+	22	73.3	08	26.7	30	100.0
χ^2 = 16.91; df=2; P<0.001						
Economic Status (in rs.)						
Upto 1500	51	36.4	89	63.6	140	100.0
1500-3000	63	52.9	56	47.1	119	100.0
3000+	47	77.0	14	23.0	61	100.0
Total	**161**	**50.3**	**159**	**49.7**	**320**	**100.0**
χ^2 = 28.57; df=2; P<0.001						

It is evident from the above table that majority 50.3 per cent of respondents reported that there problems been solved and credited at thana or tehsil diwas while remaining 49.7 per cent denied about such type of facts. The respondents who have positive response regarding solution of problem at thana diwas or tehsil diwas, the male respondents (57.5 per cent) were more in comparison to the female respondents (43.1 per cent). Caste wise distribution shows that out of total respondents who were accepted for getting solution of problems maximum 79.0 per cent were from general castes followed by 61.9 per cent were from OBC's castes while only 29.0 per cent from SC/ST's caste groups respectively. In this matter the highly educated respondents were found to bc more followed by the respondents educated at primary to high school level and illiterate respectively. It is also observed that the proportion with increase in the economic status of the respondents the proportion of opinion regarding the solution of problems also in a increasing trend.

The statistical test signifies the fact that the difference in proportion of respondents regarding the solution of problem at Tehsil or Thana Diwas between male and female and among various castes, education, and economic status is obtained to be highly significant.

The respondents who denied the facts that their problems not solved on Thana or Tehsil Diwas mostly belongs to female, SC/ST's, illiterate and individual of low socio-economic status.

Table 6.6: Profile of Respondensts and their Awareness Towards Solving Various Problems in A Better Way

Solving problems in better way	*Caste wise distribution of Respondent*							
	SC/ST		*OBC*		*General*		*Total*	
	No.	*Per cent*	*No.*	*Per cent*	*No.*	*Per cent*	*No.*	*Per cent*
1. Village member	57	39.3	47	41.6	33	53.2	137	42.8
2. Officer (Adm.)	51	35.2	56	49.6	22	35.5	129	40.3
3 Naxalite	-	-	-	-	-	-	-	-
4. NGO	17	11.7	4	3.5	3	4.8	24	7.5
5. 1+2	20	13.8	6	5.3	4	6.5	30	9.4
Total	**145**	**100.0**	**113**	**100.0**	**62**	**100.0**	**320**	**100.0**

$\chi^2 = 17.71$; df=6 ; $P<0.01$

From the above analysis, it is cleared that 42.8 per cent of respondents were accepted that the village representatives solve their problem in a better way. Out of which minimum 39.3 per cent were from SC/ST's caste maximum 53.2 per cent were from general castes, rest 40.3 per cent, 9.4 per cent and 7.5 per cent of respondents reported to the Bureaucrats, both bureaucrats and Gram Pradhan and people of NGO's respectively. Surprisingly, it is noted that no respondents in the selected area were in favour of naxals organisation to solve their problems in better ways. The difference in the proportion of respondent's perception regarding solution of various problems in better way is found to be statistically significant.

It shows that village representative as well as village Pradhan or administrative offices are the major of solving people's problems in the study area.

Table 6.7: Profile of Respondents and their Awareness towards Disputes Solving in Rural Areas

Solving various disputes	*Caste wise distribution of Respondent*							
	SC/ST		*OBC*		*General*		*Total*	
	No.	*Per cent*	*No.*	*Per cent*	*No.*	*Per cent*	*No.*	*Per cent*
1. Govt.off	44	30.3	52	46.0	35	56.5	131	40.9
2. NGO	0	0.0	9	8.0	2	3.2	11	3.4
3. Naxalite	0	0	0	0	0	0	0	0
4. Gram-pradhan	71	49.0	48	42.5	20	32.3	139	43.4
5. 1+4	30	20.7	4	3.5	5	8.1	39	12.2
Total	**145**	**100.0**	**113**	**100.0**	**62**	**100.0**	**320**	**100.0**

The above table reveals that majority 43.4 per cent and 40.9 per cent of respondents opined that the village representative and administrative officers solved rural problems and disputes in better way. Out of which general castes individual given most preference to government officers, while SC/STs people to village representatives in solving the general disputes. Only 3.4 per cent and 12.2 per cent of respondents accepted for that purpose to NGO and government officers along with village representatives respectively.

We may conclude from the result that majority of respondents were of the opinion that village representative and government officers solve their problems as well as rural disputes in the study area.

Table 6.8: Profile of Respondents and their Awareness Towards Solution of Problems

CASTE	*Yes*		*No*		*Total*	
	No.	*Per cent age*	*No*	*Per cent age*	*No.*	*Per cent*
SC/ST	82	56.6	63	43.4	145	100.0
OBC	46	40.7	67	59.3	113	100.0
GEN	7	11.3	55	88.7	62	100.0
$\chi^2 = 36.64$; df=2; $P < 0.001$						
SEX						
Male	57	35.6	103	64.4	160	100.0
Female	78	48.8	82	51.2	160	100.0
$\chi^2 = 5.65$; df=1; $P < 0.05$						
EDUCATION						
Illiterate+	88	58.3	63	41.7	151	100.0
up to high school	39	28.1	100	71.9	139	100.0
Inter+	8	26.7	22	73.3	30	100.0
$X^2 = 30.37$; df=2; $P < 0.001$						
Family monthly income (Rs.)						
Upto	80	57.1	60	42.9	140	100.0
1500-3000	39	32.8	80	67.2	119	100.0
3000+	16	26.2	45	73.8	61	100.0
Total	135	42.2	185	57.8	320	100.0
$\chi^2 = 23.53$; df=2 ; $P < 0.001$						

It is perceptible from the above table that 42.2 per cent of respondents opined that the naxalites struggle for the poor, Dalits and marginalised section of society. Out of which the proportion of SC/STs caste groups were 56.6 per cent, OBC's 40.7 per cent and general castes 11.3 per cent respectively. It is also observed that the female respondents (48.8 per cent) were given positive response, in comparison to male respondents (35.6 per cent). Educational status wise distribution shows that maximum (58.3 per cent) of respondents who were illiterate opinion that the naxalites helps the marginalised section of society. Majority 57.1 per cent of respondents were of the opinion that naxalite always helped to poor, Dalit and marginalised section of society.

Whereas in other two family income groups Rs (1500-3000) and more than Rs 3000 it was 32.8 per cent and 26.2 per cent respectively. Statistical chi square (χ^2) test signifies the fact that there is a significant difference among in the opinion of various castes, education, incomes as well as between male and female respondents respectively.

It may be concluded that the respondents in the study area who belongs to SC/STs, OBCs and females, had lower educational and economic status were in opinion of maximum proportion for helping naxalite struggling for poorer, Dalit as well as marginalised section of society by naxalites.

Table 6.9a: Profile of Respondents and their Awareness Towards Development in Last Two Decades

Development	*Frequency*	*Per cent*
Yes	294	91.9
No	26	8.1
Total	**320**	**100.0**

The opinion of the respondents is also assists about the development during the last decade in their area and presented in the above table. It depicts that majority 91.9 per cent of respondents opined for any type of development, while 8.1 per cent had the negative response.

The respondents who were aware towards any type of development further analyzed according to the different agencies or organisation with their caste education and gender respectively and recorded in table 6.9(B). It reveals that 71.4 per cent of respondent were given credit to government machinery out of which maximum were SC/ST's caste category group followed by general and OBC's caste group and this difference is found to be statistically significant. The respondents who given credit to political leadership and NGO's were in 40.8 per cent and 20.4 per cent respectively in these sources, a increasing trend is observed with status of caste increased, but this increasing trend is not significant. It is also observed that only 1.7 per cent of respondents given credit for development in study

Table 6.9b: Profile of Respondents and their Awareness Towards Credit for the Development in the Rural Area

Credit for development	*Caste*								*df = 2*
	SC/ST (139)		*OBC (103)*		*GEN (59)*		*Total (294)*		■ : *P*
	No	*Per cent*	*No*	*Per cent*	*No*	*Per cent*	*No*	*Per cent*	
1. Govt. Machinery	104	78.8	67	65.0	39	66.1	210	71.4	6.38;<0.05
2. Pol. leadership	48	36.4	44	42.7	28	47.5	120	40.8	2.32;>0.05
3. NGO's	24	18.2	22	21.4	14	23.7	60	20.4	0.86;>0.05
4. Naxal. org.	2	1.5	0	0.0	3	5.1	5	1.7	-
	Education								*df = 2*
Credit	*Illiterate (139)*		*up to high school (126)*		*Inter+ (29)*		*Total (249)*		■ : *P*
	No	*Per cent*	*No*	*Per cent*	*No*	*Per cent*	*No*	*Per cent*	
1. Govt. Machinery	98	70.5	96	76.2	16	55.2	210	71.4	5.21;>0.05
2. Pol. leadership	44	31.7	61	48.4	15	51.7	120	40.8	9.27;<0.001
3. NGO's	28	20.1	23	18.3	9	31.0	60	20.4	2.38;>0.05
4. Naxal. org.	1	0.7	3	2.4	1	3.4	5	1.7	1.68>0.05

area to naxal organisation in which maximum belongs to general caste category.

Sex Wise Distribution of Respondent's Regarding Credit of Development

Credit of development	*Male (46)*		*Female (148)*		*Total (294)*		*df = 1* χ^2 *= P*
	No.	*Per cent*	*No.*	*Per cent*	*No.*	*Per cent*	
1. Govt. Machinery	116	79.5	94	63.5	210	71.4	9.15;<0.01
2. Pol. leadership	64	43.8	56	37.8	120	40.8	1.09;>0.05
3. NGO's	16	11.0	44	29.7	60	20.4	15.94;<0.001
4. Naxal. org.	5	3.4	0	0.0	5	1.7	-

Literacy status wise distribution of respondents opinion regarding development shows that the respondents who accepted the credit of better political leadership activities of NGO's and naxal organisation maximum were qualified either at intermediate level or more than this level and minimum were from illiterate group of people but a just reverse pattern is observed in case of government machinery that is more from primary to high school qualified respondents followed by illiterate and at intermediate and above level respectively. Statistically, the difference in proportion among various educational groups of respondents for different type of organisation concern for development is not significant except better political leadership either at village level or district level respectively.

Sex wise distribution shows that the respondents who recognised that different machinery or organisation for the development during last decade, the proportions of male respondents were found to be significantly more in comparison to female respondents with the exception of the NGO's.

In the present study, the majority of respondents was providing the credit for development in the study area to the government machinery and better political leadership either at village or district level.

Table 6.10: Profile of Respondents and their Awareness Towards the Various Required Facility Provided by the Naxalites

Facilities Provided	*Frequency*	*Per cent*
1. Yes	146	45.6
2. No	174	54.4
3. Total	320	100.0

It is apparent from the above table that 45.6 per cent of respondents were of the views that the naxal organisation provided various type of facilities for the people while remaining 54.4 per cent of respondents denied about any type of facilities provided by the naxal organisation.

A further analysis has been made regarding different types of facilities provided by the naxalite or naxal organisation according to the educational status of respondents which is presented in table 6.11. It describes that majority 56.8 per cent and 54.1 per cent of respondents were of the opinion that naxal organisation helps them financially at the time of marriage and providing safety from higher castes people. Out of which maximum were from educationally qualified primary to high school followed by illiterate respondents while minimum where from those respondents who were qualified above intermediate level. Statistically, this variation is found to be significant. 39.7 per cent and 6.2 of respondents views that the naxal organisation distributed ration facility time to time and established the primary level of schooling system respectively. Out of which maximum qualified respondents were significantly more in comparison to other qualified or illiterate subjects.

The respondents who had given their opinion regarding various required facilities provide by naxal organisation further analysis according to their gender and presented in above table. It reveals that the respondents who were given their opinion about the establishment of primary school and health centers by naxalites 100 per cent were females. Whereas the respondent recognised the ration distribution, helping at marriage and safety from exploitation of higher castes maximum proportion were from male in comparison to females respondents. Statistically, it is seeing that the difference in proportion

Table-6.11: Profile of Respondent's Opinion Regarding the Various Facility Provided by the Naxalites

	Facilities Provided	*Ill. (79)*		*upto high school (61)*		*Inter + (6)*		*Total (146)*		*df = 2* ■ *: P*
		No	*Per cent*	*No*	*Per cent*	*No*	*Per cent*	*No*	*Per cent*	
1.	School	7	8.9	1	1.6	1	16.7	9	6.2	4.30;>0.05
2.	Ration distribution	25	31.6	28	45.9	5	83.3	58	39.7	7.89;<0.05
3.	Primary health	5	6.3	1	1.0	0	0.0	6	4.1	2.18;>0.05
4.	Marriage	34	43.0	44	72.1	1	16.7	79	54.1	15.26;<0.001
5.	Safety from higher caste	40	50.6	42	68.9	1	16.7	83	56.8	8.77;<0.05

is significant only in case of ration distribution and help in marriage ceremony respectively.

Table 6.12: Profile of Respondent's Opinion Regarding the Various Facility Provided by the Naxalites

Various Facilities Provided	*Male(46)*		*Female(100)*		*Total(146)*		*df = 1* $\chi^2 = P$ *continuity correction and fisher's exact test.*
	No.	*Per cent*	*No.*	*Per cent*	*No.*	*Per cent*	
1. School	0	0.0	9	9.0	9	6.2	2.99;>0.05
2. Ration distribution	34	73.9	24	24.0	58	39.7	32.78;<0.001
3. Primary health	0	0.0	6	6.0	6	4.1	1.56;>0.05
4. Marriage	36	78.3	43	43.0	79	54.1	15.78;<0.001
5. Safety from higher caste	25	54.3	58	58.0	83	56.8	0.17;>0.05

We may concluded that the people of the study area were in needs of equal food grain distribution at right time, financial and moral support in marriage ceremony, as well as the safety from the exploitation of various caste categories.

Table 6.13: Profile of Respondents and their Awareness Towards Problem Solving by the Political Representatives After General Election

Respondent view about solution	*Sex wise*					
	Male		*Female*		*Total*	
	No.	*per cent*	*No.*	*per cent*	*No.*	*per cent*
1. Yes	21	13.1	37	23.1	58	18.1
2. No	126	78.8	98	61.2	224	70.0
3. Can not say	13	8.1	25	15.6	38	11.9
Total	**160**	**100.0**	**160**	**100.0**	**320**	**100.0**

$\chi^2 = 11.70$; df = 2; $P<0.01$

The above table reveals that about three-fourth (70.0 per cent) of respondents reported not to take any interest regarding solution of their problem by the various political leaders after elections. While remaining 18.1 per cent and 11.9 per cent of the respondent had the positive response and neutral attitudes regarding such type of matter.

The difference in proportion of respondents view about taking interest to solve their problems after election is obtained to be statistically significant.

Table 6.14: Profile of Respondents and their Awareness Towards the Solution of Problem (Naxalism) By the Political Leaders and Political Parties

Respondent view on Naxal problems	*Sex wise*					
	Male		*Female*		*Total*	
	No.	*per cent*	*No.*	*per cent*	*No.*	*per cent*
1. Yes	47	29.4	31	19.4	78	24.4
2. No	69	43.1	85	53.1	154	48.1
3. Can not say	44	27.5	44	27.5	88	27.5
Total	**160**	**100.0**	**160**	**100.0**	**320**	**100.0**

$\chi^2 = 4.95$; df = 2 ; $P>0.05$

Sex wise distribution of respondents awareness towards taking interest by the political parties or political leaders for elimination of naxalism is presented in the above table, which reveals that about half (48.1 per cent) of respondents were of the views of not taking any interest to solve naxalism, 24.4 per cent opinion for taking interest while 27.5 per cent of respondents did not comment about any view. It is also observed that the female respondents (53.1 per cent) had given negative response in more proportion than male respondents (43.1 per cent) but statistically, the difference is not significant.

The results shows that majority of the people in the study area were not happy with the activities of political parties and political leaders about the elimination of naxal problem.

Table 6.15: Distribution of Respondents Knowledge about Intellectual Sympathy Towards Naxal Movement

Support from others	*Frequency*	*Percentage*
1. Yes	79	24.7
2. No.	96	30.0
3. Can not say	145	45.3
Total	**320**	**100.0**

$\chi^2 = 10.19$; df = 2; $P<0.01$

The present table reveals that out of total respondents about one-fourth (24.7 per cent) of respondents accepted the fact that there are some sympathy of intellectual regarding naxal organisation and movement due to which the elimination of naxalism is not possible while remaining 30.0 per cent and 45.3 per cent of the respondents either they refused for such type of intellectual sympathy or confused regarding the matter.

Table-6.16: Profile of Respondents and their Awareness Towards Naxalites Helped by Others Countries and Separatist Organisation

Support from others	*Frequency*	*Percentage*
1. Yes	46	14.4
2. No.	111	34.7
3. Can not say	163	50.9
Total	**320**	**100.0**

The above table reflects that only 14.4 per cent of respondents were of the opinion that the separatist organisation of the country and as well as of other countries help the naxal organisation whereas about half 50.9 per cent did not have any comment and remaining 34.7 per cent of respondents did not accept such type of help either from our country separatist organisation or other country respectively.

Table 617: Profile of Respondents and their Awareness Towards Elimination of Naxalism by Government Development Measures and Role of Criminals in Naxal Movement

Variable	*Yes*		*No*		*Total*	
	No.	*per cent*	*No.*	*per cent*	*No.*	*per cent*
1. Modernisation of police force to fight naxalite	178	55.6	142	44.4	320	100.0
2. Can government development and force police solve naxal problem	183	57.2	137	42.8	320	100.0
3. Misutilisation of naxalism by political leaders and pol. parties involvement of criminal in name of naxalism	217	67.8	103	32.2	320	100.0

It may be concluded from the above results that majority of respondents did not answer correctly regarding the help to the naxal organisation by separatist organisation and other countries may be because of unawareness about separatist organisation, low literacy rate socio-economic status and fear of police and naxalite both.

It is evident from the above table that more than half of the respondents (55.6) were reported that the modernisation of police force is done for fighting and elimination of naxalism. While remaining (44.4 per cent) did not agree with the facts, it is also seen that 57.2 per cent of respondents reported that the elimination of naxalite problem may be due to development programmes and police force policy both whereas 67.8 per cent of respondents were of the views that the political parties as well as political leaders are using criminals on the name of naxalism. The respondents who were not agree with these two types of facts were observed to be 42.8 per cent and 32.2 per cent respectively.

It may be concluded that majority of the respondents accepted to the modernisation of police force to fight against naxalite and utilisation of criminals on the name of naxalism as well as elimination of naxalite problem by implementing the various development programmes and policy respectively.

Table 6.18: Profile of Respondents and their Awareness Towards Political Leaders Involvement in the Naxalite Movemetn

Caste wise	*Caste Wise*							
	SC/ST		*OBC*		*GEN*		*Total*	
	No.	*Per cent*	*No.*	*Per cent*	*No.*	*Per cent*	*No.*	*Per cent*
1. Yes	136	93.8	55	48.7	21	33.9	212	66.2
2. No	0	0.0	27	23.9	11	17.7	38	11.9
3. Cannot say	9	6.2	31	27.4	30	48.4	70	21.9
Total	**145**	**100.0**	**113**	**100.0**	**62**	**100.0**	**320**	**100.0**

$\chi^2 = 102.20$; df = 4; $P < 0.001$

Education wise	*Education Wise*							
	Illiterate		*upto high school*		*Inter+*		*Total*	
	No.	*Per cent*	*No.*	*Per cent*	*No.*	*Per cent*	*No.*	*Per cent*
1. Yes	105	69.5	95	68.3	12	40.0	212	66.2
2. No	15	9.9	13	9.4	10	33.3	38	11.9
3. Cannot say	31	20.5	31	22.3	8	26.7	70	21.9
Total	**151**	**100.0**	**139**	**100.0**	**30**	**100.0**	**320**	**100.0**

$\chi^2 = 16.77$; df = 4; $P < 0.01$

It is reveals from the above table that more than two-third (66.2 per cent)of respondents were of the views that the political leaders are not interested for the elimination of naxalism for their own benefits out of which 93.8 per cent were from SC/STs followed by 48.7 per cent and 3.9 per cent from OBC's and general caste category respectively. About one fourth (21.9 per cent) of respondents has no idea about such types of comments in which general castes (48.4 per cent) were more than OBC's (27.4 per cent) and SC/ST's (6.2 per cent) respectively. The difference in the proportion among various caste categories regarding the self benefits, leaders not interested to eliminates the naxalites is statistically, highly significant education wise distribution shows that with increasing of educational status of the study subjects, the proportion of opinion about the elimination of naxalism for self interest or self benefits are in decreasing patterns and this decrease is found to be statistically highly significant.

The result clearly shows that the respondents belong to SC/ST's and illiterate were against the activities of the village level or district level leaders respectively.

Table 6.19: Sex Wise Distribution of Respondent's Knowledge about Attack by Naxalites on Police and Administrative Machinary

Respondent view on nax. attack on police		*Sex Wise*					
		Male		*Female*		*Total*	
		No	*Per cent*	*No*	*Per cent*	*No*	*Per cent*
1.	Police Exploitative nature	116	72.5	66	41.2	182	56.9
2.	Police provide Safety to people	19	11.9	15	9.4	34	10.6
3.	To shows dominance on Administration.	17	10.6	21	13.1	38	11.9
4.	Don't know	8	5.0	58	36.3	66	20.6
Total		**160**	**100.0**	**160**	**100.0**	**320**	**100.0**

$\chi^2 = 43.55$; df = 3; $P < 0.001$

It is apparent from the above table that out of total study subjects, 20.6 per cent of respondents did not give any reasons regarding attack by naxalites on police administration and government machinery while maximum 56.9 per cent of subjects opinion that the police exploitative policies responsible for attack by the naxalites. It is also observed that the police force provides safety to the rural people and to show the dominance on administration were the main reasons which reported by 10.6 per cent and 11.9 per cent of respondents respectively, the proportion of male respondent were found to be more in comparison to female respondents for considering all types of reasons except about showing domination to administration and any type of reasons but statistically difference is highly significant.

Table 6.20: Sex and Caste Wise Distribution of Respondent's Opinion Regarding Collecting of Levy, Extortation Money by Criminal on the Name of Naxalite

	Sex	*Levy/Extortion Money*							
		Yes		*No*		*Can not say*		*Total*	
		No	*Per cent*	*No*	*Per cent*	*No*	*Per cent*	*No*	*Per cent*
1.	Male	15	09.4	134	83.8	11	06.9	160	100.0
2.	Female	74	46.2	70	43.8	16	10.0	160	100.0
	Total	**89**	**27.8**	**204**	**63.8**	**27**	**08.4**	**320**	**100.00**

$\chi^2 = 60.12$; df = 2; $P < 0.001$

	Caste	*Levy/Extortion Money*							
		Yes		*No*		*Can not say*		*Total*	
		No	*Per cent*	*No*	*Per cent*	*No*	*Per cent*	*No*	*Per cent*
1.	SC/ST	57	39.3	82	56.6	06	04.1	145	100.0
2.	OBC	23	20.4	81	71.7	09	08.0	113	100.0
3.	Gen.	09	14.5	41	66.1	12	19.4	62	100.0
	Total	**89**	**27.8**	**204**	**63.8**	**27**	**08.4**	**320**	**100.0**

$\chi^2 = 27.41$; df=3; $P < 0.001$

The above table reveals that more than one fourth of respondents (27.8 per cent) were accepted for collecting levy and extortion money by criminals on the name of naxalites out of which the proportion of females were found to be more (46.2 per cent) than male respondents (09.4 per cent). The remaining respondents (66.8 per cent and 8.4 per cent) were not agree with such type of levy extortion money and did not provide any opinion regarding the matter respectively. The difference view proportion between male and female respondent's views regarding levy or extortion money is obtained to be statistically highly significant.

The finding reveals that (46.2 per cent) female and (39.3 per cent) SC/ST's respondents were accepted the fact of collecting levy and extorting money by the criminals of that area in the name of naxalites.

ECONOMICAL

Table 6.21 :Profile of Respondents and their Awareness Towards Various Government Programmes

Sex wise	*Awareness*					
	Yes		*No*		*Total*	
	No	*Per cent*	*No*	*Per cent*	*No*	*Per cent*
Male	118	73.8	42	26.2	160	100.0
Female	95	59.4	65	40.6	160	100.0
$\chi^2 = 7.43$; df =1; P < 0.01						
Caste wise	*Yes*		*No*		*Total*	
	No	*Per cent*	*No*	*Per cent*	*No*	*Per cent*
SC/ST	86	59.3	59	40.7	145	100.0
OBC	77	68.1	36	31.9	113	100.0
GEN.	50	80.6	12	19.4	62	100.0
$\chi^2 = 9.08$; df =2; P < 0.05						
Educational Status	*Yes*		*No*		*Total*	
	No	*Per cent*	*No*	*Per cent*	*No*	*Per cent*
Illiterate	91	60.3	60	39.7	151	100.0
Upto High School	99	71.2	40	28.8	139	100.0
Inter+	23	76.7	07	29.3	30	100.0
Total	213	66.6	107	33.4	320	100.0
$\chi^2 = 5.42$; df =2 ; P < 0.05						

The above table describes that more than two third (66.6 per cent) of respondents were aware towards various types of employment and development programmes of government whereas remaining 33.4 per cent were unaware of governmental measures. Among the aware respondents, the proportion of male (73.8 per cent) was more than female (59.4 per cent), the respondents of general caste were more (80.6 per cent) aware followed by OBC's (68.1 per cent) and SC/ST's (59.3 per cent) respectively.

Education wise distribution shows that awareness was more among the Inter plus (76.7 per cent) followed by upto high School (71.2 per cent) and illiterate (60.3 per cent) respectively.

The difference in terms of gender and caste was found to be statistically significant whereas the difference among various educational status was statistically not significant.

Table 6.22: Profile of Respondents and their Awareness Towards the Implementation of Government Programme Mnrega

MNREGA	*Sex Wise*					
	Male		*Female*		*Total*	
	No.	*per cent*	*No.*	*per cent*	*No.*	*per cent*
Yes	159	99.4	157	98.1	316	98.8
No	01	00.6	03	01.9	04	01.2
Total	**160**	**100.0**	**160**	**100.0**	**320**	**100.0**

$\chi^2 = 1.01$; df =1 ; P >0.05

The above table depicts that majority (98.8 per cent) of respondents were known about the government programme 'MNREGA' in which proportion of male (99.4 per cent) were slightly more than the female respondents (98.1 per cent). Statistical chi-square (X2) test proves the fact of no significant difference.

($\chi^2 = 1.01$; df =1; P >0.05)

Table 6.23: Profile of Respondents and their Awareness Towards Job Card Mnrega

Sex Wise	*Awareness about Job Card MNREGA*					
	Yes		*No*		*Total*	
	No.	*per cent*	*No.*	*per cent*	*No.*	*per cent*
Male	60	37.5	100	62.5	160	100.0
Female	117	73.1	43	26.9	160	100.0
$\chi^2 = 41.07$; df =1; P <0.001						
Caste Wise	*Yes*		*No*		*Total*	
	No.	*per cent*	*No.*	*per cent*	*No.*	*per cent*
SC/ST	74	51.0	71	49.0	145	100.0
OBC	75	66.4	38	33.6	113	100.0
GEN.	28	45.2	34	54.8	62	100.0
$\chi^2 = 9.25$; df =2; P <0.05						
Education Wise	*Yes*		*No*		*Total*	
	No.	*per cent*	*No.*	*per cent*	*No.*	*per cent*
Illiterate	109	72.2	42	27.8	151	100.0
Upto High School	64	64.0	75	54.0	139	100.0
Inter+	04	13.3	26	86.7	30	100.0
Total	**177**	**55.3**	**143**	**44.7**	**320**	**100.0**
$\chi^2 = 43.61$; df =2 ; P <0.001						

It is evident from the above table that more than half of the respondents (55.3 per cent) have the Job card prepared by respective gram panchyat out of which majority 73.1 per cent were female respondents and only 37.5 per cent were male. Caste wise distribution shows that 66.4 per cent of respondents belong to OBC's were accepted for the availability of Job card followed by SC/ST's (51.0 per cent) and general castes (45.2 per cent) respectively. It was also observed that with incre3asing in the educational status of respondents. A decreasing trend in proportion of respondents is registered in connection to the presence of Job card. The difference in proportion regarding the presence of Job card among the respondents of various educational and caste status as well as between male and female respondents are found to be statistically highly significant.

We may conclude from the results that OBC as well as SC/ST's caste group of individual and illiterate with low-socio-economic status were benefited in maximum proportion in the study area.

Table 6.24: Profile of Respondents and their Awareness towards Employment in Mnrega

Sex Wise	*Awareness*					
	Yes		*No*		*Total*	
	No.	*per cent*	*No.*	*per cent*	*No.*	*per cent*
Male	109	68.1	51	31.9	160	100.0
Female	124	77.5	36	22.5	160	100.0
$\chi^2 = 3.55$; df =1; P >0.05						
Caste Wise	*Yes*		*No*		*Total*	
	No.	*per cent*	*No.*	*per cent*	*No.*	*per cent*
SC/ST	125	86.2	20	13.8	145	100.0
OBC	86	76.1	27	23.9	113	100.0
GEN.	22	35.5	40	64.5	62	100.0
$\chi^2 = 57.40$; df =2; P <0.001						
Education Wise	*Yes*		*No*		*Total*	
	No.	*per cent*	*No.*	*per cent*	*No.*	*per cent*
Illiterate	123	81.5	28	18.5	151	100
Upto High School	101	72.7	38	27.3	139	100.0
Inter+	09	30.0	21	70.0	30	100.0
Total	**233**	**72.8**	**87**	**27.2**	**320**	**100.0**

$\chi^2 = 33.48$; df =2 ; P <0.001

It is apparent from the above table that out of total respondents surveyed about three-fourth 72.8 per cent of respondents were accepted for getting the employment through MNREGA in their respective villages out of which the proportion of females respondents (77.5 per cent) were found to be more in comparison of male respondents (68.1 per cent). Caste and educational status wise distribution reveals that with increased in caste and educational status of the respondents, a decreasing trend in the proportion of respondents about getting the employment facilities through MNREGA was registered. The statistical chi-square (X2) test proves the facts that there are significant difference in the proportion of getting employment through MNREGA in their respective villages among various caste and educational status groups respectively.

Table 6.25: Profile of Respondents and their Awareness Towards No. of Days Employed In Mnrega

Sex Wise	*No. of Days Employed in MNREGA*					
	(100 days)		*(Less than 100)*		*Total*	
	No.	*per cent*	*No.*	*per cent*	*No.*	*per cent*
Male	19	17.4	90	82.6	109	100.0
Female	54	43.5	70	56.5	124	100.0
Total	73	31.3	160	68.7	233	100.0
χ^2= 18.39; df =1 ; P <0.001						
Caste Wise	*Yes*		*No*		*Total*	
	No.	*per cent*	*No.*	*per cent*	*No.*	*per cent*
SC/ST	43	34.4	82	65.6	125	100.0
OBC	20	23.3	66	76.7	86	100.0
GEN.	10	45.5	12	54.5	22	100.0
Total	73	31.3	160	68.7	233	100.0
χ^2= 5.19; df =2 ; P >0.05						
Education Wise	*Yes*		*No*		*Total*	
	No.	*per cent*	*No.*	*per cent*	*No.*	*per cent*
Illiterate	32	26.0	91	74.0	123	100.0
Up to High School	34	33.7	67	66.3	101	100.0
Inter+	07	77.8	02	22.9	09	100.0
Total	**73**	**31.3**	**160**	**68.7**	**233**	**100.0**

χ^2= 10.89 ; df =2 ; P <0.01

The results clearly indicates that majority of the respondents belongs to lower socio-economic status and lower caste and lower status groups are getting employment and working as a laborer group in MNREGA programmes in their respective villages.

It is analyze from the above table that the respondents who were accepted for getting employment through MNREGA, it is very important to get information about the number of days employed in this programmes. According to this 100 days employment must be provided to them by MNREGA in their respective villages, the result clearly shows that the respondents who got the employment through MNREGA, maximum 68.7 per cent were reported to get job less than 100 days in which male proportion (82.6 per cent) was significantly higher than the female proportion (56.5 per cent). Caste wise distribution reflects that majority 76.7 per cent of OBC's respondents reported to get employment less than 100 days followed by respondents of SC/ST's (65.6 per cent) and general caste groups (54.5 per cent) respectively. But the difference is statistically not significant. It is also seen that there is an increasing trend in the proportion of respondents for getting 100 days employment is registered with increasing in educational status and this variation found to be statistically highly significant.

We may conclude that qualified respondents, belongs to general caste category and females workers were mostly benefited by getting 100 days employment in MNREGA programme in the study area.

Table 6.26: Profile of Respondents and their Awareness towards 100 Rupees Wages Per Day

Sex Wise	*Awareness*					
	Yes		*No*		*Total*	
	No.	*per cent*	*No.*	*per cent*	*No.*	*per cent*
Male	44	40.4	65	59.6	109	100.0
Female	70	56.5	54	43.5	124	100.0
χ^2 = 6.01; df =1; P <0.05						
Caste Wise	*Yes*		*No*		*Total*	
	No.	*per cent*	*No.*	*per cent*	*No.*	*per cent*
SC/ST	56	44.8	69	55.2	125	100.0
OBC	54	62.8	32	37.2	86	100.0
GEN.	4	18.2	18	81.8	22	100.0
χ^2 = 15.79; df =2; P <0.001						

(Contd...)

Education Wise	*Yes*		*No*		*Total*	
	No.	*per cent*	*No.*	*per cent*	*No.*	*per cent*
Illiterate	72	58.5	51	41.5	123	100.0
upto high school	42	41.6	59	58.4	101	100.0
Inter+	00	00.0	09	100.0	09	100.0
Total	**114**	**48.9**	**119**	**51.1**	**233**	**100.0**

$\chi^2 = 15.34$; df =2 ; P <0.001

The above table describes the awareness towards government programme MNREGA whether 100 days employment with 100 Rs. per day wages must be provided to the rural individuals or not. In the present table it is visualised to assess the opinion of respondents regarding getting facilities of right wages, it is found that about half (48.9 per cent) of respondents accepted to get 100 Rs per day wages in which females respondents (56.5 per cent)s were significantly more than male respondents (40.4 per cent) majority 62.8 per cent of respondents belongs to OBC's were in favour of getting 100 Rs. per day wages while such opinion was given by only 44.8 per cent and 18.2 per cent respondents of SC/ST's and general castes groups respectively and this difference is observed to be highly significant. Educational status wise analysis shows that only 58.5 per cent of illiterate respondents, 42.6 per cent of respondent qualified upto high school and no any respondents qualified upto intermediate and above were accepted to get 100 Rs/days wages through MNREGA job works. The difference is found to be highly significant.

It may be concluded that illiterate respondents as well as maximum OBC's and SC/ST's respondents were in favour of getting 100 Rs per day wages through MNREGA.

Table 6.27: Profile of Respondents and their Awareness Towards not Getting Full Wages in Mnrega

Sex Wise	*Sex Wise*					
	Male		*Female*		*Total*	
	No.	*per cent*	*No.*	*per cent*	*No.*	*per cent*
Grampradhan	52	80.0	11	20.4	63	52.9
B.D.O.	-	-	-	-	-	-
Both (1+2)	11	16.9	42	77.8	53	44.5
Can not say	02	03.1	01	1.9	3	2.5
Total	**65**	**100.0**	**54**	**100.0**	**119**	**100.0**

χ^2 44.51 ; df =2 ; P <0.001

In the above table the question was asked to the respondents' awareness towards not getting full wages in MNREGA. The collected information is analysed and recorded in table 6.27. It reveals that out of total respondents who had not received full wages of their work, majority 52.9 per cent were blamed to gram pradhan out of which the proportion of male respondents (80.0 per cent) were higher in comparison to the females respondents (20.4 per cent). Only 2.5 per cent of respondents did not reported any opinion regarding this matter and remaining 44.5 per cent of respondents opined that grampradhan, village representative along with B.D.O.s or the responsible representative/officers for not providing full wages for their MNREGA work in which proportion of females (77.8 per cent) were more than the proportion of male respondents (16.9 per cent). The difference in opinion about not receiving the full wages per day in MNREGA work between males and females is highly significant.

Table 6.28: Profile of Respondents and their Satisfaction Towards Family Monthly Income

Sex Wise	*Respondent's Satisfaction about Income*					
	Yes		*No*		*Total*	
	No.	*per cent*	*No.*	*per cent*	*No.*	*per cent*
Male	37	23.1	123	76.9	160	100.0
Female	31	19.4	129	80.6	160	100.0
$\chi^2 = 0.67$; df=1; P >0.05						
Caste Wise	*Yes*		*No*		*Total*	
	No.	*per cent*	*No.*	*per cent*	*No.*	*per cent*
SC/ST	14	09.7	131	90.3	145	100.0
OBC	30	26.5	83	73.5	113	100.0
GEN.	24	38.7	38	61.3	62	100.0
$\chi^2 = 24.84$; df=2; P <0.001						
Education Wise	*Yes*		*No*		*Total*	
	No.	*per cent*	*No.*	*per cent*	*No.*	*per cent*
illiterate	22	14.6	129	85.4	151	100.0
upto high school	32	23.0	107	77.0	139	100.0
Inter +	14	46.7	16	53.3	30	100.0
$\chi^2 = 15.86$; df=2; P <0.001						

(Contd...)

Monthly Family Income(Rs)	*Yes*		*No*		*Total*	
	No.	*per cent*	*No.*	*per cent*	*No.*	*per cent*
Upto 1500	13	09.3	127	90.7	140	100.0
1500-3000	30	25.2	89	74.8	119	100.0
3000+	25	41.0	36	59.0	61	100.0
Total	**68**	**21.2**	**252**	**78.8**	**320**	**100.0**

$\chi^2 = 27.29$; df=2; $P < 0.001$

The above table describes that out of the total surveyed respondents, only 21.2 per cent of respondents were satisfied with their monthly Income for their livelihood in which proportion of male respondents (23.1 per cent) were found to be more but insignificant, in comparison to the female respondents (19.4 per cent). It is also observed that with increase in caste, educational as well as their monthly family income, the proportion of satisfaction level is also registered in increasing order. The difference in proportion among various caste, education status and monthly family income group regarding opinion of satisfaction with their family income is found to be statistically highly significant.

It may be concluded that the role of caste, education and their present monthly income had the important role in livelihood and assessing the living standard and assess the capacity to purchase the goods for their livelihood in the present area, the literacy status & socio-economic status is very low and caste conflict is perhaps more which may be more obstacles for development and implementing different programmes assumed by government in right way and context.

Table 6.29: Profile of Respondents and their Awareness Towards Availability of Job Card

Sex Wise	*Awareness*					
	Yes		*No*		*Total*	
	No.	*per cent*	*No.*	*per cent*	*No.*	*per cent*
Male	80	50.0	80	50.0	160	100.0
Female	78	48.8	82	51.2	160	100.0
$\chi^2 = 0.05$; df=1; $P > 0.05$						
Caste Wise	*Yes*		*No*		*Total*	
	No.	*per cent*	*No.*	*per cent*	*No.*	*per cent*
SC/ST	84	57.9	61	42.1	145	100.0
OBC	57	50.4	56	49.6	113	100.0
GEN.	17	27.4	45	72.6	62	100.0
$\chi^2 = 16.25$; df=2; $P < 0.001$						

(Contd...)

Education Wise	*Yes*		*No*		*Total*	
	No.	*per cent*	*No.*	*per cent*	*No.*	*per cent*
Illiterate	88	58.3	63	41.7	151	100.0
upto high school	58	41.7	81	58.3	139	100.0
Inter +	12	40.0	18	60.0	30	100.0
Total	**158**	**49.4**	**162**	**50.6**	**320**	**100.0**

$\chi^2 = 9.10$; df=2; P <0.05

The above table reveals that about half (49.4 per cent) of respondents were of the opinion that village gram pradhan issued the job cards to those individual of the village who given their vote to village gram pradhan in the election in which proportion of male respondents (50.0 per cent) is slightly more than the female respondents (48.8 per cent). It is also observed that a decreasing trend was observed in the proportion of opinion regarding the preparation of job cards for those respondents who vote casting to the gram pradhan as status, of caste as well as educational qualification were increased and this increase or decrease is found to be statistically significant.

Table 6.30: Profile of Respondents and their Awareness Towards Easily Availability of Loan from Govt. Agencies

Sex Wise	*Availability of Loan from Govt. Agencies*					
	Yes		*No*		*Total*	
	No.	*per cent*	*No.*	*per cent*	*No.*	*per cent*
Male	51	31.9	109	68.1	160	100.0
female	44	27.5	116	72.5	160	100.0
$\chi^2 = 0.73$; df =1; P >0.05						
Caste Wise	*Yes*		*No*		*Total*	
	No.	*per cent*	*No.*	*per cent*	*No.*	*per cent*
SC/ST	33	22.8	112	77.2	145	100.0
OBC	32	28.3	81	71.7	113	100.0
Gen	30	48.4	32	51.6	62	100.0
$\chi^2 = 13.82$; df =2; P <0.01						
Education Wise	*Yes*		*No*		*Total*	
	No.	*per cent*	*No.*	*per cent*	*No.*	*per cent*
Illiterate	31	20.5	120	79.5	151	100.0
upto high school	53	38.1	86	61.9	139	100.0
Inter+	11	36.7	19	62.3	30	100.0
$\chi^2 = 11.51$; df =2; P <0.01						

(Contd...)

Family Income (Rs)	*Yes*		*No*		*Total*	
	No.	*per cent*	*No.*	*per cent*	*No.*	*per cent*
Up to 1500	18	12.9	122	87.1	140	100.0
1500-3000	44	37.0	75	63.0	119	100.0
3000+	33	54.1	28	45.9	61	100.0
Total	**95**	**29.7**	**225**	**70.3**	**320**	**100.0**
χ^2 = 39.44; df =2; P <0.001						

The above table reflects that only 29.7 per cent of respondents aware towards getting loan easily from government banks or government agencies. Out of total in which proportion of male respondents (31.9 per cent) were slightly more as compared to the proportion of female respondents (27.5 per cent). It is seen that majority 48.4 per cent of respondents belongs to general castes category, followed by 28.3 per cent of OBC's while only 22.8 per cent of SC/ST's respondents were of the opinion to get the loan easily from government agencies. Similar type of trend was also observed in connection to various family income groups of respondents i.e. more proportion in higher economic group and minimum proportion in lower economic groups respectively. The easily availability of loans from government banks had been opinion in same proportion (38.1 per cent and 36.7 per cent) by the respondents qualified primary to high school or intermediate level or more whereas it was 20.5 per cent in illiterate respondents respectively.

Statistically, it is found that there are highly significant difference in the proportion of opinion regarding easily availability of loans from government agencies among various caste, literacy status and monthly family income groups of respondents respectively.

Table 6.31: Profile of Respondents and their Awareness Towards Vocational Training Provided by Govt. Agencies and Ngo's

Sex Wise	*Awareness*					
	Yes		*No*		*Total*	
	No.	*per cent*	*No.*	*per cent*	*No.*	*per cent*
Male	16	10.0	144	90.0	160	100.0
female	25	15.6	135	84.4	160	100.0
χ^2 = 2.27; df = 1; P>0.05						

(Contd...)

Caste Wise	E					
	Yes		*No*		*Total*	
	No.	*per cent*	*No.*	*per cent*	*No.*	*per cent*
SC/ST	12	8.3	133	91.7	145	100.0
OBC	17	15.0	96	85.0	113	100.0
GEN	12	19.4	50	80.6	62	100.0
χ^2 = 5.55; df = 2; P>0.005						
Education Wise	*Yes*		*No*		*Total*	
	No.	*per cent*	*No.*	*per cent*	*No.*	*per cent*
Illiterate	17	11.3	134	88.7	151	100.0
upto high school	20	14.4	119	85.6	139	100.0
Inter+	4	13.3	26	86.7	30	100.0
χ^2 = 0.64; df = 2; P>0.05						
Monthly Income (Rs)	*Yes*		*No*		*Total*	
	No.	*per cent*	*No.*	*per cent*	*No.*	*per cent*
Up to 1500	16	11.4	124	88.6	140	100.0
1500-3000	11	9.2	108	90.8	119	100.0
3000+	14	23.0	47	770	61	100.0
Total	**41**	**12.8**	**279**	**87.2**	**320**	**100.0**
χ^2 = 7.21; df = 2; P<0.05						

It is analysed from the above table that only a minimum proportion of respondents (12.8 per cent) were accepted any type of vocational training provided by government agencies or NGO's. Out of which proportion of illiterate were slightly more than the literate respondents as well as female respondents (15.6 per cent) than the male respondents (10.0 per cent) respectively. It is also observed that the respondents belongs to general castes (19.4 per cent) category were in more than the respondents of OBC's (15.0 per cent) and SC/ST's (8.3 per cent) caste categories but this differences is not found to be statistically significant distribution according to monthly family income project that higher economic groups of respondents more aware about to adopts such type of vocational training while it was accepted by 9.2 per cent and 11.4 per cent of those respondents who were falling in the low economic group range of Rs (1500-300) and less than (<1500) respectively and this differences is statistically significant.

The results clearly shows that the respondents of SC/ST's, illiterates and lower economic groups were again sufferer from gaining any type of vocational training and assistances provided by government or private agencies in the study area.

Table 6.32: Profile of Respondents and their Awareness Towards Naxalism as a Medium for Getting more Financial Assistance to Government Agencies

Sex	*Yes*		*No*		*Cannot say*		*Total*	
	No.	*Per cent*	*No.*	*Per cent*	*No.*	*Per cent*	*No.*	*Per cent*
Male	22	13.8	27	16.9	113	69.4	160	100.0
Female	39	24.4	46	28.8	75	46.9	160	100.0
$\chi^2 = 16.65$; df = 2; P<0.001								
Education Wise	*Yes*		*No*		*Cannot say*		*Total*	
	No.	*Per cent*	*No.*	*Per cent*	*No.*	*Per cent*	*No.*	*Per cent*
Illiterate	31	20.5	35	23.2	85	56.2	151	100.0
upto highschool	22	15.8	26	18.5	91	65.5	139	100.0
Inter+	8	26.7	12	40.0	10	33.3	30	100.0
Total	61	19.1	73	22.8	186	58.1	320	100.0
$\chi^2 = 11.31$; df = 1; P < 0.05								

The above table reveals that out of total interviewed respondents, only 19.1 per cent opined that there is really a naxalism is a great problem in this area while remaining 22.8 per cent and 58.1 per cent of respondents opined that there is no problem of naxalism it is, only one of the medium for demanding more financial assistance from the government and did not provide any opinion regarding the matter respectively. The proportion of respondents who accepted for naxalism problem and for demanding more financial assistance from the government, the female proportion (24.4 per cent) was significantly more in comparison to male respondents (13.8 per cent), while just reversed pattern was observed in case of no comment about such type of matter. On the analysis based on educational status, it is found that the respondents qualified at intermediate level or more were in higher percentages for projecting their opinion regarding real problems of naxalism and one of the medium for gaining financial assistance to government followed by illiterate and the respondents educated upto level of high school respectively. The difference in proportion of the opinion regarding both type of problems between male and female as well as among various educationally qualified group are found to be statistically significant.

The results clearly shows that more than half of the respondents did not projects any idea regarding naxalism problem in the study area or it is one of the medium for demanding more financial assistance to government, but it may be due to lower literacy status, unawareness or fear of naxalite exploitation.

Table 6.33: Profile of Respondents and their Awareness Towards Migration, Development and Displacement of People in Sonebhadra District

Sex Wise	*Yes*		*No*		*Total*	
	No.	*per cent*	*No.*	*per cent*	*No.*	*per cent*
Male	24	15.0	136	85.0	160	100.0
Female	48	30.0	112	70.0	160	100.0
$\chi^2 = 10.32$; df = 1 ; P<0.01						
Caste Wise	*Yes*		*No*		*Total*	
	No.	*per cent*	*No.*	*per cent*	*No.*	*per cent*
SC/ST	35	24.1	110	75.9	145	100.0
OBC	34	30.1	79	69.9	113	100.0
GEN	3	4.8	59	95.2	62	100.0
$\chi^2 = 15.04$; df = 2 ; P<0.01						
Education Wise	*Yes*		*No*		*Total*	
	No.	*per cent*	*No.*	*per cent*	*No.*	*per cent*
Illiterate	45	29.8	106	70.2	151	100.0
upto highschool	22	15.8	117	84.2	139	100.0
Inter+	5	16.7	25	83.3	30	100.0
Total	**72**	**22.5**	**248**	**77.5**	**320**	**100.0**
$\chi^2 = 8.75$; df = 2 ; P<0.05						

The present table reveals that about one fourth (22.5 per cent) of respondents were of the opinion that the progress of naxalism is mainly due to migration of people from other part of the country to Sonebhadra and displacement of people due to various development projects of the area. Out of which proportion of females (30 per cent) were significantly more than the proportion of male respondents (15 per cent). Such type of opinion was provided by the OBC's respondents in maximum proportion (30.1 per cent) followed by SC/ST's (24.1 per cent) and a minimum proportion (4.8 per cent) of general castes category respectively. Education wise analysis shows that majority 29.8 per cent of illiterates were of the opinion that the increased in naxalism only due to people migration from other part of country for employment coming to Sonbhadra, or displacement of people on the name of development. Whereas it was 15.8 per cent and 16.7 per cent in the respondent who were qualified upto high school and above the intermediate level respectively. The difference in proportion for providing such type of positive statement among various caste and educational status group are found to be highly significant.

Table 6.34: Profile of Respondents and their Awareness Towards Caste Based Political Parties in Naxalism

Sex Wise	*Awareness*							
	Yes		*No*		*Cannot say*		*Total*	
	No.	*Per cent*	*No.*	*Per cent*	*No.*	*Per cent*	*No.*	*Per cent*
Male	100	62.5	24	15.0	36	22.5	160	100.0
Female	61	38.1	46	28.8	53	33.1	160	100.0
$\chi^2 = 19.61$; df = 2; P<0.001								
Caste Wise	*Yes*		*No*		*Cannot say*		*Total*	
	No.	*Per cent*	*No.*	*Per cent*	*No.*	*Per cent*	*No.*	*Per cent*
SC/ST	96	66.2	24	16.6	25	17.2	145	100.0
OBC	46	40.7	31	27.4	36	31.9	113	100.0
GEN.	19	30.6	15	24.2	28	45.2	62	100.0
$\chi^2 = 30.95$; df = 4; P < 0.001								
Education Wise	*Yes*		*No*		*Cannot say*		*Total*	
	No.	*Per cent*	*No.*	*Per cent*	*No.*	*Per cent*	*No.*	*Per cent*
Illiterate	70	46.4	34	22.5	47	31.1	151	100.0
upto highschool	85	61.2	22	15.8	32	23.0	139	100.0
Inter+	06	20.0	14	46.7	10	33.3	30	100.0
Total	**161**	**50.3**	**70**	**21.9**	**89**	**27.8**	**320**	**100.0**
$\chi^2 = 22.05$; df = 4; P < 0.001								

The above table describes that majority 50.3 per cent of respondent opinion that caste based political parties is one of the important factor to increase the naxalism in this area in which maximum 62.5 per cent were males and 38.1 per cent of females with increased in the caste status group, a decreasing trend in proportion of opinion is registered in the present study. Education wise distribution projects that out of total upto high school qualified respondents 61.2 per cent were of the positive opinion followed by illiterates (46.4 per cent) and the minimum (20.0 per cent) of the respondents qualified at intermediated level or more had positive opinion regarding progress of naxalism to the caste based political parties. The differences in proportion of this opinion between male and female among the different caste and education status are found to be statistically highly significant. It clearly shows that majority of male respondents belongs to SC/ST's and minimum qualification level was accepted to the facts of caste based political parties as major cause of increasing naxalism. It may be again due to lower social status, lower educational status as well as less awareness regarding the cause of naxalism.

Table 6.35: Profile of Respondents and their Awareness Towards Role of Political Parties and Political Representative in Naxalism

Sex Wise	*Yes*		*No*		*Can not say*		*Total*	
	No.	*Per cent*	*No.*	*Per cent*	*No.*	*Per cent*	*No.*	*Per cent*
Male	114	71.2	12	07.5	34	21.2	160	100.0
Female	74	46.2	40	25.0	46	28.8	160	100.0
χ^2 = 25.39; df = 2; P<0.001								
Caste Wise	*Yes*		*No*		*Cannot say*		*Total*	
	No.	*Per cent*	*No.*	*Per cent*	*No.*	*Per cent*	*No.*	*Per cent*
SC/ST	99	68.3	29	20.0	17	11.7	145	100.0
OBC	53	46.9	12	10.6	48	42.5	113	100.0
GEN.	36	58.1	11	17.7	15	24.2	62	100.0
χ^2 = 32.53; df = 4; P < 0.001								
Education Wise	*Yes*		*No*		*Cannot say*		*Total*	
	No.	*Per cent*	*No.*	*Per cent*	*No.*	*Per cent*	*No.*	*Per cent*
Illiterate	74	49.0	33	21.9	44	29.1	151	100.0
upto high school	100	71.9	06	04.3	33	23.7	139	100.0
Inter+	14	46.7	13	43.3	03	10.0	30	100.0
Total	**188**	**58.8**	**52**	**16.2**	**80**	**25.0**	**320**	**100.0**
χ^2 =39.77; df = 4; P < 0.001								

It is reveals from the above table that more than half (58.8 per cent) of respondents were in favour that corruption, exploitative policies and maintaining distance of political representative from common people is one of the major factor for the emergence of naxalism in the study area. Out of which maximum were from upto high school (71.9 per cent) qualified followed by illiterates (49.0 per cent), majorities were from SC/ST's (68.3 per cent) followed by general caste (58.1 per cent) and maximum from male respondents (71.2 per cent) than female (46.2 per cent) respectively. The difference in the proportion of opinion regarding projection of major causes for naxalism development due to corruption, exploitation and maintaining great distance of political representative from common people among different castes, educational status and between male and female individual are found to be statistically highly significant.

It may be concluded that the male respondent of the study area belongs to SC/ST's and had the lower educational status, were facing more problems due to corruptions, caste conflict, exploitation as well as behaviour of the political representation at village level or at higher level.

Table 6.36: Profile of Respondents and their Awareness Towards Interferance of Naxalite on Various NGO'S Programme

Sex Wise	*Interference by Naxalite in NGO Program's*					
	Yes		*No*		*Total*	
	No.	*per cent*	*No.*	*per cent*	*No.*	*per cent*
Male	09	05.6	151	94.4	160	100.0
female	34	21.2	126	78.8	160	100.0
χ^2 = 16.79; df = 1; P<0.001						
Caste Wise	*Yes*		*No*		*Total*	
	No.	*per cent*	*No.*	*per cent*	*No.*	*per cent*
SC/ST	24	16.6	121	83.4	145	100.0
OBC	13	11.5	100	88.5	113	100.0
GEN.	06	09.7	56	90.3	62	100.0
χ^2 = 2.33; df = 2; P>0.05						
Education Wise Status	*Yes*		*No*		*Total*	
	No.	*per cent*	*No.*	*per cent*	*No.*	*per cent*
Illiterate	21	13.9	130	86.1	151	100.0
upto high school	17	12.2	122	87.8	139	100.0
Inter+	05	16.7	25	83.3	30	100.0
Total	**43**	**13.4**	**277**	**86.6**	**320**	**100.0**
χ^2 0.47; df = 2; P>0.05						

It is analyzed from the above table that only 13.4 per cent of respondents were accepted for any type of interference by naxalites in various types of programmes seen by the NGO's in their area. While remaining 86.6 per cent of respondents were not agreeing with such type of facts. The problems of interference by naxalites were stated by respondents of SC/ST's caste groups followed by OBC's and general castes category. While higher educationally qualified respondent favoured to this reason, it is also observed that the female respondents (21.2 per cent) were in maximum proportion than the male respondents (5.6 per cent) and this difference is highly significant.

The difference among the proportion of difference caste groups and different educational group regarding the opinion of interference by naxalites are not statistically significant. Thus, we may conclude that a small proportion of respondents maximum from the female and SC/ST's caste group side were projected their ideas about interference in various activities of the individual by naxalites may be due to fear, less awareness and exploitation specially to the female population as well as may be due to great sympathy with NGO's personals.

Table 6.37: Profile of Respondents and their Awareness Towards Police Interferance in Different NGO'S Programmes

Sex Wise	*Police Interference in NGO's Programs*					
	Yes		*No*		*Total*	
	No.	*per cent*	*No.*	*per cent*	*No.*	*per cent*
Male	16	10.0	144	90.0	160	100.0
female	31	19.4	129	80.6	160	100.0
$\chi^2 = 5.61$; df = 1; $P<0.05$						
Caste Wise	*Yes*		*No*		*Total*	
	No.	*per cent*	*No.*	*per cent*	*No.*	*per cent*
SC/ST	26	17.9	119	82.1	145	100.0
OBC	11	09.7	102	90.3	113	100.0
GEN.	10	16.1	52	83.9	62	100.0
$\chi^2 = 3.53$; df = 2; $P>0.05$						
Education Wise Status	*Yes*		*No*		*Total*	
	No.	*per cent*	*No.*	*per cent*	*No.*	*per cent*
Illiterate	24	15.9	127	84.1	151	100.0
upto high school	17	12.2	122	87.8	139	100.0
Inter+	06	20.0	24	80.0	30	100.0
Total	**47**	**14.7**	**273**	**85.3**	**320**	**100.0**
$\chi^2 = 1.52$; df = 2; $P>0.05$						

It is evident from the above table that only 14.7 per cent of respondents were of the views that the police administration interfered, in different programmes of NGO's in which proportion of females (19.4 per cent) were significantly more than the proportion of male respondents (10.0 per cent). Caste category wise distribution shows that 17.9 per cent of SC/ST's, 16.1 per cent of general caste and 9.7 per cent of OBC's respondent were accepted for the police interference in the NGO's programmes but this difference is not significant. The respondents who were qualified more than intermediate level favoured the opinion of police interference in different NGO's programmes in maximum proportion (20.0 per cent) followed by illiterates (15.9 per cent) and qualified upto high school (12.2 per cent) respectively and this variation is not obtained to be statistically significant. The result shows that the interference of naxalites as well as police administration in different NGO's programmes is reported by same proportion of respondents with near about same reasons.

Table 6.38: Profile of Respondents and their Awareness towards Decrease in Naxalism and Increased in Employment by Ngo's Programmes

Sex Wise	***Yes***		***No***		***Can not say***		***Total***	
	No.	***Per cent***	***No.***	***Per cent***	***No.***	***Per cent***	***No.***	***Per cent***
Male	40	25.0	60	37.5	60	37.5	160	100.0
Female	45	28.1	33	20.6	82	51.2	160	100.0
$\chi^2 = 11.54$; df = 2; P<0.01								
Caste Wise	***Yes***		***No***		***Can not say***		***Total***	
	No.	***Per cent***	***No.***	***Per cent***	***No.***	***Per cent***	***No.***	***Per cent***
SC/ST	31	21.4	50	34.5	64	44.1	145	100.0
OBC	48	42.5	15	13.3	50	44.2	113	100.0
GEN.	06	09.7	28	45.2	28	45.2	62	100.0
$\chi^2 = 35.59$; df = 4; P < 0.001								
Education Wise	***Yes***		***No***		***Can not say***		***Total***	
	No.	***Per cent***	***No.***	***Per cent***	***No.***	***Per cent***	***No.***	***Per cent***
Illiterate	44	29.1	38	25.2	69	45.7	151	100.0
upto high school	38	27.3	46	33.1	55	39.6	139	100.0
Inter+	03	10.0	09	30.0	18	60.0	30	100.0
Total	85	26.6	93	21.1	142	44.4	320	100.0
$\chi^2 = 7.52$; df = 4; P > 0.05								

It is perceptible from the above table that out of total respondents awareness, only one fourth (26.6 per cent) were accepted for decreased in naxalism and increased in employment due to running different programmes by NGO's whereas rest 21.1 per cent and 44.4 per cent of respondents had negative response and not answered at all about the such facts. It is also observed that those respondents who had positive opinion regarding increased of employment majority were from female respondents (28.1 per cent) than the male respondents (25.0 per cent). The respondents belongs to OBC's (42.5 per cent) were more benefited followed by SC/ST's (21.4 per cent) while the respondents from general caste (9.7 per cent) were less beneficial from NGO's programmes. A decreasing trend was observed in the proportion of respondents in connection of increasing employment due to NGO's programmes as educational status increased. The difference in proportion of opinion regarding increasing of employment and decreasing of naxalism between male and female as well as among various caste groups are found to be highly significant but among educational group it is not significant respectively.

It may be concluded that the percentage of female individual was more for accepting decrease in naxalism and increase in employment might be because of getting employment in different programmes of NGO's to raised their social-economic and moral status in their locality.

Summary

The empirical findings may be summarised as under-

- The analysis regarding vote casting in election reveals that general caste (100 per cent) vote in election followed by OBC's (76.1 per cent) and SC/ST's (84.8 per cent) and gender wise distribution males (91.9 per cent) followed by (77.5 per cent) females vote casting in election. The younger population (20-34 yrs) was maximum in comparison to other age group. The difference in proportion of vote-casting among various caste and age group as well as between male and female is highly significant.

- The major reasons for not vote-casting in election were either checked by dominant castes or pressure created by naxalite to not vote casting in election.
- Majority 74.4 per cent of male and 64.1 per cent of female respondents had views that representative of Gram Panchayat and bureaucrats recognised their problems in the meetings and tried to solve their problems.
- It is found that more than half (50.3 per cent) of respondents of rural areas were accepted for the solution of their problem at thana diwas or tehsil diwas an increasing trend regarding solution of problem were observed with increasing of caste status, educational status and economic status of the respondents in which village representative (74.4 per cent) and bureaucrat (64.1 per cent) responsible to solve their problems while no respondents were answered about solving their problem by naxalites and naxal organisation.
- Majority 42.2 per cent of respondents were reported that the naxalites struggle for the poor, Dalits and Marginalised section of society. This proportion was found to be in decreasing order as caste status, educational and economic status was increased.
- It is found that about 92.0 per cent of respondents opinion for development in their area during last decades and maximum credits were given to government machinery (71.4 per cent) followed by political leadership (40.8 per cent) the respondents who credited to government machinery qualified at primary to high school level and male individuals respectively.
- By analyzing the opinion of respondents regarding facilities provided by the naxalites views to provide various required facilities by naxalites majority 56.8 per cent, 54.1 per cent and 39.7 per cent of respondents opined that naxal organisation helps them financially, at the time of marriage, safety from higher caste people exploitation and distribution of ration facilities time to time respectively.

- It is found that about three fourth (70.0 per cent) of the study subjects reported not taking any interest regarding solving their problems by various political leaders & parties after elections. In which male respondents (23.1 per cent) were significantly more than the females (13.1 per cent).
- Majority 48.1 per cent of respondents were viewed that the political leaders as well as political parties are not taking any interest to solve the naxalism problems, out of which female respondents (53.1 per cent) were more in comparison to the male respondents (43.1 per cent).
- It is observed that 24.7 per cent of respondents of the respective area accepted that the intellectual had sympathy with naxal organisation and movement due to which the elimination of naxalism is not possible.
- The analyzed data shows that only 14.4 per cent of respondents were of the views that the separatist organisation of the country as well as of other countries helps the naxal organisation whereas 15.9 per cent and 34.7 per cent of respondents did not comment and accepts any type of help to naxalites respectively.
- It is evident from the study that majority 55.6 per cent of respondents were reported that the modernisation of police force is done for fighting against naxalites to eliminates the problem of naxalism 57.2 per cent of respondents opined that the elimination of naxalism might be due to implementation of various government development programmes and police force policies as well as 67.8 per cent blamed to political parties and political leaders for misutilisation of criminals on the name of naxalism respectively.
- It is perceptible from the observation that more than two third (66.2 per cent) of respondent reported that the political leaders are not interested to the elimination of naxalism for their own benefits in which SC/ST's castes as well as illiterate were found to be significantly more in comparison to other castes and literate groups respectively.

- It is found that majority 56.9 per cent of respondents opinion that police exploitative policies is a major reason for naxalites attack on police administration and government machinery whereas 10.6 per cent and 11.9 per cent of respondents reported that the police force provides security to common people as well as showing their dominance.
- It is also observed that about 27.8 per cent of respondents were accepted for collecting levy and extortion money by criminals on the name of naxalites out of which the proportion of females and SC/ST's castes were found to be significantly more than male and other castes group respectively.
- In the study area majority 66.6 per cent of respondent have awareness about various government programmes and policies in which male respondents (73.8 per cent) were significantly more than the female respondents (59.4 per cent) and an increasing trend was observed on increasing the social status of castes and literacy status respectively.
- About government programmes MNREGA, 98.8 per cent of respondents had knowledge in which maximum were male than females.
- In the study area majority 55.3 per cent of respondents had the job cards prepared by respective Gram Panchyat in which majority were female respondents than male and from OBC's castes respectively
- In the study area majority 72.8 per cent of respondents were reported for getting the employment through MNREGA in which illiterate, SC/ST's and females' respondents were found to be significantly more than other groups respectively. Out of total respondents who received employment in MNREGA, only 31.3 per cent were employed 100 day and remaining less than 100 days. Only 48.9 per cent of respondents received wages 100 Rs. /Day in which females proportion were more than male proportion. It is also observed that out of total respondents who did not received full wages of their work majority 52.9 per cent were blamed

to Gram Pradhan and 44.5 per cent to both Gram Pradhan and Block Development Officer respectively.

- Only 21.2 per cent of respondents were satisfied with their monthly income for their livelihood out of which proportion of male were significantly moral than the female respondents. The increasing trend in proportion of satisfaction regarding the family income is seen as status of caste, education and monthly family income increased respectively.
- The awareness of respondents about the preparation of Job cards shows that about half (49.4 per cent) respondents were of the opinion that village Gram Pradhan issued the Job cards maximum to those Individuals of the Village who given their vote to village Gram Pradhan in election in which maximum were male respondents, illiterate and belong to SC/ST's caste group respectively.
- It is found that only 29.7 per cent of respondent's opinion for getting loan easily from government Banks and government agencies and the trend was increasing order as education, income and caste status advanced.
- It is evident from the result that only 12.8 per cent of the study subjects were accepted for getting any type of vocational training provided by government agencies or NGO's out of which maximum were from general caste (19.4 per cent) literates (14.4 per cent) and from the high monthly income group (23 per cent) respectively.
- Only 19.1per cent of respondents were of the views that there is really naxalism is a great problem in study area. Out of which illiterates (20.5 per cent) as well as female respondents (24.4 per cent) were significantly more than the literates (15.8 per cent) and male respondents (13.8 per cent) respectively.
- It is found that out of total respondent only 22.5 per cent were of the opinion that the increased of naxalism is mainly due to migration from other part of the country or displacement for the development of the area. Out of which the proportion of OBC's (30.1 per cent), females (30 per cent)

and illiterates' respondents (29.8 per cent) were found to be significantly more in comparison to others respectively.

- It is also found that majority 50.5 per cent of the respondents stated that caste based political parties are one of the important factors to increased in the naxalism in study area out of which the proportion of male respondents (62.5 per cent), SC/ST's (66.2 per cent) and respondents qualified up to high school (61.2 per cent) were significantly more than the other respective groups respectively. Majority 58.8 per cent of respondents were of the opinion that corruption, exploitative policies and maintaining distances of political representatives as well as government administrators from common people is one the major cause for the progress of naxalism in the study area is also observed that only 13.4 per cent of study subject were accepted for any type of interference by naxalites on different types of programs run by the NGO's in their area in which maximum were qualified at Intermediate level (16.7 per cent), belonged to SC/ST's (16.6 per cent) and female respondents (21.2 per cent) respectively like wise 14.7 per cent respondents stated that the police administration interference in different programmes of NGO's in which also the proportion of females (19.4 per cent), SC/ST's (17.9 per cent) and above intermediate level (20.0 per cent) respondents were more respectively.
- Analysis regarding the respondents awareness about naxalism and employment generation shows that more than one-fourth (26.6 per cent) of respondents of the study area were accepted for decreasing in naxalism and increasing in employment generation due to running of various programmes of NGO's in which maximum proportion were from females (28.1 per cent), OBC's (42.5 per cent) and illiterates (29.1 per cent) respectively.

References

Asian Development Bank, Key Indicators for the Asia and the Pacific 39th Editions, Manila, 2008.

Banerjee Sumanta, In the Wake of Naxalbari; A History of the Naxalite Movement in India, Subarnarekha, Calcutta, 1980, p. 99.

Banerjee Sumanta, Ibid., p. 11.

Banerjee, Sumanta, India's Simmering Revolution, The Naxalite uprising, Selected Service Syndicate, New Delhi,1984, p. 88.

Chattopadhyaya, Sankar, Subrid, To Establish a Liberated Area (Interview with Koteswar Rao), Frontline, Vol. 26, No.22 Octber 24, November 6, 2009, p. 22-23

Dasgupta, Biplab, The Naxalite Movement Bombay, Allied Publishers, New Delhi, 1975, p. 219.

Dasgupta, Biplab, *Ibid.,* p. 11.

Dasgupta, Biplab, *Ibid.,* p. 211.

Ganpathy Interview with various Foreign Journalists, Interview with Ganapathy, Generl Secretary, CPI (Maoist), April 24, 2007.

Gopal, S., The Naxalite Movement: Impact of External Networking Cited in Ramana.

Johri, J.C., Political Ideas of Marxist Leninist Communist in India, Indian Journal of Political Sciences, Vol. XXXII, No. 2, April-June 1971, p. 179-180.

Kujur, Rajat, Child Solders of the Naxal Movement,, Insdtitute of Peace and Conflict Studies Issue Brief, New Delhi, No. 2738, Nov. 24, 2008.

Kujur, Rajat, From CRZ to SEZ : Naxal Reins of Terror, IPCS ISSUE Brief, New Delhi, No. 2271, April 21, 2007.

Kujur, Rajat, Naxalite Violence : Hijacking Train the New face of Red-Terror, IPCS, ISSUE brief, New Delhi, No. 1967, March, 16, 2006.

Kurian, C.T. Poverty, Planning, and Social Transformation, Allied Publishersd, Bombay, 1978, p. 8

Liberation, Vol. 3, No. 1, Nov. 1969.

Louisprakash, The Naxalite Movement in Central Bihar, New Delhi, Wosdvariths, 2002, p. 259.

Mankenkar, D.R., A Revolution of Rising Frustrationsd, Vikas Publication, New Delhi, 1975, p. 2

Rai, Haridwar and Prasdad, K.M., Naxalism , A Challenge to the Proposition of Peaceful Transition to Socialism Indian Journal of Political Science cited in Nimbram, Amrik, Singh, Poverty, land and violence.(An analytical study of Naxalism in Bihar, Chandhary Printing Press, Patna, 1992, p. 2.

Ramani, R.Venkata, The Naxal Strategy in Urban Area, IPCS ISSUE brief, New Delhi, No. 3047, January, 21, 2010.

Reddy, K. Srinivas, Revolutionary and Counter Revolutionary Strategties of the Naxalite and the State, 2008, p. 92, cited in P.V., Ramana, The Naxal Channenge (Cause linkages, and policy options), 2008.

Singh, Prakash, The Naxalite Movement in India, Rupa and Company, Newdelhi, 2006, p. 121-122.

Singh, Prakash, *Ibid.*, p. 123.

U.N.D.P. Report, 1999, Oxford University Press, Oxford, 1999.

Conclusion and Suggestion

The present study is based on empirical investigation of three blocks of Sonbhadra districts namely Robertsganj, Chatra and Nagwa. Of these blocks twelve villages have been selected. This district is selected because it is one of the backward districts of country, and facing Naxal problem in last two decades, government declared this district as naxal affected and allotted special packages for rural development since the last two decades. In these districts I have explored the relationship between the emergence of naxalism and social transformation which had occurred in social-economic, political and cultural life of people in last two decades.

Social transformation has multidimensional connotation. It comprehends enormous diversity in analysis among the various disciplines. It deals with social transformation in rural society especially Post Independence era suggests that the process of planned development has created diverse patterns of social transformation in different regions. It brings transition of Agrarian society, introduction of modern technology and communication, emergence of complex network of various association and institution, state intervention in adopting different measures to strengthen certain communities, groups or classes on the one hand and weakens other on the contrary.

In 1967, when naxal movement emerged in West Bengal, that time poverty socio-economic disparity are the main issue of the movement, but after traveling almost half century, this movement change its track, today naxal organisation and naxalite not fight for common people in our country but they fight for political gain and wants to rules the country. Earlier, there base is rural India but recently in last decades, it built their base in Urban India also, they used modern techniques of telecommunication, such as mobile, internet etc to mobilized people about their ideology. They also get support of separatist organisation of country and other countries like Nepal, China, and Pakistan, to create terror in India and bring hindrance and obstacles in the running of smooth parliamentary democracy of country. They want to control the country by 2050; they used new technique and networks to achieve their goals which I have discussed in my research work.

In my thesis, I have also discussed the changes that have occurred in Sonbhadra, after the emergence of naxalism to control naxalism in Sonbhadra. State Government launched various development programmes to promote their life style and how it brings change in the rural life of Sonbhadra. In my research study, I have find out the relationship between social transformation and rise of naxalism and also discussed the various aspect of rural people life in this naxal affected region and find out the sociological explanation of various social economic, political and cultural change occur in the life of rural people.

Objectives of the present study:

1. To conceptualize the process of social transformation.
2. To analyze the emergence of naxalism in the Sonbhadra district.
3. To evaluate the measures of state intervention and social transformation.
4. To observe the nature of social transformation in Sonbhadra district in a socio-historical perspective.
5. To observe government programmes implemented in sonebhadra district after Independence and particularly in last two decades.

Hypothesis:

- Greater the level of poverty and unemployment, higher the chances of involvement in naxal activities.
- Greater the political socialisation, higher the participation in naxal activity.

- Greater the state interventions in poverty alleviation and employment generation programmes greater the decrease in violent activities in the naxal regions.
- Greater the police suppression and restrictions, higher the naxal activities in region.

To find out the relationship between social transformation and naxalism, with time boundation and limitation in my mind I have selected 12 villages for my study. In my study Nagwa block is worst affected, so I have chosen 6 villages from here, and Robertsganj and Chatra having less Naxal violence so, I have chosen 3-3 villages from both block for my study.

The total member of households in 12 villages of Robertsganj, Chatra and Nagwa blocks is 3334 households out of these house-holders we have selected 10 percent as sample for the present purpose. Numerically, the ten percent of the total householders comes 333 but despite out repeated efforts we could not contact 13 householders. Hence, the present study consists of 320 samples. These samples represent one member from one household selected randomly. Both male and female members according to their availability during field surveys have been incorporated in the sample. Altogether the study consists of males and females as samples who represent their households.

In this study data obtained from both the primary and secondary sources. Statistical method used in the study to find out the result in accurately and scientifically, so that we find out the real facts of the emergence of naxalism and the changes occur in the study area after government programmes in last two decades.

Whole Research Work Divided into Seven Chapter.

Chapter one: Introduction: In this Chapter I have written the concept of social transformation, theories of social transformation such as capitalist, Marxist, Socialist and Neo-liberal theory of social transformation and its impact on Indian society, genesis of naxalite movement and its ideology, it historical perspectives and the recent changes occur in the naxal movement in contemporary time, naxalite movement in states, naxal strategy and methods of action, recently new method adopted by Naxalites, relationship between social transformation and poverty in naxal affected areas, measures of state intervention and rural transformation in India, especially in Sonbhadra district of Eastern Uttar Pradesh. Also I have focused some developmental programmes of government. Specially launched schemes in naxal affected district such as Sam Vikas Yojana, MNREGA, Bharat Nirman etc.

Chapter two: Review of literature

The earlier studies based on social transformation, rural transformation in India and work done on naxal movement and Naxalism in India both at state level as well as national level as a theoretical and empirical investigation. These studies and review of literature used in my research work for providing me important suggestion related to my study.

Chapter three: Design of Research

In this chapter I have stated the statement of problem, objectives of the study, universe of study, hypothesis, statistical method used in study, experience from field works, sources of data collection and limitations of the study etc.

Chapter four: Socio-Economic and Demographic Profile of Respondents

In this chapter I have discussed the respondents socio-economic status, age, caste, ethnic and religious status, household structure, educational status, marital status, and occupational status etc and that collected data used in the study.

Majority of (48.2 per cent) respondents were in age group of 35 to 49 years and remaining (30.9 per cent) and (20.9 per cent) of respondents comes in the age group of 20-34 years and more than 49 years. It is also observed that average age of respondents with standard Deviation is calculated (40.40 $\pm$ 12.14) years. In this equal proportion of both male and female respondents selected for the interview. (50 per cent male and 50 per cent female).

The distribution of study subject according to their caste and gender, it is found that out of total respondents majority (45.3 per cent) belonged to SC/ST's castes and remaining (35.3 per cent) and (19.4 per cent) of respondents belongs to OBC and General castes respectively. This data shows the demographic structure is study area which is almost similar in proportion.

The educational status of the respondents reflects that about half (47.2 per cent) of the respondents were illiterate in which female (66.2 per cent) were found to be more as compare to male respondents (28.1 per cent). The rest of respondents who were qualified at primary to high school level were observed to be (43.4 per cent) and higher secondary and more than this were (9.4 per cent) respectively. The results clearly shows that the educational status is very low in the present study area, specially the female population it may be due to non-availability of infrastructural development, road connectivity, low socio-economic status and lack of awareness among the masses.

The occupational status of respondents shows that more than one third (38.1 per cent) of respondents were agriculturist whereas remaining (33.1 per cent) and (28.8 per cent) of respondents were labourers and engaged in different types of activities like as service, business small scale industries, shopkeeper etc. respectively. It clearly shows that maximum respondents are either agriculturist or working as labour due to which may fall in lower socio-economic and educational status.

Monthly income wise distribution of respondents shows that maximum (43.8 per cent) had monthly income less than Rs 1500 while rest (37.2 per cent) and (19.0 per cent) of respondents had their monthly income in the range of rupees (1500-3000) and more than Rs 3000 respectively. It clearly shows that the lower socio-economic status of the individuals in rural community of the study area.

The religious status wise distribution of respondents shows that (89.7 per cent) were belongs to Hindu family while remaining (10.3 per cent) were Muslims. It shows that Hindu community is dominant and thickly populated in the selected area.

Chapter five: Rise of Naxalism and Social Transformation in Naxal Affected Areas:

In this chapter an attempt has been made to analyze the nature and process of social transformation in a rural setting especially in Naxal affected areas. In this context the gathered information analyzed and summarized as follows:-

Analysis regarding the knowledge and factors of naxalism shows that about (96 per cent) of respondents know about the menace of naxalism. They consider ideological attitudes, caste conflict, land/labour disparity and lower socio-economic status are the main factors of naxalism.

Majority (40.6 per cent) of respondents opined about social transformation in the last two decades. Female respondents were observed to be significantly higher in proportion than the male respondents. Caste wise distribution shows that General caste respondents were given importance to social transformation, whereas OBC's and SC/ST's castes respondent reported economic and political transformation in study area in the last two decades.

It is apparent from the analysis that out of total respondents who were in favour of social transformation due to naxalism, majority (67.7 per cent) reported the change, by gun and to mobilise the people in which maximum were younger group of respondents.

It is also, analyzed the fact that (51.2 per cent) of respondents reported for taking interest to solve their problem by naxalites. Out of which female proportion was found to be significantly more than male respondents. SC/ST's respondents were more in number than other castes.

It is also analysed regarding the knowledge about participation of females in naxal movement shows that only (32.8 per cent) of respondents had some knowledge about the female naxalites in their study area out of which proportion of female were more than male respondents.

The analysis regarding police behavior in the study area shows that only (16.2 per cent) of the respondents were of the views that the police administration created problems and exploited the people on the name of naxalites, in which maximum proportion was female respondents and respondents of SC/ST's caste category respectively.

It is also analyzed about the types of social transformation in the selected area which shows that out of total respondents (88.5 per cent) and (87.7 per cent) of respondents reported to economic and social transformation out of which male respondents were observed to be more in comparison to the female respondents about (86 per cent) of respondents credited to political transformation in which females were more as compared to male respondents.

Chapter Six: State Intervention Measures And Rural Development In Naxal Affected Areas

The gathered information regarding state intervention measures and rural development in naxal affected areas are analyzed and persecuted as follows:-

- Majority (74.4 per cent) and (64.1 per cent) of respondents had views that representative of Gram Panchayat and Bureaucrats recognized their problems in the meeting and tried to solve their problems.
- It is found that more than half (50.3 per cent) of respondents were accepted for the solution of their problem at Thana Diwas or Tehsil Diwas
- It is found that about 92 per cent of respondents opined for any type of development in their area during last decades and maximum credits were given to government machinery maximum were from SC/ST's castes than other caste group.
- It is also found that various facilities provided by the naxalites. (45.6 per cent) were of the views to provide facilities by naxalites majority (56.8 per cent), (54.1 per cent) and (39.7 per cent) of respondents opined that naxal organisation helps them financially, at the time of marriage, safety from higher caste peoples, exploitation and distribution of ration facilities time to time respectively.
- It is found that about three fourth (70 per cent) of the subject reported not to take any interest regarding for solving their

problems by various political parties and leaders after election.

- It is found that majority (56.9 per cent) of respondents opined to police exploitative policies as a major reason for attack of naxalites on police administration and government machinery.
- In the study area majority (66.6 per cent) of respondents had knowledge about various government programmes and policies. Such as MNREGA (98.8 per cent) of respondents had knowledge in which maximum were males than females.
- Majority 55.3 per cent of respondents had job card prepared by respective Gram Panchayat. Majority (72.8 per cent) of respondents were reported for getting the employment through MNREGA out of which illiterate SC/ST's and females respondents were found to be significantly more than other groups respectively. Only (31.3 per cent) were employed 100 days and remaining less than 100 days only (48.9 per cent) of respondents received wages 100 Rs per day in which female proportion were more than male propórtion.
- It is found that only(29.7 per cent) of respondents opined for getting loans easily from government banks or agencies and the trend was increasing order as education, income and caste status advanced.
- It is evident from the study area results that only (12.8 per cent) of the study subjects were accepted for getting any type of vocational training provided by government agencies or NGO's.
- Only (19.1 per cent) of respondent consider naxalism as a main problem in this area (22.5 per cent) consider unemployment, poverty, displacement is the major cause of naxalism. (50.3 per cent) consider caste based political parties are also responsible for naxalism.
- Only (13.4 per cent) of the study subject accepted for any type of interference by naxalites in different programmes runs by NGO's in their area.

Conclusion

- It is evident that social transformation occurs in the naxal affected areas of Sonbhadra in last two decades. General caste individuals were mostly support this view whereas OBC's caste and scheduled castes/scheduled tribes given their views to economic and political transformation after the rise of the naxalism in the study area.
- In this area, monthly people engaged in Agriculture activities or worked as laboures, mostly people worked under various government programmes and schemes as labour such as people involvement in MNREGA Bharat Nirman, etc. There schemes bring drastic change in the study area, it control the migration of people to other cities and provides employment to rural people.
- Mostly people are illiterate, poor and unemployed and they were not aware about their social, political and economic sights that why they are easy targets of both naxalites as well as Bureaucrats and forest officers exploitative policies in the study area.
- In the study area political parties and leaders not interested to show the problem of common people after general election, they not come to Sonbhadra, because they know that people are illiterates, poor and unemployed and they can be mobilized in their favour by using money, muscles and castism as weapons in the election.
- Gender discrimination and exploitative policies of forest officers, police and other officer in the study area is the other factor which also increased naxalism in the area.
- Geographical topography of the Sonbhadra and its border with four states Bihar, Jharkhand, Chhatisgarh and Madhya Pradesh also provided ground for expansion of naxalism in the area.
- Corruption, castism are the other factor which also increased naxalism in the study area.

- Caste conflicts, land/labour disparity, unequal distribution of land are the other causes which increased naxalism in the study area.
- Criminal background, political representatives and castes based political parties emergence in the study area are other reason which also increased naxalism in the study area.
- Social evils like dowry, alcoholism, prostitution etc. also put pressure on people to involve in these social evils activities for their needs. Mostly they goes to money lender for money and they exploited than they goes to bureaucrats and naxal organisation for this problem solution, lastly they get support by naxalite in their problem solution and become active supporters, both mentally and physically.
- There is lack of vocational training centre and non government organisation in the study which is other causes of emergence of naxalism in the study area.
- There is unawareness among rural people about banking system for loan and less number of banks branches also creates problems in the rural area only educated people get loans easily.

Suggestion

- There is a need of transparency, accountability and auditing in the various government programmes runs by the government in the study area and there is need to check out the balance sheet of Gram Pradhan and other block development officer time to time.
- It is necessary to creates healthy atmosphere of cooperation between common people and bureaucrats so that they easily meet them for solution of their problem.
- In the naxal affected area there is a need of proper development specially infrastructure development. This problem is not solved by brutal police suppression, only people participation in the various government schemes and programmes can solve the naxal problems.

- There is need of opening vocational training centre and spreading banking network, cooperative agencies in the rural area.
- There is need of strong Will power in the are to punished corrupted bureaucrats, forest officers and political representative etc.
- To creates awareness among rural people about their legal and social rights by the help of Non-government organisation in the study area.
- Right to information activist provided security from government machinery in the study area.
- Non-government organisation not pressured by government officer in their day to day working and these NGO's direct report to district collector.
- Building school, colleges, hospitals, roads, sanitation facilities in the rural areas and created awareness programmes by government machinery in the study area.
- Provided maximum Job opportunity to the local rural people and encouraged their personal skills such as hand made goods and handicrafts. So that they get job opportunities in their respective villages and blocks.
- With the help of Central and State government cooperation developed this beautiful district as tourist spot and provided license to local people to open store, shops, hotels and resorts show that they get job opportunity.
- Development of rural haats and handicrafts industry in the Sonbhadra districts specially forest and agro based industry so that we proved Jobs to local people of study area.

Bibiliography

Adhikari, Anindita, and Bhatia, Kartika: MNERGA Wage payments: Can we Bank on the Banks ? EPW, VolXLV, No. 1, Jan 2010.

Athavale, MC: Small Farmers Development Agencies in M.P., Jabalpur, Agro Economic Research Centre, 1973.

Ansari, A.W.: The Changing Village India, Chetna Publications, New Delhi, 1980.

Atal, Yogesh: The Changing Frontiers of Caste, National Publishing House, New Delhi, 1968.

Breman, Jan and Mundle Sudipto (Eds.): Rural Transformation in Asia, Oxford University Press, Delhi, 1991.

Basu, Pradeep: Naxalite Movement (1967-2009) Insight into Radical Left Politics, Setuprakashani, Kolkatta, 2010.

Bailey, F.G.: Caste and Economic frontier, University Press, Manchester, 1957.

Bailey, F.G.: Political and Social Change, Berkely University of California Press, 1963

Bandopadhyay, Krishna: Naxalbari Politics: A Feminist Narrative, EPW,Vol. XLIII, No. 14 April, 2008.

Bandopadhyay, D.: Rural Unrest, Yojana, February, 2007.

Banerjee, Sumanta: In the Wake of Naxalbari,A History of the Naxalite Movement in India,Subarnarekha, Calcutta, 1980.

Banerjee, Sumanta: India's Simmering Revolution: The Naxalite uprising, Selected Service Syndicate, New Delhi, 1984.

Banerjee, Sumanta: Naxalbari: Between past and future, EPW, Vol. XXXVII, No. 22, June, 2002.

Banerjee, Sumanta: Naxalite: Time for Introspection, EPW, Vol. XXXVIII No. 44, November, 2003.

Beteille, Andre: Poverty and Inequality, EPW, Vol. XXXVIII, No.42, October, 2003.

Bhatia, B.: The Naxalite Movement in Central Bihar, EPW, Vol. XL No.15, Mumbai, April, 2005.

Bharadwaj, K.: Alternative Analytical Paradigms in Theories of Development, "Breenrah Jan and Mundle, S. (Edited): Rural Transformation in Asia, Delhi, Oxford University Press, 1991.

Borooah, K.Vani: Deprivation, Violence and Conflict: An analysis of "Naxalite Activity in the districts of India, International Journal of Conflict and Violence, Vol.2, No.2, 2008.

Bhalla, B.S. and G.K. Chadha: Green Revolution and the Small Peasant; A Study of Income Distribution in Punjab Agriculture, EPW, 5 and 22 May, 1982.

Chenoy, M. Anuradha and Kamal, A Mitra Chenoy, Maoist and other armed conflict, Penguin Book India, 2010, New Delhi.

Chakravorti, S.: Redsun, Penguin Publication, New Delhi, 2006.

Currie, Bob: The politics of Hunger in India, Macmillian Press Ltd., Chennai, 2000.

Croppe, James, H.: Rural Socialogy and Rural Develoment, Vol. 87 No. 4, Dec. 1972, pp. 515-33

Chattopadhyaya, Sankar, Subrid,: To Established A Liberated Area (Interview with Koteswar Rao), Frontline, Vol. 26, No. 22, October 24 to November, 6, 2009.

Das, Raju: Geographical Unevenness of India's Green Revolution, Journal of Contemporary Asia, 1999.

Dasgupta, Biplab: The Naxalite Movement, Bombay, Allied Publishers, New Delhi, 1975.

Dhanagare, D.N.: Peasant Movement in India, Oxford University Press, New Delhi, 1983.

Duyker, Edward: Tribal Guerillas (The Santhals of West Bengal and the Naxalite Movement), Oxford University Press, Delhi, 1987.

Dhanagare, D.N.: The Green Revolution and Social Inequalities in Rural India, Bulletin of Concerned Asian Scholars, 1988.

Dubey, Abhay: Kranti Ka Atma Sangharsh, Vanee Publication, S.D.S., Dariyaganj, 1997, New Delhi.

Desai, A.R.: A New Policy for Rural Development in South Asia, C.G.Shah Memorial Trust Publication, Mumbai, 1985.

Ghurye, G.S.: Caste, Class and Occupation, Popular Prakashan, Bombay, 1961.

Guha, Ramachandra: Adivasis, Naxalites and Indian Democracy, EPW, Vol. XLII, No. 32, August, 2007.

George, P.T.: Land Reforms: Promises and Performances, Kurushetra, Vol. XXXVIII, No. 4, January, 1986.

Gopal, S.: The Naxalite Movement: Impact of External Networking, Cited in Ramana, 2008.

Gupta, Akhil: Post Colonial Development: Agriculture in the making of Modern India, Oxford University Press, Delhi, 1998.

Himanshu: Towards,New Poverty Lines for India, EPW, Vol. XLV, No.1, January, 2010.

Harris, John: Rural Development: Theories of Peasant Economy and Agrarian Change, Hut Chinson, ELBS, 1986.

Himanshu, "Recent Trends in Poverty and Inequality, Some Preliminary Results", EPW, Vol. XLII, No. 6, February, 2007.

Johri, J.C.: Political Ideas of Marxist, Leninist, Communists in India, Journal of Political Science, Vol. XXXII, No. 2, April-June, 1971.

Kumar, Ajit: History of Naxalite Movement in Bihar, Samkaleen Publications, 2004.

Kumar Ravindra: Need of Bring about rural Transformation, Kurukshetra, March, 16-31, 1983.

Kannabiran, Vasanth, Volga, Kannabiran, Kalpana: Women's Rights and Naxalite groups, EPW, Vol. XXXIX No. 45, November, 2004.

Kujur, K. Rajat: Under Development and Naxal Movement, EPW, Vol. XLI, No.7, Feb. 2006.

Kurian, C.T.: Poverty, Planning and Social Transformation, Allied Publishers, Bombay, 1978.

Kotovosky. G: Agrarian Reformed in India, New Delhi, 1964.

Kujur, K. Rajat: Child Soldier of the Naxal Movement, Institute of Peace and Conflict Studies, No. 2738, Nov. 24, 2008, New Delhi.

Kujur, Rajat: From CRZ to SEZ: Naxal Reins of Terror, IPCS, Issue Brief, New Delhi, No.2271, April, 2007.

Kujur, Rajat: Naxalite Violence ; Hijacking Train the new face of red terror, IPCS, Issue brief, New Delhi, No.1967, March, 16, 2006.

Kohli, Atul: Democracy and discontent; India's Growing Crisis of Governability, New Delhi, 1992.

Liberation: Vol. 3, No.1, November, 1969.

Louis, Prakash: The Naxalite Movement in Central Bihar, Words Smiths, New Delhi, 2002.

Lipton, Michael: Why Poor People Stay Poor, Urban Bias in World Development, London, Temple Smith, 1977.

Mehta, A.K. Shepherd, A (ed.): Chronic Poverty and Development Policy in India, Sage Publicatin, New Delhi, 2006.

Mishra, Vinod: Selected works, a CPI (ML) Publication, New Delhi, 1999.

Mishra, S.K.: Naxalwad, K.W Publishers, New Delhi, 2010.

Maheshwari, S.R.: Rural Development in India: A Public Policy Approach, New Delhi, Sage Publication, 1985.

Mehta, Ashok: Report of the Committee on Panchayati Raj Institution, Govt. of India, 1978.

Mathur, Kuldeep: Bureaucratic Response to Development, New Delhi, National Publishing House, 1972.

Mankenkar, D.R.: A Revolution of Rising Frustration, Vikas Publication, New Delhi, 1975.

Mukherjee, Mridula: "Peasant Resistance and Peasant consciousness in Colonial India," Subaltern and Beyond, EPW, 1988, Oct. 8 and 15, New Delhi.

Mukherjee, Mridula: Aditya Mukherjee and Bipin Chandra: India's since Independence, Penguin Book, India, 2008.

Mukherjee, A.P.: Maoist spring thunder; The Naxalite Movement (1967-72) K.P Bagchi and Company, Kolkatta, 2007.

Navlakha Gautam: The Naxalite, In War and in Peace, EPW, Vol. XLII No. 36, September, 2007.

Nimbram, Amrik Singh: Poverty, Land and Violence (An Analytical Study of Naxalism in Bihar), Chaudhari Printing Press, Patna, 1992.

Nayak, Namita, S: An Estimate of Poverty among Deprived Social Groups in India, 1999-2000, M.Phil, Dissertation, Submitted to Jawaharlal Nehru University, 2007.

Patnaik Utsa: Trends in Urban Poverty under Economic Reforms: 1993-94 to 2004-05, Economic and Political Weekly, Vol. XLV No. 4, January-2010

Prasad B.N.: Radicalism and Violence in Agrarian Structure, the Maoist Movement in India, Manak Publication Pvt. Ltd., 2002, New Delhi.

Patnaik, M, and Routray, J.K.: Transformation of Rural Habitat; Concept and Approach", Kurushetra, Vol. XXX, No. 8, Jan. 16-31, 1982.

Priyadarshi, Vinita: Drafting a Counter-Naxalite Strategy, Journal of U.S.I. of India, Vol. CXL, No. 580, April-June 2010.

Patanaik, Sarmistha: Does Environmental Degradation Escalates Naxalite Violence, 2009

Rana, Subir: Land, Caste and Tribal Imbroglio; A case study on naxalite movement of Uttar Pradesh, Published in Basu Pradeep edited Book, Naxalite Movement (1967-2009) Setu Prakashani, Kolkata, 2009.

Ram, Mohan: Maoism in India, Vikas Publication, New Delhi, 1971.

Ramakrishnan, Venkitesh: Taking on Maoists, Frontline, Vol. 26, No. 22, Oct. 24-Nov. 6, 2009.

Rao, V. Krishna: Communism in Andhra Pradesh (Rise and Decline), Cauvery Publications, Hyderabad, 1989.

-Rao, M.S.A: Social Movement in India, Manohar Publication and Distribution, New Delhi, 2002.

Roy, A.K.: Ideological Bases of the CPI (ML) in Indian Political Parties; Programmes, Promises and Performance (ed.) Subhash C. Kashyap and J.P. Sharma, Research, Delhi, 1971.

Ramani, R. Venkata: The Naxal Strategy in Urban Area, IPCS Issue Brief, New Delhi, No. 3047, January 21, 2010.

Reddy, K. Srinivas: Revolutinary and Counter Revolutionary Strategies of the Naxalite and the State, 2008, P.92, Cited in. P.V. Ramana, The Naxal Challenge (Causes, Linkages and Policy Options), 2008.

Ray, Rabindra: The Naxalite and their Ideology, Oxford University Press, New Delhi, 1988.

Samanta, K. Amiya: Ideological Issues in the Naxalite Movement Left Extremist Movement: An Experiment in Armed Agrarian Struggle, FIRMA, KLM Pvt Ltd. Calcutta, 2010.

Sengupta, Pramode: Naxalbari and Indian Revolution, Research India Publications, 1983.

Sahni, Ajay: The Threal within Stregthnening Internal Mechanism, U.S.I., Defence Journal, Vol. CXL, No.58, New Delhi, 2010.

Sharma, EAS: The Adivasi, The State and the Naxalite (Case of Andhra Pradesh) EPW, Vol. XLI, April 2006.

Singh, Prakash: The Naxalite Movement in India, Rupa and Co., New Delhi, 2006.

Sinha, Shanta: Maoist inAndhra Pradesh, Ghyan Publication, Delhi, 1989.

Singh, Yogendra, "Contemporary Social Transformation in India, Processes and Contradictions." Dak, T. M. (ed.), Social Transformation in India, Ajanta Publication, New Delhi, 1990.

Subramanian, K.S.: Reflections on Naxalism in Chattisgarh, EPW, Vol. XLI, No.4, January, 2006.

Singh, Mohinder: Rural Development in India, Cultural Perspectives, Intellectual Publishing House, 1992. New Delhi

Singh, N.K.: Bureaucracy, Person and Position, New Delhi, Abhinav Publication, 1974.

Singharoy, Debojeet: Role of Women in Telengana and Naxalite Movement, IGNOU, Nov. 1995, New Delhi.

Sundarayaya, P.: Telengana People's Struggle and its lesson, Communist Party of India (Marxist), Calcutta, 1972.

Suri, K.C.: Political Economy of Agrarian Distress: Economic and Political Weekly 41;15;23-29, 2006.

Singh, Ayodhyaya: Bharat Ka Mukti Sangram, Macmillian, New Delhi, 2003.

Selig, S. Harrison: India, the Most Dangerous Decade, Madras, 1960.

Tiwari, R.K.: Rural Employment Programmes in India: The Implementation Process, New Delhi, IIPA, 1990.

Tiwary, J.K., Rural Development Administration; Perspectives and Prospects, Allahabad, Chugh Publication, 1984.

Tiwary, J.K., Rural Transformation in India, Reliance Publishing House, New Delhi, 1994.

U.N.D.P.: Human Development Report, 1997, Oxford University Press, Oxford, 1997.

U.N.D.P.: Human Development Report, 1999, Oxford University Press, oxford, 1999.

Index